THE ENGLISH PIL.....
TO ROME

ARMA · REGIS · ANGLIE · ET · F

This book is dedicated to Anthony Coles who generously and enthusiastically supported the original 'Recusant Rome' tour and others which followed, and who has enabled many modern English pilgrims to discover Rome for themselves.

THE ENGLISH PILGRIMAGE TO ROME

A Dwelling for the Soul

Judith Champ

GRACEWING

First published in 2000
Reprinted 2007

Gracewing
2 Southern Ave, Leominster
Herefordshire HR6 0QF

ISBN 0 85244 373 0
ISBN 978 0 85244 373 6

Half title page illustration:
The English royal coat of arms from the title page
of St John Fisher's *Defence of Priesthood against Luther*,
published in 1525, on the eve of the breach between
Henry VIII and Rome.

Contents

Acknowledgements

Many English Roman pilgrims and friends have contributed ideas, stories, suggestions and material to this book, and even more have listened to portions of it – often amidst the traffic and noise of Rome itself! I am grateful to all of them. The project has only taken its final form as a result of the constant encouragement of Anthony Coles and the generous and constructive criticism of Eamon Duffy.

Without the hospitality of the Rector, staff and students of the English College, Rome, this book would never have been written and I am grateful to the archivists and librarians of the College who have provided me with material, and the Rector for permission to reproduce it. Thanks are also due to the Rector of Oscott College for permission to reproduce material from collections held there, and to Oscotian colleagues and students for bearing with the last stages of completion. I am happy to acknowledge the assistance of the archivists of the Jesuits at Farm St, the Dominicans in Edinburgh and the Thomas Cook Travel Archive in Peterborough (who also gave their permission to reproduce material), and also library staff at King's College, London and the University of Birmingham.

Tom Longford and Jo Ashworth at Gracewing have been cheerful, patient and helpful in ensuring the final production of this book. I have greatly appreciated their enthusiastic determination to meet deadlines, and in doing so, the timely and accurate assistance of Christopher Hilton with proof-reading and indexing.

Preface

The origin of this contribution to the vast and ever-growing literature on Rome lies in a pilgrimage to Rome which took place in September 1993. This group of pilgrims, in search of 'Recusant Rome' set out to explore the links between Rome and the church in England, particularly since the Reformation. We based ourselves at the Venerable English College and set out from there to find other Roman places which had echoed to English footsteps. Inevitably we found ourselves moving forward into the modern period of Catholic revival in England and backwards into the mediaeval world of pilgrimage and ecclesiastical power politics, as we uncovered evidence of the influence of the English church in Rome before, during and after the Reformation. As we explored some familiar and less commonplace sites in and around Rome from this particular perspective, not only did we see the city afresh, but light was shed for all of us on another dimension of the religious history of England.

What is contained here is the fruit of the research for that pilgrimage following in the footsteps of English pilgrims through the centuries, and of further explorations since. It is not a complete history of the English in Rome, but for the historian of English Christianity it may suggest clues to the influence of Rome on the life of the English church. I hope that this book will give other visitors, pilgrims and armchair travellers the possibility of sharing a different perspective on the Eternal City. It tells a number of stories which readers will find at times poignant, inspiring or entertaining, but which I hope will encourage them to explore Rome afresh in the footsteps of generations of English pilgrims.

SS Peter and Paul
29 June 1999

Foreword

From its beginnings, the story of English Christianity has been interwoven with that of the city and the Church of Rome. Christianity established itself in Britain as a by-product of Roman colonization, and the organization of the English Church under archbishops at Canterbury and York at the end of the sixth century was the direct outcome of a papal mission to Kent, led by the Roman monk Augustine. The originator of that mission, Pope Gregory the Great, had first encountered the English in the form of fair-haired Saxons for sale in the Roman slave-market, so different from the dark good looks of the native Romans that, as everyone knows, he dubbed them 'Angels, not Angles', and determined there and then to bring so fair a nation, perched at the utter edge of the civilized world, into the fellowship of Christian peoples. Gregory's initiative established a bond between Rome and England that would persist for a thousand years. The first biography of this greatest of the Roman successors of Peter was written in England, by a monk of Whitby, and to English writers Gregory remained 'Gregorius noster', 'our Gregory'. For his sake, and the sake of the Apostle whose ministry he continued, the hearts of the English remained tied to Rome by a golden thread. Rome provided the ultimate religious pattern and resource for early English Christians. Benedict Biscop, creating his great monasteries at Jarrow and Wearmouth, named them after the twin patrons of Rome, Peter and Paul, filled them with Roman icons and books, and even brought the choirmaster of St Peter's to train English monks in the Roman mode of chanting the daily offices. Troops of English pilgrims, among them the young Alfred the Great, made their way to the threshold of the Apostles, and many settled there in their own national quarter, known by the English name *Borgo*, 'The Burrough', close to St Peter's. When, in the pontificate of Nicholas I, during one of the periodic mediaeval confrontations between pope and emperor, Imperial troops disrupted a papal procession outside Constantine's basilica, it was a group of English pilgrims who rescued from the mud the jewelled relic of the True Cross. This was as it should be, for that relic had been presented to an earlier pope by Constantine's mother, Helena, herself traditionally believed to have been born in Britain.

Rome could seem the source of political legitimacy as well as sanctity: when in the mid-thirteenth century Henry III sought to bolster his regime by rebuilding the royal mausoleum and shrine at Westminster Abbey, dedicated to St Peter, he brought to England Roman craftsmen from the Cosmati workships, to decorate the sanctuary floor and the tomb of St Edward with porphyry and gold, in the Roman manner, thereby lending him some of the trappings of the Imperial power which the Popes had raised up to protect the Church.

For most of the English, and above all for the monarchy, all that came to an end at the Reformation. The English reformers rewrote the early history of their church, editing out the Roman dimension. To them the Pope was not a benefactor and father in faith, but the Antichrist, poisoning the wells of pure Gospel Christianity with superstition and innovation, and above all invading the sovereignty and usurping the spiritual supremacy of the Lord's annointed, the monarch. The pope-burnings of the annual Guy Fawkes celebrations became a symbol of the English nation's repudiation of the city and the faith of Rome.

But still the English came. For those who retained or were reconverted to Catholicism, Rome became now more than ever a place of pilgrimage. The resurgence of the

Counter-Reformation papacy and the rediscovery of Rome's early Christian past in the catacombs cast round the city a renewed aura of holiness – *Roma Sancta.* The English pilgrim hospice in the Via Monserrato, where the most famous Englishwoman of the Middle Ages, Margery Kempe, had once stayed, had been transformed in the 1570s into the Venerable English College, a seminary training priests for the mission to England and, in many cases, for martyrdom. It remained, however, hospitable to pilgrims, and there came to claim its charity not only a steady stream of the devout, well-heeled or barefoot, seeking the threshold of the Apostles, but a procession of misfits and unfortunates, Protestant as well as Catholic, marooned English sailors or penniless widows, seeking the familiarity of English voices and the comfort of a free meal and a bed for the night.

To Rome, too, came the court of the broken Stuart dynasty, the Royal family exiled for their Catholicism as well as their political ineptitude. The last Stuart claimant of the English throne, Henry Duke of York, 'Henry IX', died a cardinal of the Holy Roman Church, Bishop of Frascati, his ruined fortunes after the French Revolution propped up by a British pension, discreetly bestowed by the humane and tactful gesture of King George III.

And secular pilgrims came too: seventeenth-century writers like John Milton or John Evelyn, eighteenth-century Grand Tourists, nineteenth-century Romantics for whom the ceremonial of the Papal Court was part of the glamour of the ancient capital of the world. With the nineteenth century too, came a revival of sympathy for and attraction to the ancient faith of Rome, an attraction if anything heightened by the beleaguered condition of the popes, kidnapped and abused during the French Revolution, besieged within a shrinking Papal Territory as the modern Italy emerged. For the first time, the Pope himself became the principal icon or relic of Rome, the centre of its sanctity, and Catholics came to pay homage less to the bones of Peter than to the Vicar of Christ. By the end of the nineteenth century the Prisoner of the Vatican was beset by a hostile Italian State, but he had become a potent symbol of the crisis of faith itself, at odds with modernity and the rising tide of scepticism and secularization.

Judith Champ's learned and delightful book provides an absorbing survey of these multiple transformations of the meaning of Rome and its bishop for the people of England. She draws effectively on a wealth of evidence – historical narrative, biographical memoirs and centuries of guide-books – to tell her story. Her use of the unpublished pilgrim book of the English College in particular provides vivid and sometimes poignant vignettes of the motley stream of humanity which made its way to the threshold of the Apostles in the centuries of the Grand Tour, and the English College and the pilgrim hostels it evolved from provide a recurring centre-point in her kaleidoscopic story. But her book is more than a fascinating narrative of the changing attraction of Rome to the English, from Saxon pilgrims down to the less strenuously pious hordes of the twentieth-century package tour. It is also a packed gazetteer of the material traces of the English in Rome, enabling the reader to track their presence through the city's monuments, churches and palazzi, and to use the stones and inscriptions of Rome and its environs to recover a forgotten but fascinating story. Many books on Rome will be published in this year of bimillennial Jubilee, but few deserve so richly a wide readershipp and a long shelf life.

Eamon Duffy
Magdalene College

Chapter One

Introduction: 'Go to Rome – it will do you good!'

In the late nineteenth century, Cardinal Henry Manning admonished the eccentric English convert poet Wilfred Scawen Blunt, 'Go to Rome – it will do you good!' Despite the fact that it has not always done them good, English Christians have been going to Rome ever since Pope Gregory the Great and St Augustine of Canterbury forged the link. The English have been travelling to Rome for at least 1400 years for a mixture of religious and secular purposes.[1] Pilgrimage involving penitence, the search for miracles, indulgences and the need for spiritual aid was an obvious purpose, but was blended with curiosity (the desire to explore strange worlds; trade (dealing in art, artifacts and relics); ecclesiastical business (the need for papal sanction, training and education for the administration of the Church) and culture (the desire to absorb art, literature, theology and learning).

Rome has exercised a particular fascination for the rest of the world since classical times. It is unique among the major pilgrimage centres in its perennial associations not only with devotion, but with power and with artistic and cultural influence. Rome itself poses questions about the practice of pilgrimage to the Eternal City. Throughout the ebb and flow of 1400 years of English travellers in Rome, the pattern has inevitably changed, and different answers can be given to the perennial question – why go to Rome? Its role in the ecclesiastical life and in the imagination of

[1] J. G. Davies, *Pilgrimage Yesterday and Today: Why? Where? How?* (1988), p. 4.

1

the English has been immense and contradictory. The
English have been drawn to Rome often in spite of themselves in search of – what? Paradoxically, the English have
pursued a centuries-long love affair with Rome, despite the
fact that their national identity has been in part shaped by
Protestant rejection of Rome and all it stands for. Even
before the Reformation, England saw itself as stoutly inde-
pendent of Roman influence after the withdrawal of the
Empire.

Pilgrimage in itself, both as a physical reality and as an
analogy for human life, has a long and complex history,
not just in Christianity. Its place in the mediaeval Christian
world is well known and has been widely discussed.[2] It has
become commonplace to ascribe the practice of
pilgrimage to the mediaeval Catholic world as part of a
pattern of popular cults and devotions, of saints, indulgences, miracles and the like, largely swept away by the
sixteenth century.[3] The use of the image of pilgrimage in
devotional writings as a metaphor for the Christian life
survives from the mediaeval to the modern world and was
translated from Catholic to Protestant thinking. *The
Pilgrim's Progress* is the classic example of the allegorical use
of the pilgrimage/journey which became deeply rooted in
Protestant Christianity.

Pilgrimage does not have to be (and surely never was)
separated from the experience of journeying in strange
lands, seeking for the unknown and of shared discovery, of
openness to broader spiritual benefits and of the freedom
from everyday commitments. It can be, indeed always was,
an experience which takes place alongside and in the
midst of other aspects of travel and it should be recognized
that 'the complex and many-sided appeal of the pilgrimage
is a fact of human experience'.[4] Any notion that there was
ever such a thing as a purely and wholly religious

2   See E. Duffy, *The Stripping of the Altars* (1993), p. 191 and R. G.
    Finucane, *Miracles and Pilgrims: Popular Beliefs in Mediaeval England*
    (1977), ch. 3, *passim.*
3   D. R. Howard, *Writers and Pilgrims: Mediaeval Pilgrimage Narratives and
    their Posterity* (1980), pp. 6–7.
4   R. Delaney, 'The Seven Churches', *The Venerabile* 5 (1932), p. 380.

pilgrimage is misguided, and the happy mixture of religious and secular motives is not a cause for criticism – although it has been made such through the centuries. Spiritual nourishment can be freely obtained by pilgrims who are wary about relics and indulgences traditionally associated with pilgrimage, but are attracted to holy places, hallowed by centuries of prayer. What one recent author has written of contemporary pilgrimage is applicable to any age: 'To go to Rome, for example, is to deny daily routine, to leave known structures and to discover how divisions can be broken down and a sense of wholeness encouraged. Major pilgrimages do have an integrating effect and, at the same time, lead to a more profound comprehension of Christian identity.'[5]

Post-Reformation 'journeys' are widely supposed in most discussions to be either metaphorical inner pilgrimages or cultural tours carried out by the curious and the educated.[6] In the view of one contemporary specialist in the field of the 'Grand Tour', it evolved as a purely educational exercise, out of a reaction against the mediaeval practice of pilgrimage and a need for a non-religious justification for the growing taste for travel.[7] However, it is worth reconsidering this traditional understanding of the practice of pilgrimage, as the evidence suggests that it was not quite so straightforward. This assumption ignores the complex motives which took mediaeval men and women on the road and denies the religious impulses which have stirred in the travellers of a later age. To limit the notion of pilgrimage to an experience (seemingly archaic and remote) of relics, indulgences and penances is to deny its wider significance in European society. It is also to ignore the evidence of later pilgrimage traditions which survived the Reformation. In the ambiguity of the English post-Reformation religious world, there was room for the survival, recovery and reinterpretation of ancient traditions. To believe that there was ever a 'pure' pilgrimage tradition is equally misleading, and here again, English

5   J. G. Davies, p. 203.
6   Ibid.
7   E. Chaney, *The Evolution of the Grand Tour* (1998), p. 203.

evidence points to ambiguity. There is evidence of medi-aeval pilgrims' curiosity about the classical ruins of Rome, and of them indulging in a little antique dealing as a side-line to their visit. Chaucer, above all, reminds us that 'though pilgrimage was meant to be a penitential exercise – and indeed for some it was – many treated it as a form of tourism and earned a poor reputation for pilgrims as a whole.'[8] Early Anglo-Saxon pilgrim visitors to Rome (espe-cially kings and churchmen like Benedict Biscop) regularly purchased collections of books, artifacts and relics for churches in England. At least one English mediaeval pilgrimage itinerary was combined with a travelogue.[9] How is it possible to divide the religious experience of Rome from the artistic, social and cultural experiences? It was impossible in both the mediaeval and in the modern worlds, and the complex interaction of motives and experi-ence helped the English in particular to deal with their uncomfortable relationship with Rome over the centuries.

From Constantinian times and the 'Romanization' of Christianity, Rome has exercised a fascination and has been the focus of church institutions. English people have been drawn to Rome by all the motives already mentioned and more besides. For the English, the fascination is all the more curious as it has often been mixed with hostility and antagonism to the institutions which give Rome its *raison d'être*. Pilgrimage to Rome from England quickly caught up with and overtook Jerusalem in popularity, partly because of the shorter distance and lack of a long sea crossing. There were other reasons though, which drew pilgrims from all over Europe. Rome could offer a variety of holy sites, shrines and relics to the pious and certainly had more saints to the square mile than any other city. It offered the possibility of cures and miracles, as well as absolution when the pilgrimage was undertaken in penance. The fact that, as papal authority extended, the remission of certain sins was reserved to the Pope, made a visit to Rome not just desirable, but a necessity for some sinners. This accompa-nied the development of the indulgence system, whereby

---

[8]   M. Walsh, *A Dictionary of Devotions* (1993), p. 198.
[9]   J. G. Davies, p. 86.

the pious completion of a circuit of shrines in Rome could assure the pilgrim of a much-reduced stay in purgatory.

The crucial difference between Rome and any other centre of pilgrimage is that it was, and remains, the centre of Catholic authority. As the Roman system and Roman authority spread throughout the church, there was a growing need for monarchs and churchmen to visit Rome, for ecclesiastical and often military reasons as much as spiritual ones. More importantly, pilgrimage was used as a means of encouraging the spread of Roman order. Pilgrimage stories had a propaganda value in inculcating an appreciation of Rome as the centre of Christendom. Early Christian writers, including Bede, emphasized links with Rome and the benefits of pilgrimage to Rome in order to foster '*Romanitas*' in the church, particularly in remote areas like Britain. The image of the known world conveyed by the thirteenth-century *Mappa Mundi* makes it clear that the Mediterranean was the centre, both physically and psychologically. Encouragement of pilgrimage accompanied the assertion of papal authority over the local churches. The principle gradually became accepted that archbishops had to go to Rome to receive the pallium which signified their office.[10] They therefore would go on pilgrimage in a spirit of humility and piety, and encourage others to do likewise. It has been suggested that the early pilgrim literature contained an element of organized propaganda to attract pilgrims to Rome and point out its cultural and spiritual highlights – that in fact the '*Libri Indulgentiarum*' were a kind of mediaeval advertisement.[11]

The draw of the shrines of SS Peter and Paul was immense, but only slowly did it become true that, 'It was Peter above all that exercised the greatest pull, for to visit Rome was not only to venerate his relics but to honour his living embodiment: Peter lives on in the Pope.'[12] In fact, the veneration of the current successor of Peter and its

[10] N. K. Chadwick (ed.), *Studies in the Early British Church* (1958), p. 27.
[11] J. R. Hulbert, 'Some Mediaeval Advertisements of Rome', *Modern Philology* 20 (1922–3), pp. 403–24.
[12] J. G. Davies, p. 7.

place in the pattern of pilgrimage is relatively modern. Before the nineteenth century, only ecclesiastical visitors and diplomats would expect or desire an audience of the Pope. Mediaeval popes were often absent from Rome, but this did nothing to stem the tide of pilgrims or lessen the attractiveness of the Eternal City. Rome was eternal – popes came and went, often with great rapidity and little mourning. The primacy of Peter and the authority of the popes over Church and State was not assumed or agreed by all, and mediaeval Europe was dominated by the ensuing conflicts. Therefore Rome itself and pilgrimage to Rome took on a powerful, even savage, symbolism. The jubilee years, during which special spiritual privileges could be obtained by visiting Rome, were proclaimed by popes from 1300 onwards. They helped to formalize and to universalize the practice of Roman pilgrimage as well as inevitably aiding the commercialization and profit-making attached to mass pilgrimage. By this means, the papal grip on the keys of heaven and earth was assured, but mediaeval jubilees succeeded whether or not the Pope was in residence. The focus on the 'living embodiment' did not arise until much later and was a product of radically different perceptions of the papacy.

The calling of the first Christian Holy Year in 1300 seems to have been a response by Boniface VIII to a spontaneous outpouring of religious fervour and enthusiasm for Roman pilgrimage. Large numbers of people were instinctively drawn to Rome as the new century dawned, but the Pope did not make any proclamation until well into February. There were some claims made for centenarian pilgrims who declared that their parents had brought them to Rome for the great blessing in 1200, though the papal archives revealed nothing. No long-term planning or preparation accompanied the proclamation of the first Christian Holy Year, but it was a symbolic event for the whole of Christian Europe, evoked by the setting of Dante's *Divine Comedy* in Rome at Easter 1300, 'the holy place where sits who to great Peter's chair succeeds'.[13] The

---

[13]   Dante, *The Divine Comedy*, Canto 3.

response was overwhelming, with an alleged 30,000 pilgrims a day pouring into the city (doubling the resident population).[14]

Jubilee became a common term in the context of indulgences. The significance of indulgences, or remission from temporal punishment due to sin, has its roots in the increasingly juridical, legalistic mind-set of the mediaeval church. By the early thirteenth century the system of indulgences had become established, by which the church administered the 'store' of merit gained by Christ and the saints for the benefit of the penitent. The system had begun under Gregory the Great, and by the mid-twelfth century indulgences could be obtained at all forty of the Roman Lent 'Station Churches'. The Holy Land had become inaccessible to pilgrims in the twelfth and thirteenth centuries and Rome was undergoing something of a revival of interest. Rome, with the papal proclamation of a plenary indulgence for pilgrims, became something of a 'new Jerusalem'.

Boniface proclaimed the Jubilee on 16 February and decreed further celebrations every 100 years. It was Boniface who decreed, in *Unam Sanctam* (1302) that salvation was impossible outside the Roman Church, and part of the motivation behind the Holy Year was the assertion of papal supremacy. There is no mention in the papal bull of the concept of jubilee, or of the Old Testament tradition, and the emphasis was on individual repentance for sin and complete pardon and remission of due punishment. The conditions for such remission involved penitential visits to the major Christian sites in Rome, over a period of thirty days for residents, or fifteen days for visitors.

Increasing English involvement in the papal court and closer ties between the English monarchy and the papacy encouraged the pilgrimage traffic from England. The intimacy of Anglo-Roman exchanges were at their peak in the late fifteenth century and early sixteenth century, until the breach of the 1530s soured relations. However, it is unsatisfactory to view the history of English pilgrimage to Rome as

---

[14] B. Barefoot, *The English Road to Rome* (1993), p. 35.

a tidal flow reaching its height in the fifteenth century, only to be dammed up in the sixteenth century and replaced by Grand Tourists in the seventeenth and eighteenth centuries. Pilgrimage and the excesses often associated with it were already the object of criticism by late mediaeval writers[15] and local shrines were supplanting the great European routes in popularity before the Reformation. Rome may well have suffered from a shift in emphasis in popular piety away from traditional saints towards Christ himself and the Virgin Mary.[16] Humanist scholarship and Renaissance cultural education were already influencing the motives of fifteenth-century visitors to Rome. Italy was increasingly regarded as the source of the highest human achievements in art, music, architecture and design. By the end of the fifteenth century traditional pilgrimage practice was accompanied, or even supplanted, by the search for scholarly contacts or cultural experience. What may have been a slow process of decline was rapidly accelerated by the effects of the breach between Henry VIII and the papacy.

Its effect on pilgrimage was to stem the flow of English people who went to Rome on ecclesiastical business, to give greater credibility during the mid-1500s to Protestant critics of pilgrimage and to reverse the attractiveness of Rome as the seat of the successor of Peter. At least, that was the overall effect by the end of the sixteenth century on the majority who imbibed the ideas of reform and acknowledged the transfer of authority to the monarchy. For the Catholics who remained loyal to papal authority, the significance of Rome became even more intense as the sixteenth century went on. By the Elizabethan period, Rome came to have a very particular and contradictory symbolic significance for Catholics and Protestants.

It is arguable that the English pilgrim, influenced by changes in fashion and motivation, did not disappear but put on new clothes. The broad-brimmed hat, cloak and staff may have disappeared, but did the pilgrim? The evidence

---

[15] Duffy, *Stripping*, p. 191.

[16] R. C. Finucane, *Miracles and Pilgrims: Popular Belief in Mediaeval England* (1977), pp. 195–8.

suggests not. Catholic recusant dependence on Rome was important, although travel was hampered by legal, financial and security restrictions. The symbolic power of Rome for English recusants was also gradually limited by a perceptible change in attitude in the seventeenth and eighteenth centuries. A certain anti-papalism and desire to assert Englishness and loyalty to the Hanoverian crown characterized some aspects of the Catholic community. The secular desire for travel, the passion for Italian (especially Roman) culture and the broadening of educational horizons gradually developed into the formalized pattern of the Grand Tour. Continental travel tended to reinforce rather than erode English prejudices about Catholicism during the first half of the eighteenth century, and many travellers were convinced by the polemic which portrayed Catholicism as the source of injustice, poverty and misery.[17]

However, the Grand Tour did not necessarily exclude piety. The term itself was first coined by a Catholic priest, Richard Lassels, in 1670.[18] Driven by the same curiosity as made many mediaeval pilgrims leave home, the Grand Tourists and other less stylized travellers from England headed towards Rome. They were as likely as not to be Christians of varying levels of piety and clearly some of them were Catholics. Rome, both classical and Christian, continued to exercise a compulsion on the English mind. While the primary interest of the Grand Tourist was cultural and the idea of relics and indulgences would have made most Hanoverian gentlemen shudder, they were still very definitely Christian. Most were educated enough to have an appreciation of Christian heritage and knew the meaning of pilgrimage, even to the point where 'contact with the faith on the Grand Tour could break down hostility in a way that had been impossible earlier in the century.'[19] There were also those within the Catholic community who sustained a tradition of pilgrimage (albeit an adapted one) within and alongside the Tour. Rome was

---

[17.] C. Haydon, *Anti-Catholicism in Eighteenth Century England* (1993), pp. 26–7.

[18.] E. Chaney, *The Evolution of the Grand Tour* (1998), p. 67.

[19.] Haydon, p. 168.

important to them for different reasons. What had changed was the meaning of pilgrimage – but to what?

By the nineteenth century the gentry had been joined by the newly emergent middle classes, 'earnest people seeking a cultural upgrading.'[20] They were followed or accompanied by a resurgence of travellers imbued with the Christian ideology of pilgrimage and not afraid to call themselves pilgrims. Two factors, one secular and one religious, influenced this revival. The secular factor was the growth of cheap popular travel, initially by rail and sea. One reason for the decline in the classic pilgrimage had been the economic and social change of the agricultural and industrial revolutions which constrained the lives of the poor. Ordinary folk ceased to have the time and leisure to absent themselves for weeks or months at a time to walk to Rome and few could afford carriages. Mass long-distance pilgrimage had to wait again for the age of cheap, fast transport. In a sense the shared experience and the corporate nature of mediaeval pilgrimage has only been recaptured in the modern group tour by train, coach and latterly by aeroplane.

The religious factor in the revival of pilgrimage was the result of the changing mood of nineteenth-century Christianity in England and elsewhere. Under the influence of Romanticism, the Catholic Church rediscovered the power of holy places and shrines, the symbolism of physical objects and the potency of saints and stories in building up the Christian life. As the Church of England began to rediscover its pre-Reformation roots, openness to Rome entered its thinking and practice for the first time since the sixteenth century. In rediscovering Rome – not contemporary Rome but the city of Peter and Paul and the early Christian martyrs – it rediscovered the common heritage of all Christians. This enabled Luther's strictures against pilgrimage to be placed in context and proportion. Alongside these developments in the Church of England went the revival of English Catholic life in an assertively Roman style. Again the potent symbol of Roman authority

---

[20]   E. Swinglehurst, *Cook's Tours: the Story of Popular Travel* (1982), p. 34.

and Roman religious culture was at work. It was powerful enough to influence Newman, Manning and many other Anglican converts and to antagonize the Protestant majority. Hostility to Rome and jealousy of its power to 'pervert' Protestants was fuelled by increasing emphasis on the personality and office of the Pope.

There exists a powerful linkage between Roman pilgrimage and martyrdom. The early Christian and mediaeval pilgrims sought to follow in the steps of, and to revere the memory of Peter and Paul and the other Roman martyrs of the catacombs. The relics of the martyrs of persecution rapidly became powerful symbols of identity in the early Christian church, establishing a Christian version of the Roman cult of heroes and contradicting Jewish tradition about the impurity of corpses and death. Martyrs and relics were the treasures of the faithful, closely guarded and revered and were in themselves sources of power. Indeed, the possession of the relics of Peter and Paul (preserved in the basilica of St John Lateran) confirmed above all else to the faithful the pre-eminence of Rome among the churches. In a sense, the relics of SS Peter and Paul authenticated the papacy.[21] To go on pilgrimage was to experience 'a little martyrdom', to leave behind the everyday, the commonplace and set out, trusting only in God, in search of absolution and a ticket to heaven. The power of Rome has, in its time, created many martyrs; devotion to Rome has brought about more. Since the twelfth century Rome has increasingly controlled the proclamation and devotions attached to martyrs and other saints. Two English saints, Edward the Confessor and Thomas à Becket were among the first to be canonized by papal decree rather than local or conciliar acclamation.[22]

It is perhaps not accidental that the nineteenth- and twentieth-century revival of English interest in pilgrimage to Rome coincided with the archaeological recovery of the catacombs and with the rediscovery of the sixteenth-century English martyrs who died specifically for Rome and the Pope. The Reformation martyrs, whose stories

21. J. Bentley, *Restless Bones: the Story of Relics* (1985), ch. 2, *passim*.
22. Finucane, p. 36.

were only widely told in the second half of the nineteenth century and who were beatified in 1886 and 1895, high-light the revival of religious interest in Rome among English Catholics. This process also set the seal on papal direction and authentication of popular cults and devotions. The pilgrim piety recreated in the nineteenth century was carefully orchestrated and clerically organized. The latter-day renewal of interest in martyrs also draws attention to the devastating extremes of English attitudes to Rome over fourteen centuries. The history of English pilgrimage to Rome reflects all the elements of spiritual loyalty, ecclesiastical authority and Church/State conflict. With this in mind, one can only echo H.V. Morton's lines on the English in Rome, written in 1957, '... even today, those that have been ruthlessly educated to be chemists and physicists, and to hold down important posts in commercial combines, descend from their coaches and gaze around upon the Roman scene, so dear to their ancestors, conscious maybe that there is something to be understood and perhaps even loved.'[23]

---

[23] H. V. Morton, *A Traveller in Rome* (1957), p. 202.

Chapter Two

To the Threshold of the Apostles

The Venerable Bede, in his *Ecclesiastical History of the English People*, records the first known English ecclesiastical delegation to Rome, when Augustine sent 'the priest Laurence and the monk Peter to Rome to inform the blessed Pope Gregory that the English had accepted the Faith and that he himself had been consecrated bishop'.[1] Gregory embodied for Bede the model of the monk-bishop of which he approved, but more than that, Bede, in writing his *History*, was at pains to nurture a sense of unity centred on Rome and the Pope among English Christians. His was a history of the church modelled on that of Eusebius, and in continuity with the Acts of the Apostles. 'The main theme of the *History* was the progression from diversity to unity.'[2] Bede's moral purpose in writing his history, 'for the instruction of posterity' as he says in the Preface, was also to inculcate the idea that the arrival of Augustine was when 'the English nation received the faith of Christ'. Roman order and unity in that faith was emphasized, and Bede's encouragement of pilgrimage to Rome in his *History* and in his other writings was part of his campaign to ensure acceptance of Roman influence and order. Among his poems was one of ninety-two lines devoted to the Apostles Peter and Paul and emphasizing the significance of Rome as the resting place of both:

[1] Bede, *Ecclesiastical History of the English People*, Bk 1, ch. 27 (Penguin Classics edn 1990).
[2] D. H. Farmer, Introduction to Penguin Classics edition, p. 27.

> The glory of the Apostles
> Let us sing in due verse,
> Barjona Simon Peter
> And the dear teacher of the Gentiles.[3]

Bede asserts that English pilgrims were pouring into Rome even before the end of the seventh century, and he assumes that bishops went to Rome for consecration.[4] This assumption, made in the eighth century, cannot necessarily be relied upon for the earlier period, as the spread of Roman order and authority throughout the church was a slow process. The encouragement of pilgrimage and papal investiture of archbishops with the pallium were among the means used to secure the 'Romanization' of Christianity, and Bede was an enthusiastic advocate. The emotional attraction of the tombs of the early saints was exploited by Rome in its relationship with other local churches. The power of Rome was, in reality, the power of Peter and Paul, and did not reflect the uniformity which became commonplace in later centuries. The Roman liturgical practice translated into English monasticism by Benedict Biscop and Wilfrid was a version selected from the wide variety available in Rome. 'What was important to Northumbrians was not that they should slavishly copy the use of a particular Roman basilica, but that they should practise customs which were consonant with those practices in, or approved by, Rome.'[5] Those customs included the stational liturgy of Rome, the mobile celebration by the papal court around the city churches, by means of which the church in England was linked more closely with the universal Church and 'the city of Rome became an image, a microcosm, of what was involved in the Communion of Saints'.[6] This in turn enhanced the sense of relationship between the pilgrim and the saints and martyrs of the early

---

[3]   Quoted in G. F. Browne, *The Venerable Bede, his life and writings* (1919), p. 204.
[4]   Bede, Bk 2, ch. 18.
[5]   E. O. Carragain, *The City of Rome and the World of Bede*, Jarrow Lecture 1994, p. 26.
[6]   E. O. Carragain, p. 9.

church whose shrines he set out to venerate, and whose feasts he had commemorated so often at home. A pilgrimage to Rome thus became a real family occasion.

Augustine of Canterbury and Gregory the Great were the focus and source for Bede's *History* and the sites associated with them in Rome took on particular significance for the English. Bede's devotion to Gregory struck deep roots among the Anglo-Saxons and he became regarded primarily as the 'Apostle of the English'. His treatise *Pastoral Care* was translated into Anglo-Saxon by Alfred the Great[7] and the first life of Gregory was written by a monk of Whitby. 'That any tradition survives about the early life of Gregory is due largely to the affection in which he was held by the English.'[8] The church of S. Gregorio Magno on the Coelian Hill was built by Pope Gregory II (715–31) on the site of the monastery from which his predecessor had dispatched St Augustine in 596–7. The present church was transformed externally in 1629 by Cardinal Scipione Borghese and was internally restored in 1734, but because of its ancient associations has remained a place of pilgrimage for the English. Although S. Gregorio was never the titular church of any pre-Reformation English cardinals, three modern English cardinals have held the title – Henry Edward Manning, Herbert Vaughan and Bernard Griffin. In 1890 a committee headed by Manning launched the first attempt at excavating the site of St Gregory's home and monastery beneath the church. Manning gave the money for the preliminary archaeological work, but it was stopped, apparently by Italian government intervention.[9]

In the years immediately after Augustine there was as much traffic out of Rome as into it, consisting of pilgrims *en route* to Jerusalem or missionaries to northern Europe and Britain, but as became clear, 'England never forgot its links with the Christianity of Rome.'[10] As Rome gradually estab-

[7]   J. D. Kelly, *The Oxford Dictionary of Popes* (1986), p. 67.

[8]   A. Marett-Crosby, *The Foundations of Christian England* (1997), p. 11.

[9]   R. Lanciani, *New Tales of Old Rome* (1901, reissued 1967 New York), p. 293.

[10] Marett-Crosby, p. 47.

lished itself as an ecclesiastical headquarters and as the site of holy shrines, an expanding number of visitors arrived in the city seeking spiritual sustenance, '*ad limina Apostolorum*' (to the threshold of the Apostles) and ecclesiastical sanction at the papal court. As early as 605 Mellitus, Bishop of London, was in Rome to confer with Pope Boniface III on matters concerning the English church.[11] In part because of Gregory and Augustine, the papacy began to shift its attention from the Eastern Empire and Constantinople to the north and west. A pilgrimage tradition had grown up in Rome from as early as the time of Constantine, when the three great shrines of the burial places of St Peter and St Paul and the basilica of St John Lateran had become established as pilgrim destinations. The other main attractions were the catacombs, the burial places of early martyrs. A list dating from 354 gave the names of thirty-two martyrs revered by the Christians in Rome, and a revised list of the early seventh century had added a further seventy names.[12] By the fourth century, churches were springing up all over Rome and the catacombs were falling into disrepair. Pope Damasus (366–84), one of the most powerful advocates of Roman primacy among the early popes, restored the catacombs to demonstrate clearly that Rome's glory was Christian not pagan. He was also the founder of the church of S. Lorenzo in Damaso, later the site of his burial.[13]

Successive sieges wrecked and pillaged the catacombs and, as liturgical life in Rome was gradually transferred to the great basilicas, it became desirable to translate the martyrs' remains to the city. This process was accelerated after the Lombard destruction of 756 and by the ninth century there were scarcely any significant saints' remains in the catacombs.[14] Pilgrimage was associated primarily with honouring the martyrs of primitive Christianity, but at an early stage became entangled with an exercise of power and authority from Rome, which was not necessarily spiritual. From the very early days of pilgrimage, particularly

[11] Bede, Bk 2, ch. 4.
[12] J. Sumption, *Pilgrimage: an Image of Medieval Religion* (1975), p. 218.
[13] Kelly, pp. 32–3.
[14] Sumption, p. 218.

for the English, devotion was combined with business.

The flow of English pilgrims to Rome had begun long before the conversion of the country to Christianity was complete. Traditionally, St Wilfrid of Hexham is the first named English Christian to go on pilgrimage to Rome in *c*. 654, before making later visits on ecclesiastical business.[15] Wilfrid was a Northumbrian noble, who after a period of royal service, entered religious life and conceived a desire to 'pay a visit to the see of the Apostle Peter, the chief of the Apostles, and to attempt a road hitherto untrodden by any of our race'.[16] At the Synod of Whitby in 664, a crucial moment in the spread of Roman order, Wilfrid spoke on behalf of Roman authority, after which he was chosen by the king to be Bishop of York, as 'one willing to accept the discipline of the Apostolic See and teach it to others'.[17] His career took a difficult path between royal service and loyalty to the papacy, and his petition to the Pope in 679 against the Archbishop of Canterbury's decision to divide Wilfrid's diocese was formative in the development of the authority of the papal court. He went personally to Rome with his petition and Pope Agatho ordered his restoration to his diocese, declaring that anyone who flouted these statutes would, 'by the authority of blessed Peter the chief of the Apostles', be punished.[18] Wilfrid was to take further appeals to Rome, returning each time with 'holy relics authenticated by the names of saints, buying also vestments of purple and silk to ornament the churches'.[19] This practice of introducing Roman artifacts, as well as devotions and liturgical practices, all served to enhance the links between England and Rome. As his death approached, Wilfrid longed to pay one final visit to Rome, particularly to S. Maria Maggiore and S. Paolo, 'and there end my life', but as his health failed, he bade his monastic brethren to do so on his behalf.[20]

---

[15] A. Gasquet, *A History of the Venerable English College, Rome* (1920), p. 2.
[16] ed. and trans. B. Colgrave, *The Life of Bishop Wilfrid by Eddius Stephanus* (1985), p. 9.
[17] Colgrave, p. 23.
[18] Colgrave, p. 65.
[19] Colgrave, p. 121.
[20] Colgrave, p. 137.

Kings and ecclesiastics were among the first English and Celtic visitors to Rome. According to Bede, Oswin of Northumberland planned to go, but his death in 670 prevented him. Caedwalla of Wessex was baptized in Rome (as an adult) by Pope Sergius I (687–701) in 689. He died soon afterwards and is the only English king apart from the exiled Stuarts to have been buried in St Peter's.[21] Bede gives an account of Caedwalla's baptism and death:

> Arriving in Rome during the pontificate of Sergius, he was baptized on Holy Saturday before Easter in the year of our Lord 689, and he fell ill and while still wearing his white robes departed this life on the twentieth of April and joined the company of the blessed in heaven. At the time of his baptism, the aforesaid Pope had given him the name of Peter, in order that he might be linked by name to the most blessed Prince of the Apostles, to whose most sacred body the king's devotion had brought him from the ends of the earth. He was buried in the Apostle's church, and the Pope directed that an epitaph be inscribed on his tomb to preserve the memory of his devotion for ever and inspire all who read or heard of it to religious fervour.

> ... Safely he came from Britain's utmost shores,
> Through many peoples, over land and sea,
> Bearing his mystic gifts, to visit Rome
> And in the shrine of Peter lay them down.[22]

Caedwalla was aged about thirty at his death and was succeeded by King Ina, who gave up his kingdom after thirty-seven years and went to Rome, 'to visit the shrines of the blessed Apostles ... wishing to spend some of the time of his earthly pilgrimage in the vicinity of the holy places, hoping thereby to merit a warmer welcome from the saints in heaven'.[23] Other early British royal pilgrims included

[21] B. Barefoot, *The English Road to Rome* (1993), p. 19.
[22] Bede, Bk 5, ch. 7.
[23] Ibid.

Coenred, King of Mercia, and Offa, 'a very handsome and lovable young man',[24] heir to the East Saxons, who went together to Rome in 709 and became monks.[25] Coenred 'passing the remainder of his days in prayer, fasting, and acts of mercy.'[26] Concen, King of Powys (808–54), the last of an old line of kings, became one of the first pilgrims from a Celtic country and died in Rome.[27]

Alfred the Great was sent to Rome at the age of five in 853, by his father Ethelwulf, who was too preoccupied with domestic matters to make his promised pilgrimage. Leo IV (847–55), who helped to rebuild the Saxon hospice after destruction by the Saracens and who created the fortified 'Leonine City' around the Vatican, acted as sponsor for the young Alfred's confirmation. He gave him a letter for his father in which he wrote, 'I have gladly received your son Alfred, whom you were anxious to send at this time to the precincts of the Holy Apostles, and as my spiritual son I had him girded with the honour and the outward trappings of nobility after the manner of the consuls at Rome, because he has given himself into my hands.'[28] Although this was described by his biographer as 'a cheap dignity designed to impress ex-colonials, a diplomatic gesture to an outlying province',[29] it was clearly appreciated by Ethelwulf, who later on determined to go to Rome himself. After his wife's death he set off with Alfred around the end of 882, staying for over a year. Leo IV had died leaving the papacy in disarray. Marinus I reigned for around sixteen months, during which time he established warm relations with Alfred and Ethelwulf, out of regard for whom he exempted the Saxon hospice from taxation.[30] This may have been because Ethelwulf and Alfred were generous pilgrims, bringing gifts of silver for the common people, gold for the clergy and nobility, a gold crown and ornamented sword for the Pope

[24] Bede, Bk 5, ch. 19.
[25] Gasquet, pp. 7–8.
[26] Bede, Bk 5, ch. 19.
[27] N. K. Chadwick, *Studies in the Early British Church* (1958), pp. 95–6.
[28] P. J. Helm, *Alfred the Great* (1963), p. 36.
[29] Helm, p. 37.
[30] Kelly, p. 112.

and various items for Roman churches.[31]

The first Archbishops of Canterbury were sent from Rome to England. Nothelm, who would be elected in 735, visited Rome some time between 715 and 731,[32] when with the permission of Pope Gregory II, he searched the papal archives and found the epistles of Gregory the Great which he returned to England for Bede to use in his *History*.[33] Around the same time, Wethburga, the first known English woman pilgrim arrived in Rome.[34] Early fathers of the English church, including Benedict Biscop, founder of the great Northumbrian monasteries, and the poet and scholar Alcuin were among the first pilgrims. Biscop made five visits in all, beginning his career with a Roman pilgrimage in 653, presented by Bede as part of his monastic conversion:

> He therefore left his own country and went to Rome, where, in fulfilment of his long and ardent desire, he made sure he visited the tombs of the apostles and venerated their remains. Directly he returned home he devoted himself wholeheartedly and unceasingly to making known as widely as possible the forms of church life which he had seen in Rome and had come to love and cherish.[35]

Biscop returned for an extended visit between 665 and 669 when he collected a vast supply of books and relics for his monastery. In 671 he was in Rome again to get approval for the founding of St Peter's, Monkwearmouth. He paid two further visits, returning with more books and relics for his foundation at St Paul's, Jarrow, and with the Arch-Cantor from St Peter's basilica to instruct the monks in plainchant in the Roman style.[36] Biscop was clearly determined to

---

[31] Helm, p. 38.
[32] Barefoot, p. 19.
[33] Bede, D. H. Farmer, Introduction (Penguin 1990), p. 25.
[34] Barefoot, p. 19.
[35] E. O. Carragain, *The City of Rome and the World of Bede*, Jarrow Lecture 1994, p. 2.
[36] Anon, 'Saxons in Rome', *Venerabile* 14 (1949), p. 208.

advance Roman influence in the English church, even to the point of dedicating his monasteries to Peter and Paul. His enthusiasm was such that he inspired King Egfrith to offer him the land in 674 for the building of Monkwearmouth in honour of St Peter.[37] Alcuin was perhaps less enthusiastic, as he wrote in 798: 'Italy is an unhealthful country and grows harmful food. Therefore give most cautious thought to what, when and what kind of food you eat; and especially avoid devotion to drink, since the heat of wine usually kindles in the uncautious the flame of fever.'[38]

St Boniface's nephew Willibald, a monk of Bishop's Waltham in Hampshire, who reformed St Benedict's monastery at Monte Cassino, was one of the most travelled Anglo-Saxons of his time. He dictated an account of his travels, published as the *Hodoeporicon* – the first known English travel book, based on his journeys in Rome, Cyprus, Syria and Palestine.[39] Boniface himself, born in Devon in 675, was closely associated with Rome and the papacy and was given specific papal authority for his missions in Germany.[40] He wrote of English people who 'left their country's shores and trusted themselves to the ways of the sea and sought the shrines of the holy apostles Peter and Paul.'[41] However, he also warned against Englishwomen making the journey to Rome as there were 'few cities in Longobardia, Francia or Gaul where an English adulteress or prostitute is not to be found.'[42]

A pattern of travel, which lasted until the railways changed Europe for ever, was established early – the rich moved from one bishop's palace or monastery to another and the poor set out on foot in the traditional pilgrim's wide-brimmed hat, carrying a wooden staff, scrip, bag and wooden bowl, begging or relying on charity. Bede declared that, following the royal pilgrims, 'many English people vied with one another in following this custom, both noble

[37] E. O. Carragain, p. 3.
[38] Barefoot, p. 19.
[39] D. H. Farmer, *The Oxford Dictionary of Saints* (1987), p. 439–40.
[40] Farmer, pp. 51–3.
[41] Gasquet, p. 3.
[42] Barefoot, p. 20.

and simple, layfolk and clergy, men and women alike'.[43]
Ironically, the early pilgrims may have had an easier route
than later ones, as they had the remaining imperial roads
to follow, although one Archbishop of Canterbury, Elfsy
(or Alsine) froze to death in the Alps around 958 on his
way to obtain the pallium.[44] The granting of the pallium of
office to archbishops by the pope, and the journey to
Rome to receive it, were increasingly seen as symbolic of
papal authority over the local churches. The white collar,
woven from the wool of lambs blessed by the Pope, took on
sacred significance, being kept ready for use as near as
possible in St Peter's basilica to the burial place of the
Apostle. The authority thus given was deemed to be
directly linked with Peter. The eleventh-century frescoes in
the Roman basilica of S. Clemente portray St Clement as
Pope and Bishop of Rome, clearing wearing the pallium.

After the disintegration of the imperial Roman routes
travellers had to wait until the sixteenth century for the
roads to be as good again.[45] On reaching Rome, the
pilgrim would find little of the grandeur of the imperial
days. The population had shrunk and the occupied city was
only a fraction of that enclosed by the Aurelian walls. Much
of the land inside the walls was given over to grazing cattle
which browsed among the crumbling ruins. The Forum
itself became known as the *Campo Vaccino* (the cattle field).
Early mediaeval Rome lay in a state of decay, many of its
classical buildings ravaged by constant military attack or by
peacetime looting. The last Emperor to visit Rome,
Constans II in 663, ordered the removal of all the bronze
ties which secured the imperial buildings and the bronze
tiles from the Pantheon to provide military hardware, and
thus advanced the decay.[46] Initially it seems that the
Colosseum (first so called by Bede[47]) and the great
columns of the Forum were a source of fascination to

[43] Bede, Bk 4, ch. 7.
[44] Gasquet, p. 3.
[45] Barefoot, p. 22.
[46] V. Ortenberg, *The English Church and the Continent in the tenth and
      eleventh centuries: cultural, spiritual and artistic exchanges* (1992), p. 129.
[47] G. Masson, *The Companion Guide to Rome* (1965), p. 317.

Christian pilgrims.[48] Gregory the Great was allegedly in favour of destroying the remnants of imperial Rome to prevent the distraction of pilgrims' attention from the holy shrines.[49] While some of the major monuments, including the imperial triumphal arches and the great bath complexes, lay largely undisturbed, some classical sites were already being turned into churches. The library of Augustus in the Forum became S. Maria Antiqua, the Curia became the church of S. Adriano, and Hadrian's Mausoleum had been transformed into a combination of church and papal fortress.[50] Most famously, the Pantheon was transformed by Boniface IV (608–15) into the church of S. Maria ad Martyres, which, 'once its company of devils had been cast out, became a memorial to the company of saints'.[51] Gradually the only value of the classical ruins to pilgrims became their usefulness as viewing towers, for which owners charged, or as sources for trade in antiquities as a sideline.[52] The historian of the Anglo-Saxon hospice has argued stoutly that 'the motives which inspired the Anglo-Saxons to make the "Rome journey" were for the most part, of a notably spiritual character,'[53] but the notion of the purely devotional pilgrimage was evidently already more ideal than reality. The most recent study of mediaeval Roman pilgrimage suggests, albeit tentatively, 'that in some respects the pilgrim was not unlike his modern counterpart, the tourist, in that some of his time was also spent in sight-seeing'.[54]

By the end of the eighth century Rome was firmly established as a major place of pilgrimage for rich and poor, lay and clerical alike and was the recognized source of ecclesiastical authority exercised through the archbishops who received their pallium from the successor of Peter. Roman

---

[48] D. Sox, *Relics and Shrines* (1985), p. 26.
[49] Sox, p. 161.
[50] Ortenberg, p. 127.
[51] Bede, Bk 2, ch. 4.
[52] Sumption, pp. 222–3.
[53] W. J. Moore, *The Saxon Pilgrims to Rome and the Schola Saxonum* (Freiburg 1937), p. 82.
[54] D. Birch, *Pilgrimage to Rome in the Middle Ages* (1998), p. 116.

pilgrimage was unique in that pilgrims found their way to Rome not in search of miracles but to pay homage principally to Peter. There is no evidence that they came to him for miracles, and there are no accounts of cures at his intervention.[55] Roman pilgrimage was about absolution from sin. Peter was, quite simply, the doorkeeper of Heaven. Miracles were not needed to assert Peter's power – a power enhanced by the reservation of sins and granting of indulgences. Acknowledgement of this power is illustrated in a poem by Aldhelm, Bishop of Sherborne and a relative of King Ina of Wessex, supposedly written on entering the basilica of St Peter's:

> Here in this fair place,
> Peter and Paul, the lights of a dark world,
> The chief fathers who guide the reins of the people,
> Are venerated in frequent song.[56]

The cult of Peter spread quickly in post-imperial Europe among the Lombards, Visigoths, Franks and Anglo-Saxons, and in Rome itself as the popes gradually took control of the city.[57] What has been described as 'a vital step in the development of Rome as a pilgrimage centre' was the extensive alteration by Gregory the Great of the Constantinian shrine over the burial place of Peter to create an annular crypt which enabled large numbers of pilgrims to get close to the shrine in an orderly and safe fashion, by walking through close to the burial chamber below.[58] Devotion in England had extraordinary power, fuelled by the links forged by Gregory and Augustine and by the constant traffic in pilgrims, relics and ecclesiastical legislation. 'The major theme of St Peter's cult in England is thus easily identified as that of St Peter's possession of the keys, an authority interpreted as signifying the power of admission into Heaven. This view is clearly expressed in the iconography of St Peter, the only Apostle to have, in his

[55] Benedicta Ward, *Miracles and the Mediaeval Mind* (1982), p. 117.
[56] Browne, p. 206.
[57] Ortenberg, p. 130.
[58] Birch, pp. 32–3.

keys, a well-established attribute in art'.[59]

Anglo-Saxon pilgrims who sought the protection and intercession of Peter and his successors lodged in the 'Saxon' quarter of Rome, on the right bank of the Tiber at the foot of the Vatican Hill. A bull of Pope John VII (705–7) refers to a body of prominent English ecclesiastics dwelling near St Peter's. This was almost certainly a hospice, as it was separate from known theological schools, and the Vatican was two miles outside the inhabited city and of interest therefore only to pilgrims. The Anglo-Saxon hospice was probably the first, but other hospices serving pilgrims from northern Europe were known to be in existence by the 770s.[60] The precise dating of the foundation of the national hospices or *scholae* around St Peter's is impossible, but they were certainly there in some form by the end of the eighth century.[61] By then they were 'organized as civilian and military autonomous entities. Only in the course of time were they absorbed into the life of Rome.'[62]

The English pilgrims' hospice, possibly founded by King Ina of Wessex, was established in 799 in the area now occupied by the Arciospedale di S. Spirito in Sassia, in the present Borgo Santo Spirito. The early thirteenth-century chronicler, Matthew Paris, gives the traditional account of the founding of the hospice:

> When Ina arrived in Rome he built a house with the approval of Pope Gregory II which he called the school of the English (*Schola Saxonum*). This he did in order that the kings of England and the royal family with the bishops, priests and clergy might come to it to be instructed in learning and in the Catholic faith, lest anything might be taught in the English Church which was heterodox or opposed to Catholic unity. Thus they would return home thoroughly strengthened in the faith.[63]

[59] Ortenberg, p. 164.
[60] 'Saxons in Rome', *Venerabile* 14 (1949), p. 209–10.
[61] Birch, p. 132.
[62] R. Krautheimer, *Rome: Profile of a City 312–1308* (1980), p. 82.
[63] Quoted in Gasquet, p. 8.

Paris rather misunderstands the meaning of '*Schola*', and has created a misleading assumption that such national institutions in Rome were educational, rather than mainly pastoral and social. Moore's understanding of the *Schola* is rather that of a 'settlement or colony of Saxons'.[64] In the *Schola*, Ina built a church dedicated to Our Lady, where Mass could be celebrated for the English in Rome and in which those who died there could be buried. Ina is also credited by Paris with the institution of the collection of 'Peter's Pence' from every family in his kingdom. However, there is evidence that the hospice may be an earlier foundation improved upon, and that 'Peter's Pence' only later replaced personal royal gifts given on behalf of the kingdom. Only in the reign of Edward the Elder (successor to King Alfred) did Peter's Pence, or Romscot, become a legally enforceable annual tax.[65]

The '*burgus Saxonum*' gave its name to this quarter, still known locally as the Borgo. Not long after its establishment, during the reign of Paschal I (817–24), the *Schola Saxonum* was badly damaged by fire 'through the carelessness of some men of English race'.[66] The whole Saxon quarter was destroyed, but the Pope,

> noticing the need of those pilgrims which had crept in through the plotting of the devil's trickery, bestowed so many gifts and benefits for their needs, as he was ever accustomed to do; he supplied everything abundantly, gold and silver, clothing for their bodies as well as the rest of the nourishment needed. Also a quantity of trees to provide timber, so that they could restore their homes as required in the same place as they had been before.[67]

After the destruction of Rome by Saracen invasion in the mid-ninth century, the church of S. Maria in Sassia was

---

[64] Moore, p. 92.
[65] Moore, p. 101.
[66] ed. and trans. R. Davis, *The Lives of Ninth Century Popes (Liber Pontificalis)* (1995), p. 8.
[67] *Liber Pontificalis*, p. 8.

built in 850 and the *Schola Saxonum* was restored by Ethelwulf and Alfred with the support of Pope Leo IV (847–55) who 'presented three gold interwoven cloths, also four gold interwoven veils'.[68] King Burgraed of Mercia was buried there in 874. Much of the site of the *Schola Saxonum* or English Hospice is occupied by the present hospital of S. Spirito in Sassia. On the site of the church of S. Maria in Sassia stands the Renaissance church of S. Spirito in Sassia. Inside the church is an ancient image of Our Lady, certainly seventh- or eighth-century in date and reputed to have been a gift of King Ina. In the sacristy of the church are a number of seventeenth-century ceiling frescoes illustrating events in the early history of the *Schola Saxonum*. One depicts the founding of the *Schola* by Gregory II and Ina in 725, and another shows Charlemagne and Offa adding to it in 794. Offa also contributed to the 'Peter's Pence' tradition by donating to the *Schola* one silver penny for every yeoman family in his kingdom.[69]

Only the names of these places commemorate the fact that for four hundred years S. Maria in Sassia and the *Schola Saxonum* were the centre of English pilgrimage to Rome, until the property was taken over by Innocent III in 1201. English pilgrimage continued to flourish during the tenth century and first half of the eleventh century, when Rome was a battlefield of factions. By the mid-eleventh century the *Schola* consisted of a pilgrim community with considerable property, with a central, quasi-monastic organization centred on the church of S. Maria in Sassia. This church was closely linked with St Peter's and the appointment of its archpriest was reserved to the Pope himself. Burial near the keeper of the keys of Heaven was deemed a particular goal of pilgrimage and so, not surprisingly, the *Schola* administered its own burial ground.[70] The area in and around the *Schola Saxonum* was at the centre of a developing centre of population and trade, created simply by the demands of pilgrims and the

[68] *Liber Pontificalis*, p. 148.
[69] Gasquet, p. 10.
[70] Moore, pp. 109–11.

desire to make a living by meeting their needs, and

> By 1041, if not before, business must have been
> thriving: at that time a house was sold, 'with two shops
> to do business ... with a pergola and courtyard in
> front', in the Saxon compound ... in fact as early as
> 854 houses with storerooms and cellars, wells, gardens
> and vineyards extended between St Peter's and the
> river. By the mid-eleventh century, too, shopkeepers
> or innkeepers, *tabernarii*, were listed among the inhab-
> itants of the Leonine city, as were waiters or shop
> assistants, *servientes*.[71]

Traffic increased between Rome and the English church
as ecclesiastical government and spiritual authority became
more complex and centralized. From the ninth century
onwards the practice of 'reserved sins' which passed from
bishops to the Pope gradually developed and it became
common for popes themselves to hear pilgrims' confessions. While bishops struggled to keep local control of
their churches, the unique role of Rome as the privileged
source of ultimate forgiveness became widely accepted.
The most detailed account of an Anglo-Saxon pilgrimage is
that conducted by an Archbishop of Canterbury, Sigeric,
who went in 990, as tradition now demanded, to receive
the pallium from the hands of John XV. He left the only
complete record or diary of an Anglo-Saxon pilgrimage,
written by one of his retinue, probably during the journey
itself. His two-day itinerary is worth recording, not only for
its illustration of the churches of interest to an early
pilgrim, but also for the staggering number of churches
visited. Sigeric's systematic visiting of the city makes a
modern 'whistle-stop' tour appear positively relaxed.

The churches he visited reflected the most popular
pilgrim saints and relics to be venerated in Rome. In the
order in which he visited them, they were as follows:
S. Pietro, to pay homage to the Prince of the Apostles and
to venerate the most popular mediaeval relic of the

---

[71] Krautheimer, p. 266.

Veronicle (see p. 38, n.98); S. Maria in Sassia, the centre of the Saxon colony; S. Lorenzo in Lucina, which contained the relic of the gridiron on which this much-loved Roman saint was martyred; S. Valentino a Ponte Milvio, which belonged to S. Silvestro in Capite and gradually fell into decay after the thirteenth century; S. Agnese, the fourth-century basilica and mausoleum dedicated to Rome's most popular female saint and the location for the papal cere-mony of blessing the lambs which produced the wool for the pallia (a play on words – Agnes/Agnus Dei); S. Lorenzo fuori le Muri, the Constantinian basilica over the burial place of St Lawrence; S. Sebastiano ad Catacombes, built on the site where the bodies of Peter and Paul had rested during the Valerian persecution, and one of the few catacomb shrines not to be largely abandoned by this time; S. Anastasia, actually SS Vincenzo e Anastasia near Tre Fontane on Via Ostiense, the site of the martyrdom of St Paul; S. Paolo fuori le Muri, built over the martyr's burial place and a walled monastery to repel Saracen attacks; S. Bonifazio (SS Alessio e Bonifazio in Via S. Sabina), a joint Greek and Benedictine monastery, distinguished for its learning; S. Sabina, famous for its fifth-century doors carved with scenes from the Old and New Testaments; S. Maria in Cosmedin, the church of the *Schola Graeconum*; S. Cecilia in Trastevere, the site of the martyrdom of the second-century Christian virgin; S. Crisogono, one of the churches on the Vatican side of the Tiber, attached to a Greek monastery; S. Maria in Trastevere, traditionally founded by Pope Callistus on the site where a miraculous flow of oil burst from the ground on the day of Christ's birth; S. Pancrazio, a rebuilt church above a catacomb from where relics of the saint were sent by Pope Vitalian to King Oswin of Northumberland. Thus ended the first day on which the archbishop's party covered sixteen miles on horseback. On the second day they abandoned their horses and walked to S. Maria Rotondo, the temple of Agrippa converted untouched from the Pantheon of the Gods to the church dedicated to all Christian martyrs; SS Apostoli, where the relics of SS Philip and James were venerated; S. Giovanni Laterano which housed the most

important relics in Rome, including a fragment of the
True Cross and the Scala Santa, and where Sigeric had
lunch with the Pope; S. Croce in Gerusalemme, founded
by S. Helena, the mother of Constantine, to house the
relics of the Passion; S. Maria Maggiore, which housed one
of Rome's most visited and popular relics, that of the crib
from Bethlehem; S. Pietro ad Vincola, to venerate the
chains which bound Peter in prison, and S. Lorenzo in
Panisperna, also traditionally associated with the
martyrdom of St Lawrence.[72] The pattern of Sigeric's
pilgrimage (which did not, incidentally, include the
church of S. Gregorio) clearly followed common practice
among those who sought connection with Peter and the
early Christian martyrs. The English King Canute wrote in
1027, 'God has granted me the privilege of praying at the
shrines of blessed Peter and Paul and in every sanctuary
within the city of Rome. And this privilege I have sought
because wise men have told me that the apostle Peter has
received from God the power of binding and loosing and
carries the keys of Paradise.'[73] Gradually a fixed devotional
routine of a more manageable scale than Sigeric's developed, that of the 'Seven Churches'. These were S. Pietro, S.
Giovanni   Laterano,   S.   Maria   Maggiore,
S. Sebastiano ad Catacombes, S. Lorenzo fuori le Muri,
S. Paolo fuori le Muri and S. Croce in Gerusalemme, and
would be visited daily by later mediaeval pilgrims.

The Norman conquest obviously strengthened ties
between England and continental Europe, and symbolic
links are suggested by the grant to William the Conqueror
of the banner of St Peter for the Battle of Hastings.
Veneration for Peter in England is evident from the
continued attraction of Rome for pilgrims and also the
innumerable dedications of churches and monasteries in
his name and the centrality of liturgical and personal devotion to him in the life of the English church. 'The English

---

[72] F. P. Magoun, 'The Rome of Two Northern Pilgrims', *Harvard
Theological Review* 33 (1940), pp. 267–89. Details of these churches
and others popular with Anglo-Saxon pilgrims are discussed in
Ortenberg, pp. 132–48.

[73] Sumption, p. 227.

cult was underlaid by a considerable official, ecclesiastical and royal devotion to St Peter.'[74] The associations which the cult fostered with the papacy were to be a considerable source of discord in the early Norman period. The Norman kings deliberately kept themselves apart from Rome. Indeed they hindered communication with Rome and would not allow subjects to travel there without specific permission. This policy combined with the conditions in Rome brought about a steady decline in the English pilgrimage traffic. During the imperial/papal struggles of the eleventh and twelfth centuries Rome was often the site of fierce battles. The difficulties encountered by pilgrims are illustrated by the canon of the First Lateran Council in 1123, which aimed at securing safe passage for pilgrims, especially *Romipetae* – those who sought to reach the threshold of the Apostles.[75] The city (including the *Schola Saxonum*) was frequently battered, so the reluctance of pilgrims was understandable. Some, including Henry of Blois, Bishop of Winchester in 1150, Jocelin of Brakelond in 1174 and John, Bishop of Norwich, in 1176 preferred to risk a sea crossing rather than take their chance overland between Italy and the north, and in 1198 the Chapter of Canterbury claimed that they were unable to get documents to Rome because of war and bloodshed on the continent.[76] In 1162–3, Peter, Cardinal Deacon of S. Eustachio wrote to Thomas à Becket that the *Schola* was stricken with poverty and could barely support a few priests and laymen to serve pilgrims, but neither Becket nor the other English bishops were in any position to help.[77] By the end of the century the buildings were in ruins and were only rebuilt by Innocent III in 1201. He built a new hospital and placed it in the care of the Confraternity of the Holy Spirit (hence the change of name), but this was no longer an English foundation. Innocent had encouraged the founding of hospitals all over Europe to care for the increasing population. The *Schola Saxonum* had stood

[74] Ortenberg, p. 168.
[75] Birch, p. 7.
[76] Birch, pp. 50–1.
[77] Gasquet, p. 20.

derelict since before the start of his reign and with characteristic enterprise he began to gather resources, and set out his clear aim to create a hospital dedicated to the corporal works of mercy within the shadow of St Peter's. Its care for destitute mothers and babies was said to have its origins in Innocent's nightmare about fishermen pulling abandoned babies from the Tiber. The 'Baby Box' near the entrance, into which unwanted children could be placed anonymously, owes much to this tradition, but probably only dates from the fifteenth century.[78] It has been suggested, somewhat speculatively, that the decline of the *Schola Saxonum* which made way for Innocent's hospital indicates a changing pattern of pilgrimage in the late twelfth century. 'Pilgrims were perhaps less willing to live out their lives as exiles at the tomb of the Apostle but preferred instead to stay only a short time before returning to their homes.'[79]

Anglo-Roman relations by this time were dominated by the competition between royal and papal authority over the church in England. Tension increased as Rome emerged more clearly as the administrative and spiritual centre of the Christian Church in the western world. Gradually during the tenth century the cardinals, drawn from a number of countries to conduct the liturgy in the major basilicas instead of the parish priests of Rome, were given administrative functions and became papal consultors and advisers.[80] In 1059 they were constituted as papal electors. The attractions of power and influence meant that many of Europe's finest minds gathered in Rome for study and to administer the Church.

Among these was Nicholas Breakspear who came from a Hertfordshire family.[81] His father had spent time as a monk of St Alban's Abbey. Nicholas studied in France and became, eventually, Abbot of Avignon, where the community complained about his strictness. The Pope removed

---

[78] B. Bolton, 'Received in His Name: Rome's Busy Baby Box', *Studies in Church History* vol. 31 (1994), pp. 153–67.

[79] Birch, p. 141.

[80] P. Granfield, *The Papacy in Transition* (1980), p. 129.

[81] *Oxford Dictionary of Popes*, p. 174.

him, but seeing his talents for himself, made him Cardinal Bishop of Albano. Breakspear was only the second Englishman to be made a cardinal (the first being Robert Pullen in 1143). From 1150 to 1153 he was a very successful papal legate in Scandinavia and was elected Pope in 1154, taking the name of Hadrian IV. He was a person of lofty ideals, 'who displayed all the qualities of righteousness that should be associated with the Vicar of Christ upon earth'.[82] It was during his reign that the papal title of Vicar of Christ became widely accepted.

Hadrian was recognized as strong-willed and clear-sighted, resolutely determined to push the monarchical claims of the papacy against imperial dominance. He has been described as one of the stronger mediaeval popes who maintained a strong stance against Frederick Barbarossa.[83] From two contemporary accounts of Hadrian IV, Cardinal Boso (an English cleric, close confidante and possibly nephew) and John of Salisbury, he emerges as a man of forgiving nature, pleasing in appearance and judicious in speech. He was respected for his wisdom and learning and was a fine preacher with a mellow voice, but he was also a political ruler who did not flinch from a fight.

He wrested control of Rome from Arnold of Brescia and the republic by using the military power of the Emperor. While the perennial mediaeval disputes with the empire over the temporal and spiritual authority of the Pope and the source of imperial power (God or the Pope) were never far away, Hadrian was prepared to appease if necessary. He had little to do with English affairs as Pope, except perhaps fatefully to encourage Henry II to incorporate Ireland into the English realm. He had seen what Norman rule had achieved in England as well as in Sicily and southern Italy and hoped it could do the same for the wretched state of Ireland, ravaged by the Norsemen. Henry's request for papal sanction for his invasion was granted, according to John of Salisbury, though the document's existence is questionable.

[82] M. Foster Farley, 'Hadrian IV, England's Only Pope 1154–9', *History Today* 28 (1978), p. 530.
[83] Ibid.

Hadrian died suddenly in the hill town of Anagni where he had retreated for security. His body was returned to Rome and his tomb can be seen in the crypt of St Peter's. It is unusual, being constructed of red granite instead of the more usual marble. 'His death', wrote John of Salisbury, 'has perturbed all the peoples and natives of the Christian faith, but it has stirred our England which gave him birth with grief still more bitter, and has watered our country with more abundant tears. His death was a cause of sorrow to all good men but to none more than me.'[84] Apart from his simple tomb in St Peter's, the only other physical remnant of Hadrian IV in Rome may be the narthex of SS Giovanni e Paolo. The narthex is the oldest part of a mainly mediaeval church which has many later English associations, and is attributed to the work of the only English pope so far in the Church's history.

Confrontations between Church and State were commonplace in the eleventh and twelfth centuries but no clash sent stronger reverberations around Europe than that between Henry II of England and his Archbishop of Canterbury Thomas à Becket. It was the classic struggle for the independence of the English church from royal control, so Becket was vigorously supported by Pope Alexander III (1159–81). Following his quarrel with the King, Becket spent several years in exile (1164–70), during which time he was reputed to have visited Rome and the Pope. One account suggests that he taught for a time at the *Schola Graeconum* at S. Maria in Cosmedin.[85]

Becket's murder in 1170 shocked Christian Europe and he was hailed as a martyr for the freedom of the church from royal power. Hundreds of miracles were reported due to his intercession and devotion to him became immensely popular all across Europe, including in Rome where relics of him are preserved in S. Maria Maggiore. These relics were removed to Rome by the cardinal legates, Albert and Theodwin, sent to England by Alexander III to enquire into the murder and the alleged

[84] Ibid., p. 536.
[85] A. D. Tomei, 'Some Memorials of St Thomas of Canterbury in Italy', *Venerabile* 6 (1932), p. 59.

miracles. They apparently included an arm which was given to the Venerable English College by Gregory XIII.[86] Only three years after his death Thomas à Becket was canonized by Alexander III. His popularity eclipsed that of Anselm of Canterbury, whose canonization Becket himself had requested, supplying an account of his life and miracles by John of Salisbury. The ceremony took place at Segni in the Volscian hills south of Rome, where a plaque in the cathedral commemorates this symbolic act in the long-running and tense rivalry between royal and papal authority over the church in England.

By the time of Alexander III, the papal right to carry out canonization was generally acknowledged in the western church. Before the eleventh century this matter was largely left to diocesan bishops, but by 1200 papal recognition of saints had become the rule and requirements for canonization were formulated.[87] The first English saint so honoured by papal decree was Edward the Confessor, proclaimed by Pope Alexander in 1161. (Edward's devotion to the papacy was well recorded and his rebuilding of Westminster Abbey (dedicated to St Peter) was in commutation of a promised pilgrimage to Rome, which English political circumstances prevented him making.) The tendency to regulate and centralize the life of the church around the papacy is borne out in the institution of formal canonization processes. It was a means of controlling the excesses of popular devotion and the hagiography. Saints in the popular view were 'much more than captive cadavers'[88] and the hagiographers, often imitating or plagiarizing stories from one to another, built up tales of wonderful penances and austerity, charity, chastity, feats of healing and so on around their subjects. This was certainly not eradicated by papal control but at least the rationale of canonization was made clear, that martyrs and saints are honoured to give glory to the Lord they served. By the late Middle Ages the canonization process was as lengthy and costly as any other cause in the

[86] Ibid., p. 62.
[87] Ward, pp. 184–5.
[88] Finucane, p. 34.

ecclesiastical courts, employing mountains of evidence and an army of staff.[89] During the pontificate of Innocent III (1198–1216) the papacy exercised universal power, controlling the religious, social and political life of the West. The Pope was not only the successor of Peter or Vicar of Christ, but to Innocent he was 'the meeting place between God and Man'. He rejected the traditional papal title of Vicar of St Peter, and made it clear that the Pope was rather, Vicar of Christ. No restriction therefore could be placed on papal power. In 1215 he tried to control public demand for relics by insisting that all newly-found relics be authenticated by Rome, but the addiction to relic-collecting was too strong for this to be really effective. Increasingly, attempts were also made to regulate the cults of saints and to prevent the worship of saints.

During the thirteenth century, in the midst of violent struggles for control of the papacy, a second English pope became a real possibility in the person of Robert Somercote, whose memorial is in the church of S. Crisogono. The church was built in 1123 by Giovanni de Crema, Pope Honorius II's legate in England, and the present high altar dates from then. Somercote's memorial is difficult to find and almost impossible to read, due to its position near a spotlight. It is a small plaque above the door in the left aisle and reads (in translation), 'Here rests in the Lord, Robert of happy memory, Cardinal Deacon of S. Eustachius, Englishman, who died on 26 September 1241'.[90]

The chronicler Matthew Paris described Somercote as the most eminent of the cardinals and he was a strong candidate at the papal conclave of 1241. He was educated in Bologna, and in England came under the patronage of Archbishop Stephen Langton. He may have been confessor to King Henry III. Entering the service of the papal Curia, he was appointed cardinal by Gregory IX (1227–41) in 1238 and given the titular church of S. Eustachius. He is said to have defended the faith of the English against accusations brought before the Pope.

[89] Finucane, ch. 2 *passim.*
[90] Translation from H. Vidon, *The Pilgrim's Guide to Rome: discovering links with past English-speaking pilgrims and residents* (1975), p. 143.

Somercote was the only cardinal who did not abandon Gregory in his violent struggle with the Emperor Frederick II. When imperial troops invaded Rome, the Pope fled accompanied by Somercote to Spoleto, where he died. The conclave which followed was a bizarre affair. Held in the midst of crisis, only twelve cardinals were able to attend the conclave and Cardinal Orsini, effectively dictator of Rome, kept the cardinals imprisoned for sixty days in appallingly squalid conditions. Somercote died during the conclave and was widely rumoured to have been poisoned to prevent his election. The elected candidate (Celestine IV) was also sick during the conclave and reigned for only sixteen days.

The climax of universal papal power came half a century later with the promulgation of the Bull *Unam Sanctam* (1302) by Boniface VIII (1294–1303) which asserted that subjection to the Roman Pontiff was necessary for salvation. Not surprisingly, therefore, the routes to Rome from the north became busier. The average journey from England in the thirteenth century took six weeks on horseback and much longer on foot.[91] The first Holy Year or Jubilee, declared by Boniface VIII in 1300, gave an enormous boost to Roman pilgrimage. Two million pilgrims were said to have visited Rome that year and similar exaggerated claims were made for subsequent mediaeval Holy Years.[92] Conditions were hopelessly overcrowded and provisions and accommodation expensive. Many people were trampled in the crowds and a monk of St Mary's Abbey, York, named William of Derby was killed in the crush of people venerating the Veronicle during the Holy Year.[93] The popular enthusiasm which apparently led to the calling of the Holy Year was indicative of an upturn in the popularity of Roman pilgrimage. Popes of the thirteenth century, from Innocent III onwards, had been at pains to promote Rome's relics, grant special indulgences and encourage pilgrims to go there, especially after the

---

[91] Barefoot, p. 32.
[92] Sox, p. 26.
[93] Brentano, *Rome Before Avignon* (1990), p. 54.

loss of Jerusalem to Muslim power in 1244.[94]

It became well established that the primary purpose of pilgrimage was to seek the holy, concretely embodied in a sacred place, a relic or a privileged image.[95] While such localization of holiness was often criticized in the late Middle Ages, by Thomas à Kempis among others, it is obvious that despite plagues and the Avignon papacy, 'mediaeval man went to Rome, Canterbury and Santiago de Compostela to be forgiven and blessed at the shrines of the holy'.[96] It was important to bring back mementos then as much as now, to prove that one had completed the arduous journey.

Rome was already, or was about to be, a city in which salesmen at booths around the Vatican – booths on the stairs, in the portico, and beneath the Navicella – sold painted replicas of the Veronicle, as well as figs and tooth extractions. Also at the Vatican, within the boothed periphery, pilgrims could procure lead or tin badges with the images of St Peter and St Paul on them; the pilgrims got these badges, which would show that they had been to the doorstep of the apostles, from the canons of St Peter's whose monopoly in their manufacture had been confirmed by Innocent III.[97]

The pilgrim badge had become, by the twelfth century, the prized mark of a pilgrimage completed. Each pilgrimage shrine had its distinctive badge, the palm leaf of the Holy Land, the cockleshell of Santiago de Compostela being the best known. Rome was late in developing its own badge and they took several forms, either the keys of Peter, alone or with the sword of Paul, or Rome's best-loved relic, the Veronicle.[98] Pilgrim badges and religious souvenirs were

---

[94] Birch, pp. 199–202.
[95] E. Duffy, *The Stripping of the Altars* (1993), p. 191.
[96] Sox, p. 21.
[97] Brentano, p. 54.
[98] The cloth believed to have been used by Veronica to wipe the face of Jesus, on his way to Calvary. Birch, pp. 77–9.

not the only trade made possible by the increasing tide of pilgrims to an area of Rome still remote from the main inhabited areas of the mediaeval city. The streets around St Peter's had become a bustling, hustling centre of activity, crowded with traders and customers, sources of all the necessities of life for the pilgrim and a major business centre.

> Money changers, as one would expect, crowded near the basilica by the twelfth century and probably long before; by the early fourteenth century they had set up forty-nine stands, all owned by great Roman families, on parts of the square and atrium steps. Along their stands, the straw vendors, ever since the twelfth century or earlier, provided bedding. In the atrium of St Peter's booksellers had set up their stalls; one fourteenth-century bookdealer was a Jew. Along the streets of the square were the booths of the vendors of religious souvenirs, the painters of icons and ex-votos, the sellers of phials – filled, one assumes, with oil from the lamps burning near St Peter's tomb – goldsmiths and rosary-makers; the cobblers, cloth merchants, and sellers of purses; and the small merchants of *generi alimentari*, fruit vendors, vegetable dealers, vendors of oil and spices, fishmongers. Indeed, as early as the mid-thirteenth century the tradespeople had invaded the steps leading to St Peter's, the atrium, the narthex, and even the interior of the church, apparently with the consent of the canons in charge, who drew fat rents from them ... In short, by the high Middle Ages, the square in front of the church and the atrium and its steps had become one big bazaar.[99]

---

[99] Krautheimer, pp. 266–7.

Chapter Three

The Mediaeval Heyday

Pilgrimage in the mediaeval period became formalized in the circuit of shrines to be visited and in the ritual of departure. The parish gathered at the local church for the celebration of the Mass and for the blessing of the departing pilgrims with the recitation of psalms and sprinkling of holy water. Guilds would often accompany their pilgrim members out of town and provide alms for the journey.[1] The familiar pattern of devotions which developed during the mediaeval period was built around the seven principal churches of Rome and their relics – S. Pietro (the tomb of Peter and the Veronicle), S. Maria Maggiore (the crib), S. Giovanni Laterano (the Scala Santa), S. Paolo fuori le Muri (the tomb of St Paul), S. Lorenzo fuori le Muri (the gridiron), S. Sebastiano (the catacombs), and Santa Croce (the Passion relics). These seven seem to have been a well-established circuit from earliest times, based on the huge importance of relics. Mediaeval piety was dominated by relics and 'the richness of Rome as reliquary made it a constant festa'.[2] A book on the Seven Churches published in 1694 describes it as 'a pilgrimage peradventure the most celebrated after Calvary and the Sepulchre of Christ'.[3]

By the early thirteenth century the system of indulgences

[1] R. Finucane, *Miracles and Pilgrims: Popular Beliefs in Medieval England* (1977), pp. 41–2.

[2] R. Brentano, *Rome Before Avignon* (1990), p. 85.

[3] R. Delaney, 'The Seven Churches', *Venerabile* 6 (1932), p. 379.

had become established, by which the Church administered the 'store' of merit gained by Christ and the saints
for the benefit of the penitent. Indulgences became available to those who went on pilgrimage and visited shrines
and could become a source of competition and rivalry
between popes, religious orders and sodalities. The system
had begun under Gregory the Great and by the mid-twelfth
century indulgences could be obtained at all forty of the
Roman Lent 'Station Churches'. Gerald of Wales gained all
the station indulgences on his visit in 1195.[4] He maintained that, of all pilgrimages, the Welsh preferred to go to
Rome and that having reached St Peter's they prayed most
devoutly.[5] Such indulgences were hard-earned. Gerald
made three pilgrimages in all; in 1199 taking a circuitous
route to avoid trouble, and in 1203 with great difficulty
escaping the mobs of Frankish robbers and royal officials
only too happy to arrest enemies of Philip Augustus, who
was at war with King John over the succession to the throne
of England.[6] Plenary indulgences (remission of full
temporal punishment due to sin) could be gained by
pilgrims visiting the Roman basilicas in a Holy Year. It was
the indulgence system which first gave rise to the publication of guide books to Christian Rome. There already
existed, for the benefit of travellers, accounts of the
remains of ancient Rome under various forms known as
the *Mirabilia Urbis Romae* (The Wonders of the City of
Rome). This ran into numerous editions and one of its
more sophisticated readers was an Englishman, Master
Gregory, who visited Rome at the beginning of the thirteenth century and wrote his own account, *De Mirabilibus
Romae*. He was impressed by the classical buildings and the
remains of the Roman water system, but did not swallow all
that the guidebooks contained and was contemptuous of
the unlettered pilgrims who did.[7]

4   Sumption, p. 230.
5   G. Williams, 'Poets and Pilgrims in fifteenth–sixteenth century
    Wales', *Transactions of the Honourable Society of Cymridorion* (1992–3),
    p. 80.
6   D. Birch, *Pilgrimage to Rome in the Middle Ages* (1998), pp. 51–2.
7   Sumption, p. 225.

However, as the indulgence system developed, pilgrims needed lists of the shrines and indulgences or spiritual value attached to each. This need was met by the *Libri Indulgentiarum*. The most famous *Liber* was the *Stacyons of Rome*, which was evidently popular, having survived in six editions. It has been described as a sort of mediaeval advertisement commending the value of pilgrimage to Rome as against Jerusalem or Santiago de Compostela.[8] The *Stacyons of Rome* dates from about 1370, but other *Libri Indulgentiarum* were in existence from the beginning of the fourteenth century. From the end of the fourteenth century new editions of these works in verse or prose came out in every major language. At the same time books of a more personal kind, but appealing to the same market, began to appear. The most famous English guide was John Capgrave's *Ye Solace of Pilgrims* (1450), which built upon both the *Mirabilia* and the *Libri Indulgentiarum*. The fifteenth century also saw an upsurge in the Celtic tradition of religious literature, manifested in poetry about pilgrimage.

> Pilgrimages were one of the most highly prized ways of showing devotion to the extraordinarily well-loved cults of the saints and seeking the latter's favours. So assured a place had they in the affections of the populace that it was inevitable that they should find an honoured and secured niche in the most distinctive form of native expression – the contemporary verse.[9]

Welsh poems referring to the Roman pilgrimage at this period are numerous. One poet of 1480 commented that Rome was 'a privileged place for pilgrims even though the way there was long and hard', and there were certainly Welsh-language versions of *Libri Indulgentiarum*.[10]

Other hospices beside that of S. Maria in Sassia developed to serve the pilgrim, including St Bartholomew's on Tiber Island. Here, one English pilgrim, Rahere, the court

[8]   J. R. Hulbert, 'Some Mediaeval Advertisements of Rome', *Modern Philology* 20 (1922–3), pp. 403–24.
[9]   G. Williams, p. 72.
[10]   Ibid., p. 85.

jester of Henry II, stayed during his pilgrimage. He contracted malaria like many others and was nursed back to health at S. Bartolomeo. As a thanksgiving on his return to London he built a priory for the Canons Regular of St Augustine, with a hospital attached – now the famous London teaching hospital of Bart's. Rahere is buried in the church of St Bartholomew the Great in London. Hospices were not always numerous enough to cope with all the pilgrims and, inevitably, serving the pilgrim trade became a business venture providing a major source of the city's revenue. In the thirteenth century the greed of pilgrim lodging-keepers had to be controlled by statute. One of the senators, Angelo Malabranca heard that innkeepers around St Peter's were violently forcing pilgrims into their lodgings – even after they had quietly settled down for the night elsewhere! He issued an edict in 1235 permitting pilgrims to stay where they wished and buy their provisions wherever they chose. Anyone forcing them to do otherwise was heavily fined.[11] The English pilgrims may well have been among those who were victims of such extortion after the loss of the English hospice in 1201. A group of English priests continued to live in Rome and serve the church of S. Pantaleo which lay in Rione del Parione near Via Arenula. Its modern site is in the corner of the Corso Vittorio Emmanuele near the Museo di Roma. This site was possibly given by the Pope to the remaining residents of the *Schola Saxonum* as recompense for the loss of their property. It remained in the hands of English priests until 1243 and was in the area of Rome which became known as the English quarter, where the later hospice was founded in 1362. There is no evidence of S. Pantaleo being used as a hospice.[12]

The year 1350 saw another jubilee year, which was an immense success despite the absence of the papacy in Avignon and attempts to stop English and French pilgrims going to Rome. This is the clearest indication that the mediaeval pilgrim was not particularly interested in the

[11] Brentano, p. 55.

[12] B. Linares, 'The Origin and Foundation of the English Hospice', *Venerabile* 21 (1962 Sexcentenary Volume), pp. 17–18.

presence of the Pope. His absence did not stem the tide of pilgrims to the shrine of Peter, and when in residence, there are no accounts of pilgrims seeking audience. A hospice serving some English pilgrims existed from about that year in Trastevere, under the care of the Chapter of the church of S. Crisogono. The hospice stood on the site of 22 Via Genovesi, at the corner of the modern Viale Trastevere.[13] The area has long since been rebuilt and no trace of the hospice building survives.

In 1396 John Whyte, a wealthy English merchant resident in Rome, offered to restore the dilapidated buildings for the use of poor pilgrims. The Chapter accepted the offer and gave use of the property to him and his heirs in perpetuity. In 1397 John Whyte made over his house in the Arenula district to the hospice, which provided much of its income. The house was on the site of the present Palazzo Farnese and was evidently large and valuable. In the middle years of the fifteenth century it was used as the residence of the King's Proctor, appointed by the monarchs to handle business in the Roman Curia. Whyte probably died in 1405 and may have been buried in S. Crisogono.[14]

There was a cluster of Holy Years at the end of the fourteenth and early fifteenth centuries, with one in 1390, as a result of Urban VI's decision to hold them every thirty-three years, in commemoration of Jesus' age at his death. This was a blatant attempt to win round Roman support for the papacy after the return from Avignon. 1390 was a delayed 1383 celebration, but was a fiasco due to the continued presence of anti-popes and the consequent division of Europe. In 1400 the presence of groups of religious fanatics, mystics of a bizarre kind and flagellants aroused considerable interest. There were said to be 120,000 of them in Rome for the Holy Year, advocating for the first time as part of the Jubilee, peace and reconciliation, freeing prisoners and conciliating enemies. This was not an aspect of the tradition which became mainstream. 1400 was also the first time when the term 'Holy Year' began to

[13] Vidon, p. 142.

[14] J. Ibbet, 'The Hospice of St Edmund in Trastevere', *Venerabile* (1962), p. 85.

supplant that of 'Jubilee', though there are those who decline to count 1400 as a true Holy Year in the sequence, since no Bull of Proclamation exists, but there is evidence of Jubilee pilgrimages. Nevertheless, in 1423, Martin V did not miss the opportunity to count thirty-three years from 1390. One has an inescapable sense that these Jubilees were more about papal standing and popularity and Roman incomes than about repentance and charity. Jubilee was a focus of ill-will and animosity between the locals, who were fed up with the disorder in the city and the pilgrims who were fed up with being ripped off, so the need for pilgrim hospices like those for the English was a very real one.

The hospice of St Edmund, known as the *Hospitalis Anglicorum*, was served by an English and Welsh confraternity which quickly merged with that running the hospice of St Thomas in Via Monserrato after 1362. After the decline in the number of pilgrims during the Reformation, the lease on St Edmund's was taken over by a Roman Archconfraternity of Charity (1602). The chapel remained open and was served from the English College until 1664.[15] St Edmund's in the fourteenth century was clearly not able to meet the needs of the growing number of English pilgrims to Rome. The 1350 Holy Year highlighted the need, when many visitors had difficulty finding reasonable accommodation. As Parks commented, 'It was the turn of the laity ... to look after pilgrims.'[16]

This was done by means of a Guild of English residents through the good offices of John and Alice Shepherd, rosary sellers, who enabled the setting up of the new English hospice in Via Monserrato. The rosary sellers (who presumably, like modern-day traders in the pilgrimage market, sold all manner of souvenirs) were numerous in Rome and clustered around Via dei Coronari, conveniently near the Via Pellegrino which took the pilgrims from the Lateran to St Peter's. The Shepherds' ownership of property suggests that the pilgrim trade was a successful one in which to make money. The society or guild existed before

15 Ibid., p. 91.
16 G. B. Parks, *The English Traveller to Italy* (Rome, 1954), p. 358.

1362 and decided to buy a house to provide for pilgrims in the city and to shelter the 'poor, infirm, needy and wretched persons from England'.[17] The Shepherds sold their property to the Guild in 1362 and offered their services to care for the pilgrims who stayed there. There was a tradition (almost certainly legendary) that a young pregnant woman walking necessarily slowly had become detached from her fellow pilgrims, became lost in the woods above the hospital of S. Spirito and been torn to death by wolves. The childless Shepherds were allegedly so moved by the story that they determined to do something. However fanciful the legend, it conveys the danger and discomfort of mediaeval pilgrimage and the Shepherds' familiarity with it. By 1383 the hospice had five houses in a row and three plots of land. Two of the houses were substantial properties, one having a tower and its own well, and all of them had gardens.[18] The last house was acquired by the will of John Palmer, an English pilgrim. His was one of the fifteen known English wills proved in Rome between 1368 and 1445 which benefited the hospice.[19] It was soon joined administratively by the Trastevere hospice of St Edmund and the two hospices combined into a single unit.

In the late fourteenth century there appears to have been a resident English colony in Rome of at least a hundred, most of whom lived in and around the Rione Parione or Arenula.[20] They mostly made a living as merchants, cobblers or rosary sellers (who were numerous), though English carpenters, tailors and goldsmiths could also be found. This began to change in the fifteenth century as lawyers, curial officials and diplomats gradually supplanted the tradesmen, both as local residents and as members of the hospice confraternity.[21] However the heyday of papal employment for the English was probably under Urban VI and Boniface IX

[17]   Quoted in *Venerabile* (1962), p. 27.
[18]   J. Allen, 'Englishmen in Rome and the Hospice', *Venerabile* (1962), p. 54.
[19]   Ibid.
[20]   Ibid., pp. 46–7.
[21]   Ibid., p. 48.

(1378–1404).[22] After the end of the schism things changed, but there was a continuous presence of Englishmen in the Curia. Some occupied their time studying law to fit them for employment. Others lingered in Rome without permanent employment, in the hope of a post and absorbed the atmosphere of humanist culture which shaped the Renaissance. Nevertheless, the curial Englishmen were very few in number by the mid-fifteenth century despite England's broadly pro-papal attitudes. The significant Englishmen in Rome in 1422 may have numbered only seventy-five, but by 1433 were as few as twenty, partly due to the gradual 'Italianization' of the Curia.[23]

Among the English churchmen whose talents obtained him a post in the Curia was Robert Easton, whose tomb is to be found in S. Cecilia. His memorial, near the entrance, bears much later decoration and a wholly inaccurate inscription. Easton was never Bishop of London, as the memorial states. The original inscription ran as follows, 'In this church lies a father famed in all the arts, a great theologian, and cardinal. England gave him a country, this blessed edifice of the Church a title and death at last a home. 1397.'[24]

Easton's is a painful story of a victim of papal ambition and cruelty in the worst days of the mediaeval papacy under the schism of 1378–1417.[25] He was a Benedictine monk of Norwich Abbey, who studied at Oxford and gained a reputation as a scholar of Greek and Hebrew. He was recalled from Oxford in 1356 to help in preaching and in 'silencing the mendicants', which made him familiar with controversy, particularly over apostolic poverty, endowments and disendowments with the Franciscans. In 1366 he was back in Oxford as Prior of Students, but two years later he accompanied Archbishop Langham to Rome

[22] M. Harvey, *England, Rome and the Papacy 1417–64: the study of a relationship* (1993), p. 26.
[23] Ibid., p. 42.
[24] H. Vidon, *The Pilgrim's Guide to Rome: discovering links with past English speaking pilgrims and residents* (1975), p. 139.
[25] *Oxford Dictionary of Popes*, p. 228.

to oppose Wycliffe's appeal against dismissal. Easton wrote a treatise against Wycliffe and Lollardy as well as a life of St Bridget, a Latin translation of the Bible and numerous works of controversy. After a brief return to England with letters for Edward III, he settled in Rome where he was appointed cardinal by Urban VI in 1381. His titular church was S. Cecilia and at the same time he was nominated by the Pope as Dean of York.

From then on, Easton's successful career became a nightmare. In 1384 Urban VI moved the Curia to Nocera, when the anti-Pope Clement VII invaded the Papal States. There the quarters were cramped and life for the curial cardinals, who were effectively prisoners, was very unpleasant. The Pope's manic behaviour gave rise to plotting among the cardinals to form a council of regency. Urban's 'main preoccupation was a petty, endlessly shifting struggle, punctuated by explosions indicative of his mental instability, over the Kingdom of Naples which he wished to secure for a worthless nephew'.[26] Easton and five other cardinals were brought before the Pope, accused of plotting, imprisoned and tortured. The Emperor Charles IV, in league with the cardinals, besieged Nocera. Urban escaped to Genoa but took with him his six miserable prisoners, continuing their torture at every opportunity.

Five of the cardinals were executed at Genoa. Easton survived by smuggling a letter to the English Benedictines, who went immediately to the King. England had continued to support Urban's papacy against rival claims, so a royal plea for clemency was heeded. Urban released Easton, but stripped him of all his titles and dignities. One of the first acts of Urban's successor, Boniface IX in 1389, was to restore Easton to his office and benefices and to write him a letter of commendation to England. After returning briefly to his native country, Easton settled in Rome where he died on 15 September 1397.

In the meantime the English hospice, founded by the Guild in 1362 was dedicated to the Blessed Trinity and St Thomas the Martyr (i.e. Becket) and grew quickly in status.

---

[26] Ibid.

From the earliest days it was known as 'the hospice of the English' and seems to have been maintained in an orderly fashion despite the general decay and disorder of Rome surrounding it.

The earliest surviving account (and the only pre-Reformation account) of an English pilgrim to Rome who stayed at the hospice was that of Margery Kempe, an East Anglian mystic and contemporary of Julian of Norwich.[27] She was in Rome from August 1414 to Easter 1415 and clearly made an impact. Her religious enthusiasm was often expressed noisily and exuberantly, getting on the nerves of her fellow pilgrims. Some would not have her company for a hundred pounds and others tried to be rid of her by abandoning her in Venice. However she was rescued and proceeded to Rome where she was received at Via Monserrato, 'and there she received communion every Sunday with great weeping, violent sobbing and loud crying and was highly beloved by the Master of the hospital and all his brethren'.[28] Her fellow pilgrims were less sympathetic and had her put out of the hospice and refused the sacraments. However, she gradually won round both the Romans and her fellow countrymen by her great works of charity in the city and evident piety. News of this reached the hospice and the Master and brethren 'asked her if she would go to them again, and she should be more welcome than she ever was before, because they were very sorry that they had barred her from them'.[29]

Rome and the hospice began to recover from the effects of the schism in the second half of the fifteenth century and rebuilding began in Via Monserrato in 1449. By a grant of Eugenius IV in 1445, the hospice had its own burial ground and its chaplain had the right to hear confessions of all but reserved sins. In the mid-fifteenth century it had a chapel with splendid and expensive fittings, a women's chamber, a nobles' and a poor men's chamber. All pilgrims were to be sheltered for three days, the poor for eight days and the sick were kept until death

27 *The Book of Margery Kempe* (Penguin Classics, 1985).
28 *The Book of Margery Kempe*, p. 116.
29 Ibid., p. 130.

or recovery.[30] This ordered hospitality continued until the late eighteenth century.

By 1450 there were allegedly 1022 pilgrim hostels in Rome, but many of them were too expensive for the average pilgrim. The popes (along with their patronage) were firmly placed back in Rome and stability had been recovered. Pilgrimage was boosted by this and by the arrival of 'new' relics including those of St Monica from Ostia and the huge popularity of the Veronicle.[31] A Welsh pilgrim poet Robin Leia devoted his account of Rome mainly to this pure white cloth ('*ylliain purwyn*')[32] and it was often portrayed instead of the classic crossed keys on the pilgrim badges worn by those who had completed the journey. 1450 was also a jubilee year and reckoned one of the more successful of the mediaeval Holy Years, with an estimated 40,000 pilgrims a day pouring into Rome.[33]

No records survive of the number of English pilgrims attending in the Holy Year. It was a year of unrest in England and plague broke out in Rome in midsummer. With the hospice half rebuilt and apparently gaining something of a reputation for inhospitality, 1450 may not have been a bumper year for English pilgrims.[34] However, 1450 did see one remarkable English visitor to Rome, the Augustinian Friar John Capgrave who published that year *Ye Solace of Pilgrims*. He made notes as he toured Rome and included a good deal of information on the contemporary state of Rome.[35] Among the curiosities he describes was the story of the building of the Pantheon dome, which was done by filling the inside with earth in which money was buried. When the dome was complete the Romans were invited to carry away as much soil as they wished and keep the money they found. Capgrave says that he saw a vault built in the English hospice in the same way.[36]

[30] Harvey, p. 54.
[31] Sumption, pp. 250–1.
[32] G. Williams, p. 87.
[33] Parks, p. 354.
[34] *Venerabile* (1962), pp. 58–9.
[35] Harvey, pp. 62–3.
[36] G. Hay, 'Pilgrims and the Hospice', *Venerabile* (1962), p. 330.

The number of pilgrims in the fifteenth century became so large, even outside jubilee years, that the handling of their transportation became an attractive business venture and royal licences were eagerly sought. As one scathing commentator remarked in relation to an appeal to Henry VI for a licence to carry pilgrims, 'Pilgrims at this time were really an article of exportation. Ships were every year loaded from different ports with cargoes of these deluded wanderers, who carried with them large sums of money to defray the expense of their journey.'[37]

The Holy Year of 1500 marked a significant development in the practice and in the spiritual symbolism attached to the Jubilee. It was on this occasion that the event which has come to symbolize above all the meaning of Jubilee was first enacted – the opening of a Holy Door. Gates or doors of course are used in scriptural imagery and were important in the liturgy of the early church. A public sinner was not allowed to pass within the gates and a repentant sinner was met at the gate and reintroduced to the community by the bishop. Catechumens were kept beyond the gate until their entry into full communion. There was some reference to opening of doors and holy doors in 1450, but for the first time at Christmas 1499, Alexander VI carried out the formal ceremony of opening the Holy Door of St Peter's, marking a recovery of the links with the Hebrew tradition of Jubilee. The prayers were taken from Scripture and the Hebrew jubilee year, including Psalm 118, 'Open for me the gates of righteousness, this is the gate of the Lord ...'. Not only did this add to the solemnity of Holy Year, but gave it a biblical resonance that seems to have been largely lacking in previous occasions. The other great feature of 1500 was the installation of Michelangelo's Pietà in St Peter's. These late mediaeval Holy Years and the presence of collection boxes outside the Holy Door, combined with the sight of St Peter's vergers collecting money from around the high altar with rakes, combined to provoke many of the reformers' critiques of pilgrimage, indulgence selling and

---

[37] Quoted in C. Howard, *English Travellers of the Renaissance* (1914), pp. 3–4.

the ways of Rome. Luther commented acidly that the Holy
or Golden Door was so called because it brought so much
gold to the pope.

The English hospice was at the peak of its splendour,
prosperity and popularity by the time of the last mediaeval
jubilee of 1500, although it could only accommodate a
relatively small proportion of the pilgrims. That year 750
English pilgrims were received. The hospice could sleep a
little over a hundred people; those who could not be
accommodated would be given money. The greatest
number of guests recorded in this period was 169 present
on Passion Sunday 1525. A distinction was made between
nobiles and *pauperes*. The former would include clergy,
professional men, ship's captains, merchants and gentry –
many would be in Rome on business but would combine it
with pilgrimage. The *pauperes* who were accommodated
separately and in poorer conditions included small
tradesmen, servants and some sailors. The sick were also
catered for and indeed buried in the hospice cemetery.
Eighteen victims of plague were buried there in 1482.[38]
Residents in the hospice were given meat every day but
Friday and Saturday, which were days of abstinence, and in
Lent they were given fish every day. Wine was provided
from the hospice's own vineyards, though imported from
further afield for festive occasions.

On the patronal feast of St Thomas, all the English in
Rome were entertained to a festive meal and solemn High
Mass. An imaginative recreation of the scene, based on
college records and accounts, evokes a flavour of the occasion.

> The church was a feast of colour in cloth and drapings
> and in painting. Everything possible was done to add
> to the glory of the scene on such occasions as the feast
> of St Thomas. For the celebrant there was 'a rede
> cheseble braynched with gold with a very fyne albe
> and ames and stole and fanne [maniple]' with tuni-
> cles and apparelled amice and alb to match for two

[38] *Venerabile* (1962), p. 102.

other ministers. If a bishop he would wear the hospice mitre 'set with perys and counterset stonys estymed at 150 docketts'. Hired trumpeters in the organ loft sounded forth as he entered, and the church in its festive robes of all colours seemed to join in the fanfare. Twenty hangings emblazoned with various coats of arms festooned the walls, while on each side of the church were suspended seven banners bearing the arms of England. Above, the ceiling was ornamented with a regular design. From the beam ends painted heads of saints looked down, while here and there the arms of England stood out in relief and colour ... As the bishop walked up the aisle he would see before him the high altar with its own curtains and frontlets. Highest above it hung a red cloth or baldachin with a yellow lining. Below on the front of the altar, were two cloths of green silk lined with blue, wrought with images of the life of St Thomas. At the foot of the altar stood two great candlesticks, over seven feet high, made of polished latten. On the altar itself were two others of latten about three feet high, and also eight small candles of wood, carved and painted white and gold. The missal rested on a cushion of tawny silk. If John Sherwood, Bishop of Durham and Chamberlain of the hospice, was pontificating, he would probably have used one of the old handwritten Sarum missals, rather than a modern printed one ... Sherwood may well have used the costly chalice of silver and gilt, weighing twenty ounces one quarter, presented by the Duchess of York. It was not as heavy or valuable as that given by the Abbot of Abingdon, but the rank of the donor made it worthy to be used on such occasions ... After Mass on St Thomas's day the whole congregation would retire to the hall. Beakers and glasses stood on a credence just inside the door. The high table was arrayed with the plate of the hospice, candlesticks of silver, again given by the Duchess of York, and also a basin of silver with a rose engraved on the bottom. There was wine from Corsica, Terracina and Calabria;

as the bishop drained his cup he would read on the bottom '*Vinum laetificat cor*'.[39]

The desire for learning, encouraged by the spread of humanism, added a new dimension to pilgrimage and England gradually took up an educational justification for travel to replace the religious one. Erasmus was drawn to Rome and tempted to stay by the learned company he found there. English humanists all headed for Italy. Indeed, 'whoever had keen wits, an agile mind, imagination, yearned for Italy.'[40] Humanist ideals flourished in England even as they began to go into decline in Italy. Henry VII's foundation of the Savoy Hospital was modelled on Italian foundations, as was Colet's school of St Paul's. One of the earliest English humanists to make an impact in Rome was John Free, son of a Bristol merchant, who gained most of his education in Italy and arrived in Rome in the early 1460s. He presented the Pope with the first Latin translation of a rare Greek work on dreams by Synesius of Cyrene. His reward for this was to be appointed Bishop of Bath and Wells, but Free died in Rome before taking up his appointment.[41] Among the confraternity members in the last decade of the fifteenth century were some of the leading names of English humanism: Thomas Linacre, the classicist and physician; William Warham, later Archbishop of Canterbury; Giovanni Giglis, poet and later Bishop of Worcester; John Colet, Dean of St Paul's and William Lily who taught classics at St Paul's and was a close friend of Colet, Linacre and Thomas More.[42] The last years of the fifteenth century seem to have been something of a golden summer for the English in Rome before a sharp winter set in. By 1525 the recorded number of pilgrims had dropped to 439.[43]

Pilgrimage had never been without its critics and the

[39] Ibid., pp. 107–8.
[40] Ibid.
[41] R. J. Mitchell, *John Free: from Bristol to Rome in the fifteenth century* (1955), *passim.*
[42] V. Flynn, 'William Lily and the English Hospice', *Venerabile* 9 (1938), pp. 1–11.
[43] *Venerabile* (1962), p. 330.

motives of pilgrims were questioned by those who objected to the expense and abandonment of responsibilities at home. In the late mediaeval period, the huge popularity of the devotions such as the Five Wounds of Christ, the Compassion of Christ and especially Corpus Christi drew some attention away from the saints to the figure of Christ himself and the Eucharist. The feast of Corpus Christi spread rapidly through a number of channels and was popular in French and German dioceses before receiving official Roman approbation. It was encouraged in the late thirteenth and early fourteenth centuries by both the Cistercians and Dominicans, whose influence on European religious culture was immense.[44] Pilgrimage also became suspect for stimulating curiosity about the world, which in the eyes of some spiritual writers (such as the influential Thomas à Kempis) was a dangerous thing.[45] Only gradually did travel and the desire to know more of the world become respectable, but it also became separated from an increasingly internalized spiritual life.[46] The first well-documented English tours of Europe undertaken in an entirely secular spirit date from the late 1540s, and the first Italian grammar book in English was published in 1550.[47]

The shift from an outdoor religion to an indoor one was encouraged by Erasmus's drawing a distinction between the outward activity of travelling to shrines and the internal spiritual cultivation of Christian character. 'You wish to deserve well of Peter and Paul? Imitate the faith of one, the charity of the other – and you will thereby do more than if you were to dash back and forth to Rome ten times.'[48] These views naturally influenced practice in England though Erasmus's great friend Thomas More wrote often in defence of pilgrimage. In his *Apology*, written in 1533, he describes those who 'murmur against chantries ... pardons and pilgrimages' as having 'an inward hatred unto the profit of men's souls,

[44] M. Rubin, *Corpus Christi: the Eucharist in late Medieval Culture* (1991), p. 180.
[45] Thomas à Kempis, *Imitation of Christ*, Bk IV, 1.8.
[46] J. J. Scarisbrick, *The Reformation and the English People* (1984), p. 163.
[47] E. Chaney, *The Evolution of the Grand Tour* (1998), p. 61.
[48] Quoted in J. G. Davies, *Pilgrimage Yesterday and Today* (1988), p. 93.

beside the envy that they bear to priests'.[49] Luther moved into a fiercely antagonistic position and in 1538 Henry VIII ordered all who had spoken in favour of pilgrimage to retract.

Some holy places declined in attractiveness, though Becket's shrine at Canterbury retained enormous popularity. Many older shrines continued to draw pilgrims though, it has been suggested, less in search of physical healing than for spiritual comfort and for less overtly 'religious' reasons.[50] New shrines came into being, following traditional patterns; some flourished, some lapsed into obscurity. In the shifting fashion of piety, pilgrimage became more associated with Christ and his mother, though many of the older beliefs in miracles and indulgences were carried over. Cult centres of Christ and the Virgin could be simply erected in local churches, but it remained true that 'for many people, the idea of a physical journey on earth was still stronger than the ideal, contemplative ascent to the eternal Christian truths.'[51]

Diplomatic and royal links between England and Rome had become stronger as a result of the mediaeval power struggles of the papacy. It was traditional that English kings were honorary canons of S. Paolo fuori le Muri and that abbots of that monastery were prelates of the Order of the Garter, but in the fifteenth century the exchanges became more than symbolic. Between 1417 and 1467 the English took to keeping a King's Proctor in the Roman Curia to deal with ecclesiastical appointments and by 1464 the office was becoming regarded as permanent.[52] These proctors were often associated with the hospice, and Robert Fitzhugh (1433) and Andrew Holes (1434–40) both lived in the house left by John Whyte, then part of the property of St Thomas's hospice. The next proctor, William Grey (1446) was one of the loan guarantors for the rebuilding of the hospice and he played a great part in its running.[53]

[49]   Thomas More, *The Apology* (Yale edition ed, J. B. Trapp, 1979), p. 73.
[50]   Finucane, p. 195.
[51]   Ibid., p. 196.
[52]   Harvey, p. 8.
[53]   Harvey, pp. 13–14.

The hospice became the one institution which drew all the English ambassadors, agents and envoys together. Part of its role was as a centre through which all Englishmen, whether on business, study or pilgrimage circulated.[54]

Yet at the same time Archbishops of Canterbury had ceased to receive the pallium in person. None of the five archbishops of the fifteenth century were consecrated in Rome and only one, John Morton, went there for any purpose.[55] Also, the English cardinals ceased to live in Rome – Easton was the last one to stay there for nearly a century. In the fifteenth century no English cardinals went to Rome, even for conclaves, neither in the sixteenth century did Wolsey (even though he had papal aspirations at two conclaves). His contemporary, Christopher Bainbridge, was already in Rome as a royal envoy when he was named as cardinal. By the early sixteenth century royal links with Rome were more important than strictly ecclesiastical ones. Under Henry VII the English hospice became known as the King's Hospice. The English ambassador, on behalf of the King, took over the appointment of the Warden and Chamberlains, supplanting the elective rights of the Confraternity members.[56]

Political and ecclesiastical relations between the popes and the English Church and State were regularly dealt with by royal proctors and envoys and by the appointment of Cardinal Protectors. During the late fifteenth century many English envoys were sent to Rome; in 1487 no less than ten ambassadors of Henry VII entered Rome together and all received an audience of Innocent VIII.[57] Though only formally recognized by Julius II (1503–13), the role of Cardinal Protectors began to emerge from 1492. The first reference to any national Protector is to the English Cardinal Protector in 1492 – a reminder of Tudor enthusiasm for the papacy up to the 1520s.[58] Cardinal Francesco Piccolomini served as Cardinal Protector of England for

---

[54] W. E. Wilkie, *The Cardinal Protectors of England* (1974), p. 11.

[55] Parks, p. 337.

[56] M. Williams, *The Venerable English College, Rome* (1979), pp. 1–2.

[57] W. Maziere Brady, 'The Palazzo Torlonia', *Anglo-Roman Papers* (1901).

[58] Wilkie, p. 12.

eleven years before his election as Pope Pius III in 1503, though he survived less than a month as pope.[59]

The King's ambassador to the papacy in the late fifteenth and early sixteenth century generally lived in the Palazzo Torlonia, now located on the right-hand side of the modern Via della Conciliazione. This palazzo, designed by Bramante, was actually owned by the English kings from 1504, being given to Henry VII by Adriano Castellesi, Piccolomini's successor, in an effort to curry favour. It had been built by Castellesi, who had lived in England and held a number of English church benefices, from where the wealth came to build his palazzo.[60] In a gesture he was later to regret, Henry VIII gave the Palazzo Torlonia to Cardinal Lorenzo Campeggio who spent time in England as papal envoy. He lived in the unfinished palazzo for more than three years (1519–24) from where he took part in two papal conclaves. He was forced to write to Wolsey for money to put the place in good repair. His family continued to own it until 1609 when they sold it to the Borghese. The Campeggio reclaimed it briefly between 1635 and 1650. After numerous sales it passed to the Torlonia in 1820 and in the nineteenth century was the scene of many fashionable balls attended by the English aristocratic visitors. In between balls it was rented out to English visitors of less aristocratic cut. A party of Thomas Cook's tourists found themselves, to their surprise, accommodated there for Easter 1866 at a cost of £500 for ten days. They were conscious of the building's earlier English connections and felt they 'might indulge a little pride in the fact'.[61] John Sherwood, absentee Bishop of Durham, lived in Rome in a house rented from the hospice for twenty years, but moved into the Palazzo Torlonia when he was given the post of King's ambassador, until his death in 1493. He was buried in the English hospice. His predecessor as royal ambassador to Rome was commemorated in the church of S. Crisogono with the inscription:

[59] *Oxford Dictionary of Popes*, pp. 254–5.
[60] Maziere Brady, op. cit.
[61] *Cook's Excursionist and Tourist Advertiser*, 1 May 1866.

To David William, Englishman, Doctor of Canon Law, Dean of Menevia, Keeper of the Rolls and Envoy of King Henry VII of England, this tablet erected by William Fell, on account of his singular learning, integrity and wisdom. He died in the year 1491 on 28 September. Wales, where dwelt the early Britons, was my begetter, England my nurse, Oxford my teacher: having come to Rome as envoy and having completed twice five lustres, I died. That is all. Reader, depart.[62]

Sadly, despite being recorded so recently, this delightful inscription cannot now be found.

One of the last English royal diplomat/churchmen before the upheavals of the sixteenth century was Christopher Bainbridge, Archbishop of York and titular Cardinal of S. Prassede. Born around 1464 in Westmorland, Bainbridge was educated at Queen's College, Oxford where he was Provost in 1495 and to which he became a generous benefactor. He also studied in Ferrara and Bologna and in 1493 was resident in Rome and *Camerarius* of the hospice. He had an outstanding career in England, being treasurer of St Paul's in 1503 and Dean of York. In 1505 he became Dean of Windsor and was also Master of the Rolls until he became Bishop of Durham three years later.

Bainbridge was very much the King's man, a vigorous defender of Henry VIII's interests and apparently liable to the same violent temper as his master. In 1509 the King sent him to Rome, to the Palazzo Torlonia, as ambassador and he was among the batch of cardinals created at a consistory at Ravenna to defend Julius II against those who wanted to call a general council. Taking up his post in Rome in 1509 he was a confident and experienced character who quickly became the dominant personality in the English colony. In 1510 he effectively took over responsibility for the government of the hospice, and with supreme self-assurance carved out his niche in the Curia. 'Contentious and worldly, but forthright and single-

---

[62] Vidon, p. 144.

minded, Julius found a kindred spirit and one whose force-fully-held opinions came to blend easily with his own.'[63] Bainbridge's total dominance was only thwarted by Wolsey's enmity, which ensured that he was never appointed Cardinal Protector.

In 1514 Bainbridge was engaged in negotiations with the Pope to have Henry declared 'Most Christian King' in place of Louis XIII. His career was cut short when he was allegedly poisoned by a chaplain in his own service and an aggrieved victim of Bainbridge's temper, called Rinaldo de Modena. The poisoner was thrown into Castel S. Angelo, where he not only confessed to the murder, but said he had done it at the instigation of Giovanni Giglis, Bishop of Worcester, Bainbridge's rival at the papal court and Wolsey's puppet. The Bishop forced de Modena to retract his statement but the poisoner stabbed himself to death in prison. No charges were brought against Giglis. 'Wolsey destroyed him [Bainbridge], with the connivance of King and Pope, using Giglis as his instrument.'[64] Bainbridge, not greatly mourned, was buried in the King's hospice. The remains of his magnificent tomb can still be seen in the present church of the English College.

At this point both popular religion and the sources of ecclesiastical authority were to be wrenched apart. A poignant symbol of the wrench is St John Fisher, the only English cardinal to date canonized by the church. A great protagonist of the papal cause and of Catholic teaching against Luther, Fisher (as Catherine of Aragon's confessor) argued the case for the validity of her marriage. Fisher was already a marked man and in prison, when in 1534 the newly-elected Paul III nominated him as a cardinal and perhaps unwittingly sealed his fate. Fisher's titular church, which he never saw, was S. Vitale.

The hospice in its future was to have a unique role in the turmoil of the sixteenth century and beyond, but after Bainbridge's death it deteriorated rapidly. Giglis reported to Wolsey that the King's hospice was in a poor state, saying

---

[63] Wilkie, p. 42.
[64] Ibid.

that the few Englishmen there did nothing but eat and drink, run riot and abuse each other and that the candidates for the Wardenship in 1517 were worthless.[65] Any attempts at reform were overtaken by the sack of Rome in 1527 when the hospice was pillaged. Scarcely any records survive for the period up to 1538.

Ecclesiastical diplomacy and the best efforts of the 'Defender of the Faith' (Henry VIII) failed to get Thomas Wolsey elected as the second English pope. The King's envoys and agents, in what has been described as 'an almost hysterical intensification of Anglo-Roman diplomatic relations'[66] did their best at the conclave of 1521 and again in 1522. Despite their failures, Wolsey did have his palace built in Rome, in what is now called the Via delle Pozzo delle Cornacchie.[67] This was apparently named after a well which stood in the courtyard of the palace bearing Wolsey's coat of arms of two crows standing either side of a rose. The palace survives but not the well. Wolsey's titular church was S. Cecilia in Trastevere but he never went near Rome. By the later 1520s, Wolsey had issues other than papal ambition to preoccupy him and he worked with Lorenzo Campeggio on 'The King's Great Matter'.

Campeggio played a major role in the royal divorce case, having previously won confidence in England as papal legate in 1518 to assist in the reform of the monasteries. During his visit he was lodged at Wolsey's London house and much energy was put into impressing Campeggio and winning his friendship. Wolsey saw him as the heir apparent to the Cardinal Protectorship and therefore a necessary ally.[68] He was one of the great legal celebrities of his day and the star canonist of the Roman Curia. The son and grandson of famous teachers of law at Bologna, he was a widower from 1509 with two daughters, and three sons, two of whom became bishops and one a cardinal. He entered papal service in 1511 and was made cardinal by Leo X (1513–21). As a result of Campeggio's assistance to

---

[65] Parks, p. 364.
[66] E. Chaney, *The Evolution of the Grand Tour* (1998), p. 42.
[67] Masson, p. 165.
[68] Wilkie, p. 54.

Wolsey and Henry in 1518, not only was he given the Palazzo Torlonia but in 1524 made absentee Bishop of Salisbury. He never visited his see but his name is recorded along with all the other holders of the office on a modern marble plaque in Salisbury Cathedral. Wolsey had secured an important friend for England at the papal court. As planned, after Giulio de Medici became Pope Clement VII in 1523, Campeggio became Cardinal Protector of England – the last one to be nominated by the Crown.[69]

Edwarde Foxe and Stephen Gardiner, Wolsey's men in Rome handling the marriage case in 1528, therefore pressed for the choice of Campeggio as co-legate with Wolsey to try the case. Campeggio understood by 1528 what an impasse Clement VII's indecisiveness had created, but was 'fated to carry out the policies of less intelligent men'.[70] He did his best to achieve for Clement what he saw at the outset was impossible, but never lost sight of the fact that what mattered was the good of religion, not the Pope's convenience.

Campeggio, while anxious to reach agreement, saw the dangers of continued procrastination and agreed with Wolsey that if Henry did not get his way, then papal authority was finished in England. He was almost defeated by the Pope's half-promises to Henry and alleged advice to him to marry Anne Boleyn and trust him to ratify it later. The Pope's insistence that Campeggio try to persuade Catherine to retire to a convent was the last straw – she refused and demanded a legal decision.

Forced to take the matter to trial, Campeggio took the view that whatever arguments were placed about the validity or otherwise of Catherine's first marriage were irrelevant. The bull of Julius II of 1503, the authority of which nobody had questioned, had dispensed Henry and Catherine from all impediments and they had been free to marry in the eyes of the Church. Therefore he could do no other than declare that Henry and Catherine had been validly married and remained so. One of the lesser effects

[69] Ibid.
[70] P. Hughes, *The Reformation in England* (1950), vol. 1, p. 178.

of his decision was that Henry saw fit to deprive Campeggio of the benefice of the See of Salisbury in 1534. Campeggio returned to Rome where he died in 1539. He was buried in S. Maria in Trastevere, where his sarcophagus can still be seen in the portico, but his body and that of his son were removed to Bologna in 1571. The present inscription was not added until 1868. Without his knowledge, his world of negotiation and diplomatic compromise was replaced by that of conflict between the camps of Reginald Pole and Thomas Cromwell. 'For all his brilliance as a lawyer and a diplomat', like many of his contemporaries, 'he participated in momentous events without shaping them or seeming to catch their real significance.'[71]

As a result of the 'momentous events', the English practice of pilgrimage to Rome, intertwined with ecclesiastical business and seeking after culture, dwindled rapidly. The relationship between England and Rome, often testy throughout the mediaeval period, had reached a flashpoint. However, this was not only a clash of jurisdictions, as in Becket's time, but a fundamental and theological rejection of all that Rome represented. Among the effects which it had was to give real credibility to the undercurrent of criticism of certain aspects of popular piety, including pilgrimage. Under the influence of the Reformers, English churchmen began to reject the validity of pilgrimage, shrines and relics and to seek an internalized route to salvation. Rejection of Roman authority and animosity to the papacy meant that, above all, pilgrimage to Rome was anathema. The shrines of Peter and Paul and the early martyrs had become so closely associated with the authority claims of the papacy that it was by now impossible to separate the two. The authority of the Apostles was visible in the relics and tangible in Roman influence over religious and political life. The spiritual effectiveness of pilgrimage was denied and the power of Rome, built on the bones of Peter and Paul, was rejected. For the English, Rome had become a place where they had made themselves at home, put down roots and laid claim to property.

[71] Wilkie, p. 58.

To them it was not just (or even principally) the seat of the Pope, but it held the bones of Anglo-Saxon kings and of the favourite English martyr, Thomas à Becket. The English pilgrimage to Rome, which had been a common aspiration and a familiar ideal in mediaeval society took on a new meaning. Rome ceased to be a focus of unity and source of salvation and became a focus of division and source of discord. The pilgrim badge of the crossed keys or the Veronicle became a badge of defiance rather than a symbol of the shared experience of Christian life.

Chapter Four

Roma Sancta

As one group of Englishmen left Rome, another moved in, fleeing the influence of Protestant reform and the scourge of hostile civil power. Some survived through from the 1530s to the 1560s and beyond, but pilgrimage became supplanted by exile – a prolonged pilgrimage, and certainly penitential in its experience.

Exile, of course, became a regular (often the only) option for English Catholics after the death of Mary Tudor, and Rome was not the only haven. However, links with the Pope and representation in Rome were seen as vital to the survival and later to the recovery of English Catholic life. The hospice became crucial, both symbolically and practically. By 1538 only one decrepit member of the confraternity remained, and when this came to the Pope's attention, Paul III took action himself and decreed the election of a new confraternity. Thus from 8 March 1538 the hospice passed from royal to papal control – effective recognition that the breach with England was not temporary. Cardinal Reginald Pole, one of the most influential Englishmen in the sixteenth-century church was the obvious choice as warden of the hospice to secure its continuity and its loyalty to the papacy.

Reginald Pole was born in Worcestershire in 1500 into a family closely related to the Tudor royal family. He was educated first at Oxford, then under Henry VIII's patronage at Padua where he had an outstanding career and imbibed the influences of humanism. Soon after returning to England in 1526 he was pressed into royal service, uneasily handling material related to the divorce question. 'In 1530 he greatly angered the King by blurting out his opposition to the divorce proceedings: with the result that he was shortly afterwards permitted to leave England, fortified by a Royal pension and a commission to resume his studies.'[1] He did not see England again for twenty-three years.

After striving to bring about reunion across the widening rift between England and the papacy, Pole finally had to give up hope of compromise after the execution of More and Fisher in 1535. When tacitly asked for his support of Henry's assumption of the title of 'Supreme Head of the Church in England' his response was a treatise, usually known as *De Unitate*. It was 'an emotionally-charged attack upon the King; it is a patently sincere attempt to induce him to repent; and it impressively argues the case for Papal primacy in the Church.'[2] In 1536 he was summoned to Rome and created cardinal, with the titular church of S. Maria in Cosmedin.

From 1538 Pole and his English household were installed in Via Monserrato, but he spent many of the following years travelling on papal diplomatic business and participating in the reform of the Church. In 1545 he attended the first stages of the Council of Trent as a papal delegate and at the papal conclave of 1549 he came within one vote of election as pope. Therefore on Mary's accession in 1553, Pole was her natural choice to lead the restoration of English Catholicism. This short-lived attempt came to an abrupt end when queen and cardinal died within hours of each other in November 1558. S. Maria in Cosmedin bears no mark of Pole's presence as titular cardinal but Pole can be seen in Rome, in a painting above the sacristy door in S. Francesca Romana.[3] Possibly attributed to one of Raphael's favourite pupils, Perin del Vaga, the painting shows Pole (in black rather than Cardinal's red) in conversation with Pope Paul

[1]   D. Fenion, *Heresy and Obedience in Tridentine Italy* (1972), p. 28.
[2]   Ibid., p. 39.
[3]   R. J. Abbott, 'The Lesser Churches of Rome', *Venerabile* 17 (1956), p. 230.

III (1543–49). It was thus presumably painted *c.* 1534–6.[4] Pole also left a very curious and particular monument in Rome, or at least on the road out of the city. Along the Via Appia Antica stands the church entitled Domine Quo Vadis, commemorating the famous story of St Peter meeting a vision of Christ on the road as he attempted to escape from Nero's persecution. Pole became convinced that the chapel was built at the wrong point, and a little further along the road is a tiny circular chapel at what he believed to be the site of St Peter's vision.

Another participant in the prolonged negotiations of the sixteenth century was Edward Carne, a Glamorgan lawyer and landowner who did live to see the real significance of events. He first emerged on the Roman scene in 1529–30, representing Henry's case in the marriage dispute, and became a well-known figure in Vatican circles. His career illustrates the changing fortunes of English Catholic life in relation to Rome in the sixteenth century. Carne's life highlights the personal cost of the break with Rome for many individuals in England and Wales and the limited, difficult and often secret contact with Rome which they sustained.

Carne maintained his Catholicism throughout the religious changes and returned to Rome in 1555 as Mary Tudor's ambassador and warden of the English hospice in Via Monserrato. Wisely he remained in Rome after Elizabeth I's accession until his death in 1561. The new dangers and complexities for English and Welsh Catholics caught between Roman and royal authority and the lengths to which they were driven is illustrated by Carne's petition to visit his family in Wales. Elizabeth I agreed but the Pope and his successor apparently refused him leave to go. Only much later did it emerge that his 'detention' in Rome had been arranged by Carne himself, knowing the danger which would face not only him but his family and estate if he did return to Wales. As it was, Elizabeth's sympathy and tolerance were extended to the family of this 'papal exile' and they were left unmolested. Carne's tomb

---

[4] Masson, p. 314.

in the courtyard of S. Gregorio records poignantly the anguish of religious exile.[5] Part of it reads, in translation, 'When the schism broke out in Britain after the death of Mary, he freely endured to be deprived of his native land for the Catholic faith, and died with a great reputation for honour and true piety.'

Near Carne's monument in S. Gregorio is that of another English religious exile of the sixteenth century, Robert Peckam. His father Edward contrived to be Master of the Mint and a member of the royal household under both Henry VIII and Edward VI and then a Privy Councillor to Mary, with considerable influence at court. Robert was also a Privy Councillor to Mary, MP for Buckinghamshire and a staunch Catholic and had briefly joined Reginald Pole's retinue in Rome when he took over the hospice in 1538.[6] His Catholicism clearly became uncomfortable after the accession of Elizabeth and, claiming ill-health, he set out to travel abroad in 1564. He died in Rome on 10 September 1569. Although buried in S. Gregorio, his heart was later interred in Denham parish church, Buckinghamshire, where his parents are buried. Robert Peckam became the subject of an eponymous novel by the twentieth-century diplomat and author, Maurice Baring (published in 1930).

The events of the 1560s, culminating in Elizabeth's excommunication in 1570, combined to make Italy inaccessible to the English. All but merchants needed licences to travel and Rome itself was out of bounds. Property could be confiscated if orders to return were not obeyed. 'Thus while the good Protestant travelled abroad in terror of the Inquisition, the good Catholic or merely curious returned home in fear of Elizabeth's secret service.'[7] It might be assumed that the increasingly hostile atmosphere between Rome and England brought an end to the constant flow of pilgrims and churchmen pouring across Europe. This was not altogether true, although the numbers were greatly

[5]   J. M. Cleary, 'The Carne Monument in Rome', *Cardiff Naturalists' Society Reports and Transactions* 53 (1948–50), pp. 12–15.
[6]   *Venerabile* (1962), p. 204.
[7]   E. Chaney, *The Evolution of the Grand Tour* (1998), p. 76.

reduced. Suspect Catholics, such as Sir Francis Englefield, were punished by confiscation for remaining too long in Italy, and in 1566 Henry Fitzalan, twelfth Earl of Arundel transferred his estate to his fellow Catholic son-in-law before travelling to Italy.[8]

After the break with Rome and particularly after the excommunication of Elizabeth I in 1570 the English Catholics were faced with the seemingly insurmountable difficulty of maintaining their religious tradition of papal authority while the monarch and church of the law and the land rejected it. One means was to be the foundation of the Venerable English College out of the hospice in 1579. Under the direction of Cardinal William Allen it began the training of English priests for missionary work in their native, now hostile land. His aim and his achievement was to confront the new order in England and to create a distinctive, robust and uncompromising response among recusants to the temptation of 'acquiescent conformity'.[9] This was to give rise to a new Roman martyr tradition taken up devotionally by later generations. Allen himself was in Rome in October 1579 when he received compliments from the Pope on the good beginning made. From late 1585 until his death in 1594, the college was his home and he was buried in the crypt of the college church.[10]

The effect of the formal break with Rome on English Catholic life was, of course, profound and when the last of Mary's bishops, Thomas Goldwell retired to S. Silvestro al Quirinale in Rome, where he later died, Catholic England was at its lowest ebb. Born around 1500 of an ancient Kent family, Thomas Goldwell was a scholar of All Souls, Oxford between 1520 and 1535. He was also possibly presented to the living of Cheriton near Folkestone. Shortly after 1535, Goldwell left England and joined Reginald Pole in Padua. In 1538 he was included in the Act of Attainder on Pole and his household 'for casting off their duty to the King and submitting themselves to the Bishop of Rome'. In the

[8]   Chaney, p. 78.
[9]   E. Duffy, 'William, Cardinal Allen 1532–1594', *Recusant History* 22 (1995), p. 279.
[10] R. L. Smith, 'The Intriguing Allen', *Venerabile* 6 (1932), pp. 5–12.

same year he was among the group which accompanied Pole to Rome and the English hospice. Goldwell became *Camerarius* and began a lifelong connection with the hospice. By 1543 Pole had become protector of the hospice and Goldwell was warden.

He accompanied Pole to the conclave of 1549–50 which elected Julius III and failed to elect Pole by a single vote. Soon after, Goldwell entered the Theatine Order at Naples (a new order, founded in 1524 by Gian Pietro Caraffa, later Pope Paul IV, which was to be immensely influential in the European Counter-Reformation, although it never spread to England). He had little opportunity to take up the life of his new order. Returning to England with Pole after the accession of Mary in 1553 he assisted at Pole's consecration as Archbishop of Canterbury and was himself appointed Bishop of St Asaph. Mary later wished to see him succeed Sir Edward Carne as ambassador to Rome, but she died before completing the appointment.

After the death of Mary and Pole, Goldwell was without support in England and was soon expelled from his see. He left for Italy and lived for a time with the Theatines in Naples and in Rome at S. Silvestro al Quirinale. In 1561 he attended further sessions of the Council of Trent, encouraging moves to excommunicate Elizabeth I. He held the post of warden of the hospice until 1567. In that year he was appointed vicar of St John Lateran. From 1574 he was Vicegerent of Rome and among those he ordained was St Camillus of Lellis, founder of the Ministers of the Sick. The saint's room can be seen at the house of his order at the church of S. Maria Maddalena, not far from the English hospice. Goldwell also ordained some of the first priests and martyrs trained in Via Monserrato after the college began in 1579. At the vigil of the Immaculate Conception in 1580, Goldwell conferred the tonsure on one of the greatest composers of the period, Palestrina. It is said that Palestrina conducted a special musical service in the chapel of the Venerable English College in February 1584.[11] Goldwell, Palestrina and St Camillus were all part

---

[11] D. Crowley, 'Bishop Goldwell', *Venerabile* 5 (1930), p. 66.

of the circle of St Philip Neri, founder of the Oratory, who lived at S. Girolamo, opposite the English College. From there he would visit the college regularly and blessed the young priests as they left for the English mission. In 1580, at the age of 80, Goldwell was determined to join his young friends on the mission, aware of his role as the only surviving bishop of the old hierarchy. He and the party including Ralph Sherwin, Edmund Campion and Robert Persons got as far as Rheims, where he became ill and was unable to continue. The delay while he was nursed back to health meant that government spies would be on his trail and his age and poor health made capture inevitable not only for him but his companions. Reluctantly he returned to Rome when his health permitted and spent his remaining years at S. Silvestro. He continued to be active as Vicegerent and a plaque in the portico of S. Cecilia (which had been, ironically, Wolsey's titular church) commemorates the consecration by Goldwell of the high altar. He also consecrated the altar at S. Silvestro al Quirinale where he was buried after his death on 3 April 1585.

Maintaining the pilgrimage tradition was an important symbol of Catholic continuity and renewal. The Holy Year of 1575 was a demonstration of the Counter-Reformation revival spearheaded in Rome by Philip Neri and his circle. Gregory Martin's *Roma Sancta* published in 1580 when the memory of the Holy Year was still fresh, reflected the continued and even enhanced significance of pilgrimage to Rome, particularly for English Catholics.

Gregory Martin was 'the scholar in action'.[12] An Oxford don at St John's College, friend and colleague of Edmund Campion, he became tutor to the Earl of Arundel after resigning his fellowship in 1568. After the Earl's father's arrest in 1569 he fled to Douai and was ordained priest in Brussels in 1573. He spent the rest of his life teaching at Douai and Rheims and working at his most enduring work, the translation of the Bible into English (known familiarly as the Douai Bible). *Roma Sancta* is the product of eighteen

[12] G. Parks, in Gregory Martin (ed.), *Roma Sancta* (1969), Introduction, XI.

months spent in Rome towards the end of his short life (1542?–1582), an experience which had a profoundly moving effect on him. Part of it was published by the English College in 1583 as *A Treatise of Christian Peregrination,* or as Martin called it in a subtitle, *A Short Discourse of Pilgrimage and Relics.* This early posthumous publication by the college reflected both the esteem in which Martin was held (Allen preached at his funeral) and the desire to publish for an English readership at least a partial account of the strength of piety in late sixteenth-century Rome.

Roma Sancta, not published in its complete form until 1969, offers a comprehensive survey of religious practice, charities and churches available to the pilgrim at the height of the Tridentine Reformation. It is a systematic account, probably based in part on information on religious institutions provided by Goldwell as Vicegerent of Rome. He drew on the record of the 1575 Holy Year published by the Dominican Angelo Pientini and on a Rome guidebook, *Le Cose Meravigliose dell'Alma citta di Roma,* which had an appendix written before 1560 by an Englishman, Thomas Shakerley, who was a papal organist and chief musician to the Cardinal of Ferrara.[13] The 1575 edition of this had re-edited Charles Borromeo's advice on the proper conduct of pilgrims, which Martin translated and included in his text. Martin suggests that the clergy were increasingly leading the way in maintaining the pilgrim tradition, but other evidence (even in his own work) suggests that it remained predominantly a lay-organized activity. The continued popularity of pilgrimage among nationalities for whom it was practicable was indicated by the fact that the Pope had reduced the number of days on which the pilgrim circuit of the 'Seven Churches' should be completed from fifteen to two, in order to reduce crowds and lessen the strain on hospices.[14]

Martin, aptly, was probably the first English pilgrim to stay at the hospice after its change of status to the Venerable English College in 1579. He appears to have

[13] Chaney, p. 76.
[14] Parks, Introduction, *passim.*

been in Rome during 1580 and early 1581 and was elected chaplain of the hospice.[15] The Pilgrim Book of the hospice was quite deliberately restarted in 1580 in view of the fact that, 'although it does not explicitly appear in the Bull yet the Pope declared by word of mouth that this college was bound to receive and maintain the English pilgrims according to the statutes of the hospice'.[16] The first recorded pilgrim was Thomas Arundell (later first Lord Arundell) who, on the patronal feast of St Thomas of Canterbury, 29 December 1580, 'was on this day admitted as the first guest, and remained with us for three days'.[17]

Roma Sancta fulfils the role of guidebook for the English pilgrim, listing and describing the 'Seven Churches' and their relics and then the other important churches in Rome. Martin then goes on to record the personal piety, the preaching and the devotions he has seen in Rome, as evidence of the power of the new spiritual forces at work. In Book II he records the charities, confraternities and religious houses of Rome – a unique record of Counter-Reformation religious life. Among these institutions was the English hospice, converted by order of Gregory XIII into the English College. Martin tells the story of its foundation and goes on to set out the pattern of life in the newly-formed seminary.[18]

It is clear from the space given by Martin to a history of jubilee years and an account of the most recent one in 1575, that pilgrimage to Rome still flourished in the wake of the Reformation but also that he shared the determination of the Tridentine reformers to reassert the triumph of popular Catholicism. The purpose of the jubilee year was unequivocally defined as:

> Now then, that the whole people of God might have some solemn time generally to invite them and move them to crye to God al together for an universal remission, to joyne together in prayer, in travail, in hart

---

[15] A. Gasquet, *A History of the Venerable English College, Rome* (1920) p. 64.
[16] Gasquet, p. 78.
[17] VEC Archives, Liber 282.
[18] Parks, pp. 112–14.

and intention; to satisfie al at once, so far as they can, and for the rest to crave pardon al at once; to meete and assemble together out of of the world in the head citie of Christianitie; to protest their unitie of faith, and charitie of minds in so great diversitie of nations; to solace and comfort and confirm one another in devotion and true religion against Pagans, Jews and Heretikes; to make one campe as it were marching under the ensign and standard of Christ crucified; for these and suchlike goodly and godly causes, the Catholike Church (taught alwaies by the Holy Ghost), ordained the yere of Jubilee, now kept every twenty-fifth yere. Wherein his Holiness proclaimeth a ful pardon to al pilgrims that goe to Rome.[19]

He lends authority to his own account of the Jubilee and of pilgrimage by quoting an extensive passage from St Charles Borromeo's vigorous exhortation to pilgrims of 1575.

Borromeo, Bishop of Milan for twenty years until his death in 1584, was one of the dominant creative figures of the Counter-Reformation. He was the first resident bishop that Milan had seen in eighty years and the reforms which he instituted there became a model for dioceses across Europe.[20] Borromeo had close links with the English exiles in Rome and Douai[21] and his influence on the rebirth of English Catholicism was formative. Goldwell was briefly his Vicar-General while at the Council of Trent in 1562 and Griffith Roberts, a Welsh scholar and one of Goldwell's archdeacons in Bangor, became his secretary and chaplain. Roberts served Borromeo faithfully for the rest of his life. In 1580 Ralph Sherwin, Robert Persons and Edmund Campion, the first group to leave the college in Rome for the English mission with Goldwell, visited Borromeo en route in Milan. They stayed for eight days and Sherwin and Campion preached each day. According to Persons,

---

[19]   Parks, p. 222.
[20]   *Oxford Dictionary of Saints*, pp. 55–6.
[21]   Gasquet, p. 54.

He had sundry learning and most goodly speeches with us, tending to the contempt of this world and perfect zeal in Christ's service, whereof we saw so rare an example in himself and his austere and laborious life; being nothing in effect but skin and bone, through continual pains, fasting and penance; so that without saying a word, he preached to us sufficiently and we parted from him greatly edified and exceedingly animated.[22]

It became established routine that the English missionaries broke their journey at Milan. Owen Lewis, co-founder with Allen of the English College, became Borromeo's Vicar-General, friend and confidante and was with him as he died.

Given the close links between the great reforming bishop and the English exiles, it is not surprising that Gregory Martin knew him and appreciated his writings. In his Holy Year exhortation quoted by Martin, Borromeo encouraged his contemporaries by reminding them of the ancient tradition of pilgrimage to Rome.

It was an old custome and practice of good Christians, with great religion to make concourse from al partes to the place where the Relickes of Saincts and other [of] their monuments were: but specially to Rome, where bicause the blessed Apostles Peter and Paul [and] other innumerable saincts of God were martyred, and their sacred bodies and Relickes rested there, great multitudes of al nations went thither to obtain the prayers of them and intercessions to God, and to honour also those bones and those limmes, which when they lived in flesh, were the habitation and temple of the Holy ghost, and which were to be raised again most graciously unto immortal life.[23]

In addition he urged upon them the particular contemporary value of the witness of pilgrimage, 'in these our

[22] Quoted in Gasquet, p. 84.
[23] Parks, p. 224.

unhappie times, when Heresie impugneth this holy worke, the religious fervour of devout Pilgrimage be somewhat cooled and diminished'.[24] In the midst of this, he argued that pilgrimage to Rome was an important sign of loyalty to the Church, but more importantly, it was not enough just to visit Rome and the holy sites. 'You must joyne hereunto true and perfect penance, so that you make this journey in the grace of God, and with such mortification of your flesh and senses, as may serve for the satisfaction of your sinnes.'[25] Borromeo reasserted the most rigorous tradition of pilgrimage, as an act of penance, unmixed with humanist motives of travel and cultural improvement. Rejecting the 'internalizing' spiritual tradition of Thomas à Kempis, Borromeo wanted to rebuild the tradition of public, corporate, physical acts of devotion. This brought a new dimension to the purpose of pilgrimage (or enhanced one scarcely thought of) that of pilgrimage as witness to Catholicity and symbol of rejection of its opponents. It also thereby re-emphasized the link between pilgrimage and martyrdom. Pilgrims to Rome had always sought and revered places of Christian martyrdom and venerated relics of martyrs of the imperial persecution. Now the Church was under persecution again, fresh martyrs' blood was being shed. The assertion of continuity and the martyr tradition were vital elements in pilgrim devotion.

Gregory Martin was in Rome when his friend Campion and his companions began their pilgrimage back to England and martyrdom in spring 1580, around the time when he was writing or contemplating *Roma Sancta*. The language of Borromeo's advocacy of pilgrimage clearly echoed in his head as he wrote for an English readership of Roman piety in action and of pilgrimage to the city. He would also have known that from 1580, the church of the hospice/college became not only a place of rest for pilgrims while they sought indulgences in Rome, but a pilgrim shrine in itself. By a decree of Gregory XIII, a plenary indulgence could be obtained by all who prayed in the college church for the conversion of England to

24 Ibid.
25 Ibid., p. 226.

Catholicism. This is the earliest known official commendation of such prayers and by making the church a source of
remittance of punishment, Pope Gregory placed it among
the pilgrim churches.[26] Within a year Ralph Sherwin was
dead and it had the association with martyrdom which
traditionally gave rise to pilgrim shrines. English pilgrims
thereafter not only had their own hospice, but their own
martyrs' shrine in Rome. It was around this time (between
1580 and 1583) that a lay pensioner of the college, George
Gilbert (an exile and pilgrim himself) commissioned the
series of pictures in the church of deaths of English
martyrs from 1535–83.[27] The martyr tradition of the
college itself very quickly began to enter the English
Catholic psyche. It is perhaps not surprising therefore that
in 1582 one of the first band of missionary priests who had
left in 1580, Leonard Hyde, escaped his captors and
returned to Rome as a pilgrim. On 20 June 1582 he and his
brother, along with Sir Geoffrey Pole and his son, were
admitted to the hospice as pilgrims.[28] When they left
England, Sherwin was already dead and Luke Kirby
tortured and in prison awaiting execution. Hyde must have
entered the college church with its new illustrations on the
walls with a fresh and urgent sense of martyrdom. He and
his companions no doubt fulfilled the requirements for
the plenary indulgence. The promise of martyrdom played
an essential part in the spiritual formation of the priests at
the English College, and by May 1582 (only five months
after his martyrdom) Cardinal Allen was distributing frag-
ments of Edmund Campion's bones as relics.[29]

After the Reformation, while for English Catholics Rome
was becoming even more significant as the centre of faith
and source of missionaries, visiting Rome was difficult and
dangerous for non-Catholics. For Catholic missionaries it
was the return journey which was dangerous, but for

---

[26] Anon., 'Broadsheet of 1580', *Venerabile* (1934), pp. 431–2.
[27] Gasquet, p. 122.
[28] A. Gasquet, *Obit Book of the Venerable English College* (Rome 1929), pp. 51–2.
[29] Duffy, *Recusant History* 22 (1995), p. 279.

Protestants under Elizabeth and James I attempts were made to regulate travel, and they could only visit Rome in defiance of a government ban. Yet a surprising number did so. The English College continued the tradition of hospitality and non-Catholic visitors as well as Catholic were welcomed, sometimes unwisely. A more sinister and hostile visitor to Rome at the same time as Gregory Martin was Anthony Munday, who went to Rome in 1578–9, probably driven by curiosity and wanderlust. His companion Thomas Nowell had Catholic sympathies and in fact was received into the English College as a scholar. Following his dismissal in 1583 he turned spy against the Catholics in England. Munday was also later to have a moderately successful career as an anti-Catholic spy, as well as a playwright.[30] His were not the endeavours of a principled Protestant but of a self-serving chancer.[31]

Using Nowell's contacts, Munday and he crossed continental Europe and managed to work their way into the English College, first as pilgrims and then as students. On the basis of his three months in Rome, Munday published in 1582 *The English Romayne Life*, a savage account of the college and of pilgrimage to Rome. The two charlatans were greeted warmly by those whom Munday was later to dupe and conspire against, 'Master Dr Morris [Morris Clynnog] the Rector of the house came to us, to whom we delivered the letter sent to him on our behalf from Paris, which when he had read, he said we were welcome, allowing us the eight days entertainment in the hospital, which by the Pope was granted to such Englishmen as come hither.'[32] It is clear from Munday's words, that the hospice tradition of three days' hospitality for the wealthy and eight days for poorer pilgrims was still in place in 1578, although the keeping of the Pilgrim Book did not resume until the end of 1580. The sustaining of this tradition in the height of hostility between Rome and England

---

[30] P. J. Ayres (ed.), 'Anthony Munday', *The English Romayne Life* (1980), Introduction.

[31] M. Williams, 'Anthony Munday', *Venerabile* (1946), pp. 36–44.

[32] *English Romayne Life*, p. 23.

and the most energetic pursuit and persecution of seminary priests is remarkable, even naïve, and left the college and its alumni open to the abuse of treacherous friends like Munday.

Munday gives a revealing and cynical description of pilgrims in Rome visiting the 'Seven Churches' for the showing of relics. He comments on the range and number of relics and 'the multitude of people that come thither to see them', for instance at S. Maria Maggiore 'an old rotten crib or manger', Aaron's Rod 'in the form of a Bishop's staff', hair 'that grew on Our Lady's head', the finger of St Thomas 'which he thrust into the side of Christ', the point of the spear which pierced Christ, 'certain pieces of money' said to be those of Judas, 'an old rotten piece of wood' from the Cross, and thorns 'which sometime, as they say were on the crown of thorns wherewith Our Saviour was crowned'.[33] He remarks on the popularity of the devotions, especially among English pilgrims, but it must be noted for what purpose and audience he is writing – it would appeal to an English Protestant readership in the 1580s to be told that English Catholics were being duped in this way. 'At all these Seven Churches there are a number more relics than I can well remember, which maketh the people resort to them almost daily; and our Englishmen, they are as zealous in these matters as the best and believe that those relics are the very certain things whereof they bear the name, so great is their blindness and want of faith.'[34]

His savagery did not stop at the pen for he gave evidence against Edmund Campion and Luke Kirby, despite which the hospice doors remained open. Another Elizabethan Protestant traveller welcomed at the English College, despite the real danger which might ensue, was Fynes Morison, a Protestant Lincolnshire lawyer who travelled Europe and the Middle East between 1591 and 1597. After his return he published his *Itinerary*, in which he recounts his travels including his visit to Rome in 1593. On arriving

---

[33] Ibid., pp. 55–6.
[34] Ibid., p. 57.

in the city he went to the English College and sought the protection of Cardinal Allen. He was received kindly and offered guided tours of Rome as well as instruction in the Catholic faith! Despite their kindness, he took the precaution of moving his lodgings regularly to avoid the visits of unwelcome clerical guides, and disguised himself as a Catholic Frenchman when he sought an audience with Cardinal Bellarmine.[35] 'The conception of travel one gathers from Fynes Morison is that of a very exciting form of sport, a sort of chase across Europe, in which the tourist was the fox, doubling and turning and diving for cover, while his friends in England laid three to one on his death.'[36]

The government ban on visiting Rome was widely ignored as travel generally became a popular pursuit among the wealthier English and was increasingly regarded as beneficial to mind and body. It must be said, though, that fear and suspicion of Catholicism, the Pope and Jesuits meant that for many the beneficial effects stopped at the Alps. Lord Burghley, who had pushed his son to Italy in the early days of Elizabeth, warned his own children at the end of his life, 'suffer not your sons to go beyond the Alps'.[37] He failed to prevent his grandson's visit, and although he sent thanks to Cardinal Savelli for his safe return, it was believed that he had become a Catholic.[38] The extended travels in Italy and subsequent conversion to Catholicism, of Burghley's son-in-law the Earl of Oxford, led to an Elizabethan edict recalling all English subjects, 'living beyond the seas under the colour of study and living contrary to the laws of God and the Realm'.[39] Clearly it was a source of frustration that 'the Renaissance had set men travelling to Italy as to the flower of the world. They had scarcely started before the Reformation called it a place of abomination.'[40] The effect

[35] W. Purdy, 'Fynes Morison', *Venerabile* 6 (1934), pp. 364–6.
[36] C. Howard, *English Travellers of the Renaissance* (1914), p. 95.
[37] Quoted ibid., p. 73.
[38] Chaney, p. 81.
[39] Chaney, p. 82.
[40] Howard, p. 73.

was not to last long and the idea of encountering Jesuits and cardinals became an added thrill for the Protestant traveller of the seventeenth century. By the 1590s travel was becoming safer and easier and alongside the Catholic exiles, Protestants also began to defy the restrictions, which were finally lifted (except for Rome itself) in 1604. As recusant life developed in England, while loyalty to the Pope remained crucial and the seminary priests from Rome and elsewhere were regarded as a lifeline, so also emerged the resilient independence of the English Catholic community. For many, the distance from Rome and the minimizing of papal authority became the key to toleration and later to relief from the penal laws. Questions of ecclesiastical jurisdiction dogged the English recusants during the seventeenth and eighteenth centuries as they tried to formulate *ad hoc* administrative tools.

One of the most striking examples of an English appeal to Rome to resolve an issue of ecclesiastical jurisdiction, and frustration as a result, was that of Mary Ward. With immense courage and stubbornness she founded her religious institute of women in the teeth of opposition from the English clerical authorities. She and her companions were advised by Mary's supporter the Spanish Infanta, whom they visited in Brussels, to travel to Rome in the physical dress and guise of pilgrims for safety's sake. A nearly contemporary portrait of Mary Ward exists of her in dark brown dress and cloak, topped by a broad-brimmed hat and carrying a staff.[41] If her dress is anything like authentic in the portrait – and there was presumably something identifiable as 'pilgrim's garb' – this suggests that the traditional dress of the pilgrim had survived the Reformation. The Caravaggio painting of Our Lady of the Pilgrims in the church of S. Agostino suggests likewise. It is also not surprising that a group of women, pilgrims or otherwise, needed male company on the journey. A priest (trained in Rome) and a layman accompanied them. They arrived in Rome on Christmas Eve 1621 in order to

---

[41] H. Peters, *Mary Ward: a World in Contemplation*, translated by Helen Butterworth (1994), pp. 310–11.

petition the Pope for approval of the institute. A rather romanticized but nonetheless evocative account of their arrival imagines the scene as follows:

> On Christmas Eve they entered Rome. The city glittered with myriad lights; pilgrims from all nations poured through the squares; triumphal arches and garlands of green swayed from balcony to balcony. The procession, with the Pope in the midst, streamed singing and praying to the Lateran; prelates and guards, monks and gentiluomini, torchbearers, beggars, clerics, street arabs, horsemen, litters, coaches, thronged every street and alley, and all the bells of the Eternal City carolled and clamoured beneath the starry heavens. Nobody noticed the little group of dead-tired, silent pilgrims among the vast crowds. Before they sought a hostelry for the night, Mary went to the Gesù and spent two hours on her knees before the tomb of S. Ignatius. They found accommodation near the Ponte Sisto, close to the English College.[42]

The Pope was unwilling to approve the institute but permitted the women to open a school in Rome so that he and the cardinals could judge for themselves their way of life. In June 1622 Mary Ward petitioned for permission for the school, despite a lack of Italian language and money and the presence of famine and epidemic in Rome. The school opened in October in a house on the corner of Via Monserrato and Via Montoro adjoining the English College and was a great success. It was a two-storey property, part of the court of the Princes Savelli which gave its name to the notorious prison which had adjoined. The community consisted of four sisters who had travelled with Mary Ward plus four other unknowns and their two male travelling companions. They often attended Mass at the English College and several of the community had

---

[42] I. G. Coudenhove, *Mary Ward* (n.d.) quoted in Edmund O'Gorman, *Our Islands and Rome* (1974), pp. 7–9.

brothers or other relatives among the students.[43] In 1627 the sisters presented a silver chalice to the College.[44] Support from the English College was in the teeth of opposition from English secular clergy, whose representative in Rome John Bennet did his best to discredit them in his reports. As a result in Catholic circles in England they were held to be immoral, in Rome ridiculous. The continued support of the Jesuit superior of the English College, Thomas Fitzherbert, was a mixed blessing, as he believed that Bennet's attitude to the English women was coloured by his antagonism to the Jesuits.[45] The school itself attracted 100–150 girls, nearly all poor and illiterate, but did not survive many years as the institute was suppressed in 1631. A modern plaque in the English College church commemorates the death and burial there of four of the community – Barbara Ward (Mary's younger sister who died of smallpox after only a year), Barbara Babthorpe, Elizabeth Cotten and Catherine Dawson. While in Rome, Mary Ward and her companions developed a particular devotion to an image of the Madonna in S. Maria Maggiore. They placed themselves under the protection of Our Lady of the Snows and when finally papal approval for the institute was obtained, the first novices were professed in 1634 in S. Maria Maggiore.[46]

It is clear that English links with Rome, including a depleted pilgrimage tradition survived the Reformation under considerable difficulty. For the English Catholics of the sixteenth and seventeenth centuries, pilgrimage became more clearly associated with exile and certainly for the missionary priests the pilgrimage to the place of martyrdom was back to England. Rome began to take on a new role in the imagination as well as the theology of both Catholicism and emergent Protestantism. It became an

---

[43] M. Edelburga Eibl IBVM, 'Mary Ward and her Roman School', *Venerabile* 19 (1959), pp. 345–53.

[44] Agnellus Andrew, 'Mary Ward – another English College Saint?', *Venerabile* 28 (1985), pp. 9–19.

[45] Peters, p. 388.

[46] M. Oliver, *Mary Ward 1585–1645* (1959), *passim*.

object of curiosity and derision for its retention of traditional religious practice and a source of apprehension as the source of a newly-aggressive Catholicism. This did not quite eradicate the imaginative hold which Roman culture had on the English. Throughout the sixteenth and seventeenth centuries there were always those, on both sides of the religious divide, who hoped for reconciliation. Pilgrimage became more difficult. The shrinking numbers of English Catholics and the lack of parochial structure made it almost impossible to organize group travel for this purpose. The public advocacy of pilgrimage brought risk of persecution, the ritual associated with it was lost and travel for Catholics rarely safe. Yet the battle to retain elements of pre-Reformation Catholic life (evidenced in the deliberate reconstituting of the English College Pilgrim Book) was bred of a conscious determination to confront the new order. Pilgrimage, martyrdom and Rome were powerfully symbolic for the English.

A Roman votive flask of the type commonly found in the catacombs, sought by pilgrim/souvenir hunters from the earliest
days of pilgrimage to Rome, and a source of controversy in the
nineteenth century (see p. 177).

Courtesy of Oscott College

Stained glass window in Canterbury
Cathedral showing the murder of Thomas
à Becket in 1170, the most dramatic clash
between the papacy and English royal
authority in early mediaeval Europe (see
p. 34).

Courtesy of Oscott College

A shield bearing the English and French arms quartered. Dating from 1412, it hung above the entrance to the English Pilgrim Hospice from then until the seventeenth century.

Courtesy of the Venerable English College

The tomb in the English College Church of Cardinal Christopher Bainbridge, Tudor royal envoy to the papacy between 1493 and his murder by a rival churchman in 1514 (see p. 59).

Courtesy of the Venerable English College

A plan of the centre of the city of Rome in 1576, showing the Castel S Angelo and Hospital of Santo Spirito on the left and the Pantheon at the top.

Courtesy of the Venerable English College

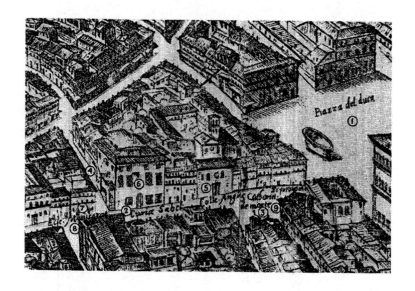

Mary Ward's First Roman School

From a plan of Rome by Antonio Tempesta 1593

1. Piazza Farnese
2. Via Monserrato
3. Piazza della Rota
4. Via Montoro

5. English College and Church
6. Curia Savelli
7. Mary Ward's School
8. S. Maria di Monserrato

9. S. Girolamo della Carità

A detail of the area around the English College in 1593, showing
the college and Mary Ward's School (see pp. 81–3).

Courtesy of the Venerable English College

The buildings of the English College, taken from an illustrated life of Pope Gregory XIII dated 1596. The dragon on the tower is taken from his coat of arms and is to be found in the college arms.

Courtesy of Oscott College

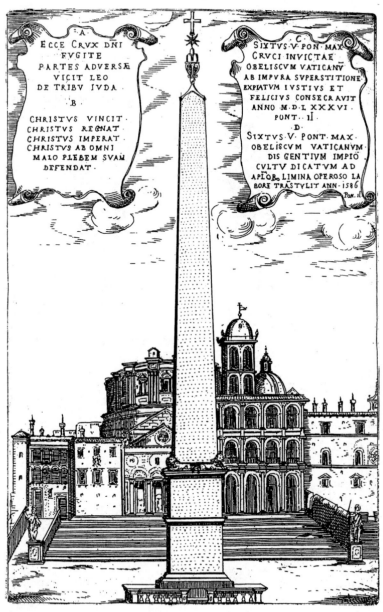

An engraving of St Peter's Square in 1586, showing the incomplete dome of the new basilica and the obelisk moved there from the place of Peter's execution.

Courtesy of Oscott College

Cardinal William Allen (1532–1594), founder of the English College which secured the provision of missionary priests for England and preserved the hospice tradition of pilgrim hospitality (see pp. 72–3).

(see pp. 72–3).

Courtesy of the Venerable English College

VEDUTA DELLA GRAN PIAZZA E BASILICA VATICANA.

Roma presso Domenico Pronti Incisore.

N.° 1

VEDUTA INTERNA DELLA BASILICA DI S.P.° IN VATICANO.

Roma presso Domenico Pronti Incisore.

N.° 2

Plates 10–14 depict the Seven Churches (S Pietro, S Giovanni Laterano, S Maria Maggiore, S Sebastiano, S Lorenzo fuori le Muri, S Paolo fuori le Muri and S Croce in Gerusalemme) which were the focus of pilgrim devotion from mediaeval to modern times (see p. 40).

Courtesy of Oscott College

VEDUTA DELLA BASILICA DI S. Gᴺⁱ IN LATERANO

Roma presso Domenico Pronti Incisore .

n. 3.

VEDUTA INTERNA DELLA BASILIᶜᴬ DI S. Gᴺⁱ IN LATERANO

Roma presso Domenico Pronti Incisore ,

n. 4.

VEDUTA DELLA BASILICA DI Sᴬ. MARIA MAGGIORE.

Roma presso Domenico Pronti Incisore

n.5.

VEDUTA INTERNA DELLA BASILICA DI Sᴬ. Mᴬ. MAGGIORE.

Roma presso Domenico Pronti Incisore.

n.6.

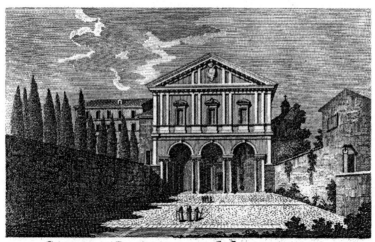

CHIESA E BASILICA DI S. SEBASTIANO.

In Roma presso l'Incisore Domenico Pronti N.º 7

CHIESA E BASILICA DI S. LORENZO FUORI LE MURA

N.º 8

CHIESA E BASILICA DI S. PAOLO APOST.

In Roma presso l'Incisore Domenico Pronti N.º 5

CHIESA E BASILICA DI S CROCE IN GERUSALEMME

N.º 6

VEDUTA DELLA PIAZZA DEL POPOLO

PORTA FLAMINIA DETTA DEL POPOLO.

Roma presso Domenico Pronti Incisore

English pilgrims entering from the north of Rome would arrive through the Porta Flaminia and their first view of Rome would be the elegant Piazza del Popolo. In 1850, Cardinal Nicholas Wiseman's letter *From Without the Flaminian Gate* was a source of controversy in England (see p. 152).

PALAZZO DELLA CANCELLARIA APOSTOLICA nº41.

PALAZZO COLONNA.
Roma presso Domenio Pront inc.

Nº 42.

The Palazzo della Cancelleria was the residence of Cardinal Henry
Duke of York (see p. 117).
The Palazzo Colonna was the residence in Rome of John Talbot,
16th Earl of Shrewsbury (see p. 155).

Courtesy of Oscott College

Chapter Five

Royal Ambassadors and Sentimental Travellers

Catholic recusants, of course, fled into exile from England and many of those aspiring to the missionary priesthood found their way to Allen's seminary in Rome. However, even in the early seventeenth century there can be seen hints of wealthy Catholic travellers combining elements of pilgrimage with the emergent 'Grand Tour'.[1] The disruptions consequent on the Reformation had put an end to the incipient Grand Tour from England, but by the early seventeenth century it was under way again. In 1614 Thomas Howard, Earl of Arundel (who sat lightly to his family faith, though he died a Catholic) began to put together his famous art collection in Italy, with the help of the architect Inigo Jones who was also a Catholic. This has been described as arguably the most significant Grand Tour ever undertaken, as much for the impetus it gave to Inigo Jones's own classically-inspired work as for the fact that the Earl and Countess of Arundel were the foremost art collectors in England before the eighteenth century.[2] While Arundel was waning from Catholic allegiance, others like Sir Tobie Mathew (whose ordination Arundel may have attended) set out as Protestant tourists and returned as Catholic pilgrims. Mathew 'was among those who took their part in laying down the careful rubric of the Grand Tour',[3] but he was received

[1] These are discussed by Edward Chaney in ch. 8 of his *Evolution of the Grand Tour* (1998), pp. 203–14.
[2] E. Chaney, *The Evolution of the Grand Tour* (1998), p. 208.
[3] D. Mathew, *Sir Tobie Mathew* (1950), p. 13.

into the Catholic Church while in Italy. While on the road he met up with other travelling recusant gentlemen, including Sir George Petre, and he travelled with Sir George Gage. Arundel and other connoisseurs employed Mathew and Gage's diplomatic and artistic expertise, and their Catholicism proved useful in making connections for their patrons with Italian art collectors and Flemish painters like Rubens and Van Dyck. Gage was believed to be the foremost English connoisseur of his day, and to have particular influence with the Flemish masters.[4]

A year after his first visit to Rome in 1605, when he had been greatly impressed by meeting Robert Persons at the English College, Mathew became a Catholic. Perhaps in recognition of the college's influence in his decision, he made a gift of 11,000 scudi for missionary purposes. Out of this, vineyards and a farmhouse were bought at La Magliana, which the college owned until 1917. After a brief period in England, partly in prison, Tobie Mathew returned to Rome in 1611 and studied theology at the English College. In 1614 he was ordained by Cardinal Robert Bellarmine, but kept it secret almost to the end of his life. The rest of his career was an extraordinary mix of court intrigue, diplomatic activity and travel, including unsuccessful attempts to negotiate a marriage between Prince Charles and the Infanta Maria of Spain, which earned him his knighthood.[5] Having revealed his priesthood in 1640, he fled for his life to Ghent where he died in 1655.[6]

Under Charles I the boom in foreign travel among the English received virtual official approval and a number of visitors like Hugh Popham recorded their cordial welcome in Rome. He arrived in February 1639, dined at the English College with the Protector of England, Cardinal Barberini, who he described as 'the gallantest gentleman in the whole world'.[7] Even before the Civil War, 'the journals and

4   Chaney, p. 209.
5   Chaney, p. 209.
6   Anon, 'Sir Tobie Mathew', *Venerabile* 15 (1950), pp. 37–40.
7   J. Stoye, *English Travellers Abroad 1604–1667* (revised edn. 1989), p. 122.

papers of English travellers after 1630 nearly all testify to the cordiality of their reception in central Italy'.[8] Another traveller on whom hospitable treatment at the English College left a lasting mark was Robert Dormer, Earl of Carnarvon, who dined a the college en route to and from Constantinople in 1634. Born a Catholic, he had been forced to abjure as a boy on the death of his father. Facing his own death from mortal wounds on the battlefield of Newbury in 1643 he recalled the kindness he had received at the English College in Rome, despite his Protestantism. He was reconciled to the Church and begged the King to ensure a Catholic upbringing for his son.[9]

Among other Protestant visitors who were entertained with courtesy at the English College were the Puritan poet John Milton who was there in 1638–9, and the diarist John Evelyn in 1644. The poet Richard Crashaw became a Catholic not long before reaching Rome and was given the status of pilgrim at the English College.[10] Evelyn spoke of being 'well acquainted' with the superior of the college and mentions other English visitors including Lord John Somerset, brother of the Marquis of Worcester, who had apartments in the nearby Palazzo della Cancelleria, Patrick Carey, the brother of Lord Falkland, and two doctors, Bacon and Gibbs, who were attached to the household of Cardinal Capponi. Crashaw, Carey and Gibbs were part of a distinguished circle of English recusant poets resident in Rome.[11]

On 18 February 1645 Evelyn visited the English College and also saw the nearby hospice of Pellegrini della Santa Trinita, one of the largest pilgrim hospices. He was much impressed by what he saw there.

> In the hospital of the Pellegrini della Santa Trinita I had seen the feet of so many pilgrims washed by

---

[8] Ibid.
[9] Anon, 'Robert Dormer and the Venerabile', *Venerabile* 18 (1958), pp. 230–1.
[10] K. Haggerty, 'The English College and Richard Crashaw: Puritan, Poet, Papist and Priest', *Venerabile* 30 (1991), pp. 17–27.
[11] Chaney, ch. 10.

princes, Cardinals and noble Romans and served at table, as the ladies and noble women did to other poor creatures in another room. 'Twas told us that no less than 444,000 men had been thus treated in the jubilee of 1600 and 25,500 women, as appears by the register.[12]

This hospice had been the product of an enhanced appreciation of the need for charitable aid for pilgrims in Rome evident in the largely unsuccessful 1550 Holy Year (remarkable otherwise only for the approval by Julius III of the Society of Jesus founded by Ignatius Loyola). St Philip Neri founded the Confraternity of the Blessed Trinity, which is believed to have given shelter to as many as half a million pilgrims during that year. Accommodation and food were free and every pilgrim was waited upon, cared for and washed, as a 'guest of God'. He received a dinner of meat and soup, a warm and clean bed, a breakfast of warm milk and would be accompanied to the pilgrim churches before receiving provisions for the road home. St Philip would go as far out of Rome as the Milvian Bridge to meet pilgrims and invite them to his hostel. One of the features of Santa Trinita was the active involvement of the wealthy and aristocratic in the care of pilgrims, and generations of English Catholic visitors enrolled in its membership.[13] This is the first indication of the inversion of rich and poor and the service of the powerless by the powerful which has become associated in more modern times with our concept of Jubilee. The aristocracy would imitate Christ in literally and metaphorically washing the feet of the poor.

James Alban Gibbs is often described as a 'Scotsman, educated at Oxford', but in reality his career appears a little more complicated. He was the son of William Gibbes of Bristol, a convert to Catholicism and physician to Henrietta Maria, wife of Charles I, whose court was full of Catholics. James was born in 1611 near Caen, Normandy

[12] ed. W. Bray, *Diary of John Evelyn* (1818), p. 136.
[13] See the account of Pauline de la Ferronays in ch. 8.

and was educated at the Jesuit college of St Omer's and at the famous medical school in Padua. He became a well-known and popular figure in Rome as a Latin poet and tutor to the Duke of Modena's son and as a physician. He practised at the hospital of Santo Spirito to which he took Evelyn and his party. Evelyn regarded him as an 'incomparable poet'.[14] In 1657, Alexander VII appointed him Professor of Rhetoric at the Sapienza University, Rome's oldest. Remarkably, in 1673, Gibbs was awarded the degree of Doctor of Physic by the University of Oxford. He died in Rome and was buried in the Pantheon. The inscription, now disappeared, read:

> James Alban Gibbs, Doctor of Oxford and at the same time, strange to relate, a Catholic, Imperial Poet Laureate, Professor Emeritus of Rhetoric in the Pontifical University, English by race, French by birth, he passed his life in Italy. He chose to die in the city that is all men's country, and to be buried in the church of all the saints, awaiting with them eternity, not of fame, but of life. He died on 26 June 1677 in the 66th year of his age. Benedetto Gibbs, his heir, placed this tablet in deep grief.[15]

As some of the heat went out of Anglo-papal relations following the accession of Charles I and his Catholic queen Henrietta Maria, it became possible to re-establish quasi-diplomatic relations between Rome and the English court. It was hoped in Rome that the weakness and division of English Protestantism in the 1630s could be exploited and Charles I's conversion achieved, to the obvious advantage of the Catholics. Three papal envoys in succession were appointed before the Civil War put paid to Roman hopes – Gregorio Panzani (1634–7), George Conn (1637–9) and Carlo Rosetti (1639–41).

Buried in the church of S. Lorenzo in Damaso is George Conn, a Scottish priest from Aberdeen. He was a trusted

[14] Chaney, p. 227.
[15] H. Vidon, *The Pilgrim's Guide to Rome: discovering links with past English-speaking pilgrims and residents*, 1975, pp. 26–8.

servant of Cardinal Barberini, a powerful papal nephew who had been appointed Cardinal Protector of England and has been described as 'like him in his mix of superficial culture, snobbery and ambition'.[16] Conn had lived abroad, mainly in Rome as a canon of S. Giovanni Laterano for twenty-six years. He and William Hamilton, the English envoy sent to Rome, had much in common: 'both were Scots, both enjoyed excellent reputations as diplomats and both were handsome men trained to smile their way past opposition'.[17] He took up residence in London in 1636 and was well treated by Charles I, to whom he was a close friend. Cultivating Charles with gifts of Italian Renaissance paintings, Conn did his best to bring about his conversion and reconciliation with Rome. His efforts were supported by the Queen who was trying to bring up her son as a Catholic and who was surrounded by a circle of overt or private Catholics at Court.

For the short time he was in London, Conn apparently replaced Archbishop Laud as the most important religious adviser at Court. He negotiated vigorously with Charles, particularly in relation to the oath of allegiance to the Crown, which required Catholics to declare the Pope's deposition of Elizabeth I as 'impious and heretical'. In return, Charles expected concessions from Rome on a range of issues including communion under one kind, celibacy of the clergy and papal deposing power.

Ultimately his vigorous campaign to achieve relief of the restraints on Catholics aroused opposition, as did his proselytizing at Court. The opposition to Conn became public when the influential Lord Newport, Master of the Ordnance, complained that his wife had been converted by Conn. He insisted that curbs be placed on papal agents at Court and that the Queen's chapel be closed. Her influence prevented any effective measures being taken, but by 1638 Charles's popularity was at a low ebb and riots were occurring against Catholics, Laudian high churchmen and the Queen's Romanizing activities. Conn's perhaps ill-

[16] H.O. Evennett, *The Spirit of the Counter Reformation* (1968) (Postscript by John Bossy), p. 144.

[17] M. J. Havran, *Catholics in Caroline England* (1962), pp. 143–4.

judged and often rashly-executed mission to England lasted until 1639. He returned to Rome 'soured in mind and sick in body' and died a few months later.[18] As England collapsed towards civil war, the King's cause was taken up in Rome by an unofficial delegate, Sir Kenelm Digby. Born in 1603 in Gayhurst, Buckinghamshire and brought up a Catholic, Digby had been educated at Oxford, completed the Grand Tour and embarked on a naval career. In 1630 he became a member of the Church of England, only to return to Catholicism in 1635. He was a great friend of Sir Tobie Mathew and came into contact with George Conn at Court. With acquaintances made through Conn in 1639 he evolved a plan to raise funds from Catholics to defend the King's position – only to find himself summoned before Parliament to answer for his conduct.[19] In the early months of 1645, Digby travelled with his two sons and a companion, Thomas White, to Rome. He was received warmly and, in flamboyant style, presented the King's cause to the Pope. Emphasizing the loyalty of English Catholics to Rome and the great services which Henrietta Maria had rendered the Church, Digby assured the Pope of the imminent conversion of Charles and England to Catholicism.[20] To aid the King in defeating his enemies, Digby asked the Pope for 500,000 scudi. His flamboyant style and the scandalous behaviour of his travelling companion White did not help to convince the Pope, who was not persuaded of Charles's intention to convert. Digby's mission came to an end in November, when Innocent X offered 100,000 scudi in return for complete toleration for Catholics in England and signs of real success for the royalists in the Civil War. There was no likelihood of either.[21]

Digby was forced to return in 1647 on an even more fruitless mission and, wearied by the whole business, he left for England in January 1648 in ill-health. Having achieved little, he was condemned by the King's opponents for conniving and plotting with the papacy and criticized by

[18] A. Dures, *English Catholicism 1558–1642* (1983), p. 79.
[19] R. T. Petersson, *Sir Kenelm Digby: Ornament of England 1603–65* (1956), p. 152.
[20] Petersson, pp. 215–16.
[21] Ibid., p. 218.

Catholics for having bungled the attempt.

Inevitably, as Conn's and Digby's failures illustrate, ecclesiastical links with English Catholics were entangled with questions of royal authority. The accession and abdication of James II, the last Catholic king of England (1685–88), was to bring the issue to a head. Under James II, for the first time in 150 years, a royal ambassador to Rome was appointed. This created difficulties in Rome. The Pope had sent a discreet, private ambassador to London, but James II had insisted on receiving him with full diplomatic honours. He now expected the same in return. The choice of the Earl of Castlemaine was 'not felicitous',[22] as he was chiefly known as the husband of Charles II's favourite mistress. His status was not settled when he arrived in Rome and for this reason he was met privately two miles outside the city by Cardinal Philip Howard, the Protector of England, and taken to his palazzo at the English College.[23] This arrangement did not last long when Howard found the college Rector and Castlemaine engaged in secret whisperings and clandestine meetings. Within days the Rector was on his way back to England and the ambassador installed in a palazzo belonging to the Doria Pamphili in the Piazza Navona. Over the gate hung two shields twenty-two feet in diameter which attracted such attention that a pamphlet was produced to explain their meaning! One showed Britannia paying homage to the Church, assisted by an elderly male figure representing 'Christian Zeal', a female figure representing 'Prudence' and the figure of Hercules trampling Envy as 'Royal Valour'. There was also an altar, with the Book of the Gospels resting on the shoulders of two Turks, one holding a mutilated copy of the Koran. The scene was completed by two sphinxes, the Tiber and branches of laurel symbolizing the victories of the Church. The other shield contained the coats of arms of England, France, Ireland and Scotland, the garter, lion, unicorn, helmet, crown, ermine mantelet, in a shield supported by two angels. Then another Hercules, with club

---

[22] G. Anstruther, 'Life of Cardinal Philip Howard OP', (unpublished MS in the Dominican Provincial Archives, Edinburgh).

[23] R. Lanciani, *New Tales of Old Rome* (1901, reissued 1967), pp. 285–6.

and banner bearing 'Dieu et Mon Droit', a matron representing Britannia, St George spearing a seven-headed hydra
representing seven leaders of rebellion, including the
Catholic traitor Titus Oates. Hercules and Britannia were
trampling the rebels Colledge and Cromwell. This one was
completed by sphinxes, the Thames and laurels. These
extraordinary displays were erected by the 'secret' English
ambassador to the Holy See![24]

On the day appointed for the formal presentation of
credentials, Rome was brought to a standstill by the celebrations and processions. A massive banquet, rounded off
by a fancy-dress masquerade drive down the Corso,
preceded the formal events on 8 January 1687. On the day
itself, Castlemaine's carriage was escorted on a circuitous
route to the Quirinale led by thirty-two outriders and 335
carriages. A week later the newly-accredited ambassador
gave his state banquet in the gallery of the Pamphili palace.
On the table were eighty silver trays supporting lions and
unicorns of sugar and 190 separate dishes were served.[25]

Despite keeping Rome agog for weeks, the embassy of
Lord Castlemaine was not long lived. Diplomacy was not
his forte and at only his second papal audience he resorted
to bullying and hectoring Innocent XI. When on 3 May he
threatened the Pope that if his royal master's wishes were
not met, the ambassador would be forced to leave Rome,
the Pope courteously reminded him that May was a cooler
month for travel than June.[26]

The career of Cardinal Philip Howard OP was closely
enmeshed with the Stuart royal family and illustrates the
perils of English Catholic relations with royal and papal
power in the seventeenth century. Howard contrived a
career as both royal servant and papal servant, while
playing an active part in the restoration of Catholic life in
England. He pursued this career mostly in Rome, as
Cardinal Protector of England and royal agent in Rome.

In the Dominican church of S. Maria Sopra Minerva, his

[24] Ibid., pp. 286–8.
[25] Ibid., p. 291.
[26] J. F. Champ, 'Philip Howard OP, Rome and English Recusancy', *New Blackfriars* 76 (June 1995), p. 277.

titular church, Howard is buried. His tomb is not easily visible, being in the pavement of the choir, the fourth from the centre on the right side of a semi-circle of tablets, now largely obscured by the organ console. At his own insistence, it is a flat stone with a plain inscription, without adornment or word of praise:

> To Philip Thomas Howard of Norfolk and Arundel, Cardinal Priest of S. Sopra Minerva of the Holy Roman Church, of the saintly family of the Order of Preachers, Archpriest of S. Maria Maggiore, Protector of Great Britain, Grand Almoner of England, father of his country and of the poor. His sons of the English Province of the same Order, being named his heirs, placed this tablet in mourning for their most excellent father and restorer, with the approval of the eminent cardinals of the Holy Roman Church, Paulutius of Altieri, Francis of Nerli, Galeatius Marescottus and Fabrutius Spada, the executors of his will. He died on 20 June in the year of our salvation 1694 at the age of 64.[27]

Philip Howard was the great-grandson of St Philip Howard, first Earl of Arundel, who died imprisoned in the Tower for his faith. He took vows as a Dominican in 1646, was ordained six years later and returned to England to collect funds for his first Dominican foundation at Bornhem in Flanders. In 1674 he was created cardinal and from then on lived in Rome, where he was known as the Cardinal of Norfolk. At first his titular church was S. Cecilia, but he was translated to Sopra Minerva in 1679. He was the first English cardinal created since Allen, eighty years before, succeeding Barberini as Cardinal Protector of England and Scotland in 1679, with general oversight of institutions and appointments. He was the first ever English-born Protector and his appointment makes clear the need for the papacy at this time to maintain real contact with the English Catholics, through a person who knew the realities of the

[27] Vidon, p. 154.

seventeenth-century recusant mission.

Alongside the Grand Tourists, ambassadors and cultural visitors to Rome from England, there flourished a persistent tradition of religious pilgrimage encouraged by Howard. The pilgrim book of the English College runs continuously in three volumes from 1580 to 1767.[28] What is remarkable is that, although visitors such as Milton and Evelyn were often noted, a clear distinction was often made between them and the true pilgrims. Many of the pilgrims of the seventeenth and eighteenth centuries were not wealthy but arrived in need of alms and often of medical care. The ancient tradition of poor pilgrims receiving eight days' charity in the hospice was the accepted practice. So commonplace was this that in some cases it was simply noted that pilgrims received 'the ordinary charity of the college'.[29] Pilgrims were expected to arrive with letters of testimonial, and practice seems to have tightened up in the late seventeenth century. On 22 January 1682 'Robert Pugh of Ipswich and John Durridge of London came from Naples and having no kind of testimonial were at first refused entertainment till his Eminence the Cardinal Protector [Philip Howard OP] sent them with an order to admit them to the ordinary charity of pilgrims.'[30] Howard had a reputation for the generosity of his welcome to all English visitors and pilgrims, rich and poor alike.[31] Many of the pilgrims who were received at the English College in the 1680s were taken on his recommendation, including Thomas Watkins of Monmouthshire who arrived on 20 December 1680 'to the ordinary charity as pilgrim' but stayed for three months 'by express order of the Cardinal Protector'.[32]

Early in 1685 he created his new palace for formal use adjoining the English College, extensively rebuilt and refurbished at great cost. The work done under Howard's direction created the college buildings much as they can be seen today. His apartments were built on the site of the

[28] VEC Archives Liber 282, 283, 292.
[29] Liber 283.
[30] Ibid.
[31] J. F. Champ, *New Blackfriars* 76 (June 1995), pp. 268–79.
[32] Liber 283.

Corte Savelli prison, acquired by the college in exchange for other properties. Among Howard's visitors was Gilbert Burnet, historian and later Bishop of Salisbury under William and Mary. On his visit in 1685 he claimed to have found most of the cardinals opposed to the extremism of the Stuarts. He discussed Anglican orders with one cardinal and had a number of conversations with Howard of whom he said, 'he hath all the sweetness and gentleness of temper that we saw in him in England, and he retains the unaffected simplicity and humility of a friar amidst all the dignity of the purple'.[33]

Howard remained loyal to the Stuarts and was a close adviser to James II before and after his exile. He was aware of the dangers facing the new king in 1685 and urged a policy of caution but with little success. Before and after 1688, James did his best to ignore or circumvent Howard's advice, until he needed money in 1690. Howard was treated roughly by the Stuarts, including attempts to replace him as Protector with Rinaldo D'Este, a relative of the Queen. Nevertheless he continued to demonstrate public support by organizing celebrations in Rome on the accession of James II and the birth of the Prince of Wales – short-lived celebrations as it turned out.[34]

Loyalty to the Stuart cause carried its own costs and among those who left England in the wake of the Stuarts was Philip Michael Ellis OSB, Vicar Apostolic of the Western District.[35] The one lasting benefit of James II's reign for English Catholics was the appointment of Vicars Apostolic in 1688 to administer the English mission. As Vicars Apostolic and not Bishops in Ordinary, they were direct papal appointees, with little local jurisdiction by right. This was later to prove problematic and by the end of the eighteenth century direct papal rule, albeit exercised vicariously, was not seen by all English Catholics as an unmixed blessing.

[33] M. L. Clarke, 'British Travellers to Rome in Tudor and Stuart Times', *History Today* 28 (1978), p. 751.

[34] B. Foley, *Some Other People of Penal Times* (Lancaster, 1991), p. 27.

[35] G. Hay, 'An English Bishop in the Volscians', reprinted from the *Venerabile* 19 (1959) in D. A. Bellenger ed. *Fathers in Faith* (1991), pp. 23–30.

The appointment of a Vicar Apostolic for England had been planned as early as 1669 and by 1672 an abortive scheme was under way to appoint Howard as Bishop and Vicar Apostolic.[36] However the matter was shelved for most of Charles's reign, but taken up rapidly on James II's accession in February 1685. Through his envoy in Rome, John Caryll, James petitioned successfully for an appointment. John Leyburn, who had been Howard's secretary, was appointed Vicar Apostolic for England in August 1685 and was joined by three other appointees (Philip Ellis OSB, Bonaventure Giffard, and James Smith) in early 1688. The system of government by Vicars Apostolic lasted till the mid-nineteenth century, but by the end of 1688 James II was in exile, and Ellis and Giffard were in Newgate gaol.

Ellis was born in 1652, the third son of an Anglican clergyman, and was a schoolboy convert, known to his schoolfellows as 'Jolly Phil'. He was educated first at Westminster, then at St Gregory's Douai, not, as was rumoured, kidnapped by the Jesuits and whisked off to St Omer's.[37] He came of a remarkable family: one brother became Under-Secretary of State to William III, another Secretary of State in exile to James II, and a third became the Church of Ireland Bishop of Meath. Philip Ellis himself became a monk of St Gregory's (the forerunner of Downside Abbey) and was professed in 1670.

He became court preacher to James II and established a considerable reputation as 'the most effective court preacher of his day'.[38] He exercised influence at Court and among London Catholics, urging them to seize the opportunity of religious freedom and a more prosperous future offered by James II's policies. At the same time, he tried to restrain James's policy of enforcing Catholicism and to moderate the influence of his Jesuit advisers. Ellis was a well-known figure, boldly wearing his Benedictine habit around London and responsible for the conversion to Catholicism of a large number of courtiers. His episcopal

[36] J. Miller, *Popery and Politics in England* (1973), p. 47.
[37] Bruno Navarra, *Filippo Michele Ellis* (Rome, 1973), p. 28.
[38] G. Scott, *Gothic Rage Undone: English Monks in the Age of Enlightenment* (1992), p. 14.

consecration took place in St James's Palace on 6 May 1688 and he was awarded a grant of £500 and a salary of £1000 a year from the royal exchequer.[39]

On his release from prison, Ellis followed the King into exile, first to St Germain, but from early 1693 he lived in Rome.[40] Once in Rome he acted as secretary to Cardinal Howard, living with him, either at SS Giovanni e Paolo or at the English College and attending him in his final illness. Ellis took over much of his work as semi-official royal representative of James II at the papal court and succeeded to this role on Howard's death in 1694.

The loss of his protector left Ellis in an awkward position. He was not liked at the college and in 1695 the rector petitioned the Pope to have him removed. He went to live with the Dominicans at SS Giovanni e Paolo until they left in 1697. It is not clear where he passed the next few years – perhaps with the Dominicans or his own order.[41] However, he made repeated efforts to return to England, while attempting to do what he could for the English Catholic cause in Rome.[42] Growing uneasy over his own position, despairing of ever returning to England and poised uneasily in the current dispute between the Benedictines and the Vicars Apostolic, Ellis resigned his vicariate in 1705.[43]

In 1708 Ellis's life was finally given a sense of purpose, when he was appointed Bishop of Segni. Lying south of Rome, high in the Volscian hills, Segni has been described as, 'a town like the Volscian hills from whose stone it is built. There is not much to attract one and the chief monument is a pre-Roman wall of great blocks of Volscian stone.'[44] This hardly does justice to a delightful hilltop town of steep winding streets and mediaeval stone houses, offering magnificent views of the Volscian hills all around.

[39] Ibid., p. 13.
[40] Navarra, p. 71.
[41] Ibid., pp. 77–8.
[42] B. Hemphill, *The Early Vicars Apostolic of England 1685–1750* (1954), p. 21.
[43] Scott, pp. 65–7.
[44] Hay, *Fathers in Faith*, p. 27.

It contains pre-Christian relics including the famous walls and was an episcopal see as early as 499. The tiny eleventh-century Cathedral of S. Pietro, built on a Roman site, contains remnants of thirteenth-century frescoes and has a mediaeval campanile built in part by the family of Pope Innocent III who were Counts of Segni. (Innocent himself was born across the valley at Anagni.) Its position on top of Monte Lepino caused Ellis to commend S. Pietro as a place of devotion to Mary, under the title of 'Our Lady of the Mountains'.[45] In the Middle Ages, Segni's mountainous fortified position made it a regular safe haven for embattled popes. Eugenius III (1145–53) built a palace there and in 1173 Alexander III performed the ceremony there for the canonization of St Thomas à Becket.

Philip Ellis set about his new charge as Bishop of Segni with great zeal and energy but with very little initial optimism. He wrote of the people of Segni, '... (they) are only a little more civilized than the ancient Volscii, their ancestors. They appear to take no interest in education and culture and, what is far worse, seem to be quite averse from religion. For the most part they do not even know the basic truths of the faith.'[46] From this unpromising beginning, Ellis became a model bishop, much loved and revered by his people and still regarded as a fine reforming bishop who achieved much for his see and his people.

The Pope had specifically asked Ellis to found a diocesan seminary, which he did, taking over the ruined papal palace next to S. Pietro. He built it into a combined seminary and school. (It continues as a school.) In November 1710 he held a diocesan synod which met in the cathedral of Our Lady and drew up reforms for the seminary and the diocese. He completed three visitations between 1710 and 1714 and twice arranged missions throughout the diocese.

Ellis inherited a cathedral and palace which was a laughing-stock, a dilapidated building, the only entrance to the cathedral being through the wine cellar. He constructed a proper entrance, reroofed the building and

---

[45] Navarra, *Guide Book to Cathedral of S Pietro, Segni*, p. 10.
[46] Hay, p. 27.

carried out much restoration. The cathedral now contains many beautiful works of art, including fine modern sculpture, as well as memorials to Ellis's work. He died in Segni in November 1726, greatly mourned, and was buried in the chapel of the seminary.

For the leaders of the English Catholics trying to rebuild the mission, links with Rome were vital. The value of ecclesiastical representation in Rome had been realized quickly by the Vicars Apostolic and after the death of Philip Howard, George Witham was rapidly appointed as their agent. He served from 1694 until he was appointed as Vicar Apostolic himself in 1703. His episcopal consecration took place in Montefiascone, the same small town near Viterbo where in 1719 James III contracted his dramatic marriage to Maria Clementina. Witham's successor also went on to become a Vicar Apostolic, for Scotland in 1707. From then on two men carried the English agency in Rome for the rest of the eighteenth century. Laurence Mayes served for forty years until he died in office in 1748. The agent still had to work discreetly and the coded language used conveys an air of espionage largely outdated even then. The Pope was often referred to in letters as 'Mr Abraham' and Rome itself known as 'Hilton'. For some extraordinary reason, Catholics in general were known as 'Mrs Yaxley's family'.[47] Mayes did not have an easy time of it and was often in severe financial embarrassment. Persecution had largely ceased in England but the recusants continued to live in difficulty often due to lack of resources, and requests to Rome for help to maintain clergy were often met with the same response – no money. In the 1720s the Vicars Apostolic regularly found it impossible to pay Mayes' salary and there was real danger of the Roman agency coming to an end.[48]

In the 1730s the secular clergy and Vicars Apostolic became determined to get rid of Jesuit control of the English College which had been in place since the 1580s and did not in fact end until the suppression of the Society

[47] B. Hemphill, *Early Vicars Apostolic of England 1685–1750* (1954), p. 80.
[48] Ibid., pp. 91–3.

of Jesus in 1773. This dispute led to the only visit to Rome by an English Vicar Apostolic in the eighteenth century. In 1736, Matthew Prichard OFM, Vicar Apostolic of the Western District, set out for Rome with the apparent intention of obtaining financial aid for his impoverished District or resigning. However his motives were not trusted by his brother bishops, who believed him to be pro-Jesuit in the matter of the control of the college. Therefore Mayes was urged on by the other Vicars Apostolic to greater efforts to obtain secular control.[49] At about the same time, Christopher Stonor, nephew of the Vicar Apostolic of the Midland District, arrived in Rome to study Canon Law. His uncle had made no secret of his dissatisfaction with Mayes' energy and activity on behalf of the bishops, so it was no surprise that Christopher became Mayes' assistant and succeeded him in 1748 as English agent.

Christopher Stonor was one of the most influential English churchmen of the eighteenth century and his burial place and memorial are in the church of S. Caterina della Rota in the piazza of the same name opposite the English College. His memorial gives some idea of his remarkable attributes.

> To the memory and peace of Christopher Stonor, Englishman of Oxford, a man of distinguished ancestry, formerly member of the Ecclesiastical Academy, Theologian Laureate of the Faculty of Theology at the Sorbonne, Head Chamberlain of Clement XIV and of Pius VI and granted by him the honour of Domestic Prelate, who, on account of his remarkable reputation for wisdom was appointed agent of the clergy at the Holy See by the English Catholic Bishops. He was of great service to the Church and lived a devout man for 80 years. He died on 12 April 1795. Hail most devoted man and farewell in peace.[50]

---

[49] Ibid., pp. 137–8.
[50] Vidon, pp. 147–8.

Christopher was born in 1716, the third son of Thomas Stonor and nephew of John Talbot Stonor. He spent twelve years studying at St Gregory's seminary in Paris and while still a deacon was left in charge of the college for several months in 1742. Ordained the following year, he returned to England and lived at the family home at Stonor Park with his uncle, the Vicar Apostolic of the Midland District. He succeeded Laurence Mayes in 1748 and retained the post of agent till 1790.

Initially he lived with the Cardinal Duke of York as his chaplain in Rome, but was appointed a papal chamberlain and given quarters in the papal palace of the Quirinale. His long period in office as agent covered a time of considerable upheaval in England and Rome, including the end of Jesuit control of the English College and suppression of the Society. He also saw the achievement of the first Catholic Relief Act in 1778, easing the constraints on English Catholics. In 1790 he retired to a house in Via Giulia and assisted with priestly duties at S. Caterina, where he was much loved as a man of great charm and kindliness. His friends marked their affection by paying for the erection of his monument in S. Caterina.

By the eighteenth century the Grand Tour was at the peak of its popularity and its *aficionados* appear, in many accounts of Rome, to have taken over the city from the pilgrims. Rome was the venue for tourists who sought to imbibe the classical past which inspired so much of current architectural and domestic fashion in England. Much to the distaste of successive popes, Rome was the antique shop of Europe and its statuary and the archaeological artifacts swelled the collections of many English country houses. It offered access to great art of the Renaissance and Baroque periods for those seeking artistic education and was a favourite backdrop for aspiring artists of varying levels of distinction. Travel had become desirable and beneficial for education, culture and health, and the affluent English, comfortable in the security of their country's economic and military might, set forth with gusto. The novelist Laurence Sterne poked fun at his fellow travellers and their European hosts in his (unfinished) *A Sentimental Journey through France and Italy.*[51]

> Your idle people that leave their native country and
> go abroad for some reason or reasons which may be
> derived from one of these general causes –
>> Infirmity of body,
>> Infirmity of mind, or
>> Inevitable necessity.
> The first two include all those who travel by land or
> water, labouring with pride, curiosity, vanity or
> spleen, subdivided and combined *ad infinitum.*
> The third class includes the whole army of peregrine
> martyrs; more especially those travellers who set out
> upon their travels with the benefit of clergy, either as
> delinquents travelling under the direction of gover-
> nors recommended by the magistrate – or young
> gentlemen transported by the cruelty of parents and
> guardians and travelling under the direction of
> guardians recommended by Oxford, Aberdeen and
> Glasgow ...
> Thus the whole circle of travellers may be reduced to
> the following heads.
>> Idle Travellers,
>> Inquisitive Travellers,
>> Lying Travellers,
>> Proud Travellers,
>> Vain Travellers,
>> Splenetic Travellers.
> Then follow the Travellers of Necessity,
> The delinquent and felonious Traveller,
> The unfortunate and innocent Traveller,
> The simple Traveller,
> And last of all (if you please) The Sentimental
> Traveller.

In 1734 Richard Pococke noted forty English visitors to
Rome (i.e. of any social consequence) and a report in an
English local newspaper of 1751 proclaimed that 'The

[51] Published 1768 (The World's Classics, 1928), pp. 13–15.

English Lords and Ladies who are in this city (Rome) are so numerous as to be able to form amongst themselves a society as considerable as that of the Roman Noblesse. They have hired for the purpose a palace, where there is every evening an assembly for a play, a concert of music and supper.'[52] Horace Walpole, on his arrival in Rome in 1740, wrote, 'The English are numberless. I know at Rome you will not have a grain of pity for one, but indeed 'tis dreadful dealing with schoolboys just broke loose, or old fools that are come abroad at forty to see the world, like Sir Wilful Witwou'd.'[53]

Pilgrimage passed from the mainstream of English society as a reason for travel, but, as will become clear, did not disappear completely. The religious rites of Rome, including the practice of pilgrims, were among the objects of curiosity for English visitors, as Walpole noted: 'We are just come from adoring a great piece of the true cross, St Longinus' spear and St Veronica's handkerchief; all which have been this evening exposed to view in St Peter's'.[54] A number of factors have combined to render English pilgrimage to Rome invisible in the eighteenth century. Firstly, the emphasis in contemporary and later accounts of English society on the Grand Tour; secondly, the relative size and poverty of the recusant community limited the numbers able to make the journey; thirdly, the historiography of English Catholicism has for a long time emphasized the separation of English recusancy from continental Europe, and no one has expected to find accounts of English Catholic pilgrims in Rome. Nevertheless, in the midst of the Grand Tourists and other travellers, it is possible to find pilgrims. Who is to say that among Sterne's list of 'Travellers' were not some who found themselves drawn to the pilgrim shrines of Rome, even, if only, like Walpole, out of curiosity?

English Catholic visitors in the eighteenth century can be described in four categories. There were the affluent Catholic gentry who aspired to join their Protestant coun-

---

[52] J. Black, *The British Grand Tour* (1985), pp. 2–3.
[53] C. B. Lucas (ed.), *Letters of Horace Walpole* (1904), p. 24.
[54] Ibid., p. 26.

terparts on the Grand Tour, the ecclesiastical officials who sought to reorder relations between the English recusants and Roman officialdom, the Stuart exiled court and its supporters and fourthly, a modest number of genuine pilgrims motivated by the same aspirations as their mediaeval forebears.

As religious persecution waned in England and life for Catholics became more relaxed, the wealthy aristocracy and gentry began to emulate the desire of their Protestant neighbours to broaden their horizons. Excluded from many aspects of public life, the Grand Tour gave Catholics an opportunity to share a broader culture and develop personal accomplishments.[55] Catholics had the double attraction of devotion as well as culture, which makes it more difficult than ever in this period to know whether Catholic visitors to Rome should be called pilgrims or tourists. For the less financially secure Catholic gentry, living abroad for a time was often a way of cutting costs, avoiding financial ruin and perhaps preserving family estates. Also, the engagement by Catholics in socially respectable activities such as the Grand Tour was a conscious assertion of the recusants' desire and capacity for assimilation into the mainstream of English society.

English Catholic Grand Tourists began to leave their mark on Rome in the eighteenth century. They found themselves in a very different religious atmosphere from the quiet restraint of recusant England. Roman religion was lavish, voluptuous and sensual. On the whole it was undemanding, except at Lent and Easter when penitence was taken very seriously. Despite rationalization, over 120 festivals and Sundays were celebrated in Rome in 1770, when brilliant ceremonies, lit with forests of candles, took full advantage of the splendour and elegance of the baroque churches. Only at Easter did the services cease to be occasions for the senses rather than the spirit, and in Holy Week the atmosphere changed dramatically. The churches were stripped bare, all entertainments were

---

[55] M. B. Joyce, 'The Haggerstons: the education of a Northumbrian family', *Recusant History* 14 (1978), p. 180.

closed, the city fell silent and fashionable ladies wore black.[56] Despite the immense cultural differences, even for Catholics, the English felt at home in Rome.

There were English coffee houses where English journals could be read, English inns where English cooking could be enjoyed, taverns run by Englishmen where English students met. The expensive Albergo Londra was always full of English guests; while the elegant apartments at Casa Guarneri near the Spanish Steps were occupied by a succession of English tourists. Also there were numerous English people who had made their home in Rome.[57]

English recusants in eighteenth-century Rome were enormously varied in their political, cultural and religious devotion. They included Joseph Dormer, a member of a staunch Warwickshire recusant family, and a member of the Stuart household in exile, who died of dysentery in Rome in 1764 and is buried in the church of S. Buonaventura,[58] and the Jacobite Catholic baronet, Sir Carnaby Haggerston of Haggerston, Northumberland. He and his brother were in Rome in the winter of 1777–8 when they heard of their father's death; Sir Carnaby remained in Italy and commissioned designs for a new house at Haggerston.[59] Three generations of Haggerstons made the Grand Tour, beginning in 1711.[60] William Constable of Burton Constable, Yorkshire, made several Grand Tours in order to refurbish and decorate his house.[61] Described as 'a man of liberal views and considerable learning, both in the fine arts and in natural and experimental philosophy',[62] Constable's artistic and

---

[56] M. Andrieux, *Daily Life in Papal Rome in the Eighteenth Century* (1968), pp. 120–6.
[57] C. Hibbert, *The Grand Tour* (1969), p. 149.
[58] Ingamells, *A Dictionary of British and Irish Travellers in Italy 1701–1800* (1997), p. 306.
[59] Ingamells, *Dictionary*, p. 442.
[60] M. B. Joyce, *Recusant History*, p. 180.
[61] J. Black, p. 201.
[62] Ingamells, *Dictionary*, pp. 235–6.

scientific collections came to be more important to him than his religion and he drifted away from Catholicism.[63] During the tour he made in 1769–70, he was criticized by one of the resident English clergy for his lack of devotion and disregard of his faith.[64]

James Byres, the Scottish antiquarian (1734–1817) and Thomas Jenkins (1722–98) an English painter and dealer, were at the centre of the artistic world of the Grand Tourists. Byres was from a Jacobite Catholic family, and Jenkins, born in Rome, was at the heart of the papal court.[65] Among the most important of their Catholic clients, whose collections continued after their lifetimes to have national and international importance, were Charles Townley (1737–1805),[66] whose collection formed the basis of the British Museum collections, and Henry Blundell (1724–1810) much of whose collection now belongs to the National Museums and Galleries on Merseyside.[67] Linked to these fashionable Catholic circles were two very influential Jesuits resident in Rome, the Scottish Abbé Peter Grant (1708–84), 'an amiable busybody ever anxious to attend the more distinguished British travellers';[68] secondly, Fr John Thorpe (1726–92) a Yorkshireman of a rather more rigorous turn of mind, who was much concerned at the 'great degenerancy in Catholick families' in England.[69]

One of the most important guidebooks of the period was written by a Catholic Grand Tourist whose piety was also in evidence. Henry Swinburne (1743–1803), author of *Travels in the Two Sicilies in the years 1777, 1778, 1779 and 1780*, was the fourth son of Sir John Swinburne of Capheaton Hall, Northumberland. He was educated in Europe and his writings played an important part in disseminating information for travellers in southern Europe, especially

[63] C. Bence Jones, *The Catholic Families* (1992), p. 39.

[64] Ingamells, *Dictionary*, p. 235.

[65] Their careers and contacts can be traced in Ingamells, *Dictionary*, pp. 169–72, 553–6.

[66] Ingamells, *Dictionary*, pp. 946–8.

[67] Ingamells, *Dictionary*, pp. 101–2.

[68] Ingamells, *Dictionary*, pp. 420–2.

[69] Ingamells, *Dictionary*, pp. 939–42.

[70] J. Black, p. 24.

Italy.[70] He met and married his wife in France, where she had been educated by Ursuline nuns. The eldest daughter of Henry and Martha Swinburne, also called Martha, died aged 9 in September 1778 while travelling in Rome with her parents.[71] She was buried in the chapel of the English College where she is commemorated by a bust carved by the fashionable Irish sculptor Christopher Hewetson,[72] and an extravagant memorial tablet, criticized by Fr John Thorpe for its lack of religion, which reads:

> Martha Swinburne born October 10 1769. Her years were few but her life was long and full. She spoke English, French and Italian and had made some progress in the Latin tongue; knew her English and Roman histories, arithmetic and geography, sang the most difficult music at sight with one of the finest voices in the world, was a great proficient of the harpsichord, wrote well, and danced many sorts of dances with strength and elegance. Her face was beautiful and majestic, her body a perfect model and all her motions graceful. Her docility and alacrity in doing everything to make her parents happy could only be equalled by her sense and aptitude. With so many perfections, amidst the praises of all persons from the sovereign down to the beggar in the street, her heart was incapable of vanity; affectation and arrogance were unknown to her. Her beauty and accomplishments rendered her the admiration of all beholders, the love of all those that enjoyed her company. Think then, what the pangs of her wretched parents must be on so cruel a separation. Their only comfort is the certitude of her being completely happy beyond the reach of pain, and forever freed from all the miseries of this life. She can never feel the torments they endure for the loss of a beloved child. Blame them not for indulging an innocent pride in transmitting her memory to posterity as an honour to her family

---

[71] Ingamells, *Dictionary*, pp. 916–19.
[72] Ingamells, *Dictionary*, pp. 494–5.

and to her native country, England. Let this plain character penned by her disconsolate father, draw a tear of pity from every eye that peruses it.

The diary of one of the college students records that, 'After her child was buried Mrs Swinburne used to come every feast and Sunday to hear Mass at our college; but care was taken that none of the scholars should serve it ... The Mass used to be said mostly by one of the Prefects who received (at least for some time) 3 Paulos per Mass. After Christmas she came no more.'[73]

Italy, and Rome in particular, had returned to the centre of the English cultural mentality. The flourishing of the Grand Tour meant that classical and contemporary art and artifacts found their way into English country houses, whether owned by Catholics or Protestants. English Catholic ecclesiastical relations with Rome remained awkward, but after the waning of the memories of the seventeenth-century hostility and bloodshed, the role of Rome in English recusant politics also waned. The position which Rome occupied in the English Catholic mind changed, perhaps becoming more like that of their Protestant contemporaries; less a symbolic focus of power and unity, more a source of artistic inspiration and culture. Nevertheless, the pilgrimage tradition was not drowned by the Grand Tour, and Chaney is accurate in asserting that 'the phenomenon known as pilgrimage lasted considerably longer than its successor, that which the seventeenth-century priest and former pilgrim, Richard Lassels, first identified as the Grand Tour'.[74]

---

[73] VEC Liber 815, *Diary of John Kirk*, p. 96.
[74] Chaney, p. 203.

Chapter Six

Exile and Shipwreck

The story of the English in Rome in the eighteenth century is dominated by the Stuart royal family who lived there in exile after the failure of the 1715 attempt to reclaim the throne of England. Their welcome at St Germain had worn thin, and from 1717 James III and his family lived at the Palazzo Muti in Rome. The Pope was reluctant to have the Stuarts in Rome itself but there were close bonds between the royal family and the papal family of Clement XI (Albani) and he felt constrained to offer protection. Such were the papal connections that the Pope's eldest nephew, Annibale, preached a funeral oration for James II in the papal private chapel, and later on that same nephew was succeeded as Archpriest and Prefect of St Peter's by Henry, Cardinal Duke of York (1751).[1] The Palazzo Muti was the only site in Rome apart from the Vatican and Quirinale to have a permanent papal guard of honour.[2] The exiled Stuarts became an object of constant curiosity to the eighteenth-century fashionable Europeans for whom Rome was the climax of the Grand Tour, but also something of an embarrassment to English visitors to whom they offered unwanted diplomatic assistance. Most eighteenth-century English visitors to Rome probably followed Lord Chesterfield's advice to his son if he met a Stuart in Rome.

[1] Lewis, *Connoisseurs and Secret Agents in Eighteenth Century Rome* (1961), pp. 31–3.
[2] F. McLynn, *The Jacobites* (1985), p. 164.

'Feign ignorance of him and his grievances. If he begins to talk politics, disavow any knowledge of events in England and escape as soon as you can.'[3]

The Stuart residence of the Palazzo Muti was the goal of Jacobite pilgrims. Built in 1644, it occupies the narrow end of the Piazza SS Apostoli and was known in the nineteenth century as the Palazzo del Pretendente. H.V. Morton described it as 'a dull little palace',[4] but it was apparently in the eighteenth century, 'a large square mansion of stone, standing on its own extensive pleasure grounds'.[5] For seventy years it was the headquarters of the 'King across the water'. James III and his queen, Maria Clementina, lived there and maintained a semblance of courtly life, as the Marquis of Blandford found, when invited to dine. 'There is every day a regular table of ten or twelve covers well served, unto which some of the qualified persons of his Court or travellers are invited; it is supplied with English and French cookery, French and Italian wine, but I took notice that the Pretender ate only of the English dishes and took his dinner of roast beef.' The Pope also gave the Stuarts the Palazzo Savelli in Albano as a summer retreat, where James spent many happy hours.[7]

In the same piazza as the Palazzo Muti is the church which gives it its name, SS Apostoli, which featured significantly in the lives of the Stuarts. The present church dates from 1702, so it was fashionably new when the Stuarts took up residence in Rome, although at least one later visitor was unimpressed with its baroque splendour; '... the edifice which was a monument to faith has given place to the temple of a monumental vanity'.[8]

On a pillar of the nave on the right is a memorial commemorating Queen Maria Clementina, the wife of James III, marking the burial place of her heart. After the

[3] B. Barefoot, *The English Road to Rome* (1993), p. 100.
[4] H. V. Morton, *A Traveller in Rome* (1957), p. 246.
[5] B. W. Kelly, *Life of Henry Benedict Stuart, Cardinal Duke of York* (1899), p. 12.
[6] Barefoot, p. 99.
[7] McLynn, p. 164.
[8] F. Marion Crawford, *Ave Roma Immortalis* (1903), p. 158.

failed 'Fifteen, a suitable marriage was vital for James to keep the cause alive. Maria Clementina, a Polish princess, was related to the royal houses of Austria and Spain and had influential aunts in all the courts of Europe. The marriage contract, signed in 1718, stated that the marriage must take place on papal territory and that if she was not safely delivered to the Papal States within three months, the deal was off. Maria Clementina then became the subject of the most celebrated intrigue of the eighteenth century.[9]

British pressure was put upon the Emperor to prevent his cousin's marriage to the Pretender by fair means or foul. Maria Clementina and her mother had reached Innsbruck en route for the Papal States on 3 October 1718, when they were detained by imperial warrant. The royal party were held at a palace outside the city where they were to remain until April 1719.

Factions intrigued on both sides to advance and delay the wedding. The papal nuncio became convinced that a secret abduction was the only solution and Charles Wogan, a young Irish Jacobite, set about bringing it off. Travelling under false passports, he and a small group of friends, posing as pilgrims to Loreto, travelled as far as Innsbruck.

On Thursday 27 April 1719, Maria Clementina attended Mass as usual in Innsbruck's Capuchin church, but the following day was not seen and was reported as unwell. Only two days later, when more forceful enquiries were made, did the princess's tearful mother admit that she had fled the palace during the night leaving a letter. The letter and the tears were a ruse to protect her mother from any blame, although she knew all about the plot.

Using a network of contacts across Europe, Wogan and his party had put together an elaborate escape plan. A meeting was arranged at a coach house outside the city walls of Innsbruck, where a female accomplice disguised as a countess had already retired for the night to await leave to continue her journey. At 1 a.m. the princess was taken in

---

[9]   G. Gurtler, 'Deceptis Custodibus or Liberty Lost – Liberty Regained', *Royal Stuart Papers*, 25 (1990), *passim*.

pouring rain to the coach house, where some time later the 'countess' and her maid got into a carriage which had been given clearance to pursue its journey. They fled the city under cover of darkness and filthy weather, and by 8 a.m. had reached the Brenner Pass. On the morning of Saturday 29 April, Maria Clementina stepped on to Venetian soil and safety, just a few hours after her escape had been discovered in Innsbruck.

In the meantime, Spain had gone to war with England and James was in Madrid awaiting the outcome of a Spanish-supported rising at Glensheil. In his absence the Pope himself set out to meet Clementina and a marriage by proxy was contracted on 9 May.[10] Even the menace of a British fleet off Civitavecchia did not prevent the marriage taking place at Montefiascone on 1 September 1719. Wogan and his fellow conspirators were rewarded with Roman senatorships and royal titles when the court was established in Rome.

Sadly, the romantic start did not herald either a long or a happy marriage. The strain of an impecunious court, the squabbles and dissent and the preoccupations of her melancholy husband placed an intolerable strain on Maria Clementina and the marriage. She accused him of having an affair with Lady Inverness, the wife of a courtier. For a time she left James and fled to the nuns of S. Cecilia in Via Vittorio. She eventually returned and devoted the rest of her life to her two young sons and to works of piety. Less charitably, Clementina's behaviour has been described as the 'melodramatic outburst of a neurotic, religiously maniacal woman, whose imbalanced tendencies were accentuated by life with the austere, melancholy and jealous James'.[11]

Maria Clementina died aged thirty-five in January 1735, and her funeral was an extraordinary affair, lacking nothing in royal pomp and ceremony, for all she was an uncrowned queen. Her body was taken first to SS Apostoli in procession, where, after the recitation of the Office for

[10] Lewis, p. 36.
[11] McLynn, p. 164.

the Dead, it was embalmed under the direction of the Pope's physician and dressed in the habit of the Dominicans, of which she was a Tertiary. After lying in state in the chapel of the Dominican Order, she was redressed in royal robes of purple velvet, gold and ermine and returned to SS Apostoli where thirty-two cardinals assisted in the Office for the Dead. Finally, the catafalque left for St Peter's,

> attended by members of numerous religious orders and congregations bearing lighted candles and followed by the entire Stuart household in court dress. With the hearse also went the students of the English, Scots and Irish Colleges and a detachment of the Swiss Guard. Then followed in order the officials of the Pope's household, Prelates of the Palace, Masters of Ceremonies, Protonotaries and chaplains in their carriages attended by halberdiers and mace bearers with silver maces. Last of all came ten coaches containing the Chevalier de S George, the Princes Charles Edward and Henry and their respective suites.[12]

Following the *De Profundis*, the body was again reclothed in Dominican habit and enclosed in its coffin, ready for the Requiem Mass and burial at St Peter's which followed the next day.

Despite their marital difficulties, James remained a disconsolate widower until his own death thirty-one years later. He spent many hours in prayer in SS Apostoli where his wife's heart was interred. One contemporary traveller noted after the Queen's untimely death. 'The King of England is too devout! He spends his mornings in prayer in SS Apostoli beside the tomb of his wife.'[13] As well as being the place of James's solitary mourning, SS Apostoli was also the regular venue of public prayers for the safe return of Charles Edward during and after the 'Forty-Five. Not surprisingly, it was given to the Duke of York as his

[12] Kelly, pp. 21–2.
[13] S. G. A. Luff, *The Christian's Guide to Rome* (1990 edn), p. 163.

titular church when he was ordained cardinal priest on 1 September 1748. Therefore it was also used for his episcopal ordination in 1758 when he was appointed titular Archbishop of Corinth (*in partibus infidelium*).

Both Prince Charles Edward (Bonnie Prince Charlie) and Henry (later Cardinal Duke of York) were born in the Muti, but it was rarely a happy home. Not only did Maria Clementina flee from her marriage to James and eventually die young and leave him a melancholic widower, but unhappiness followed the marriage of Charles Edward too. He was fifty-two, a defeated and disillusioned claimant to the throne and well advanced in the drunkenness and dissipation which marred his life, when he married Louisa Stolberg aged nineteen. He moved her into the Palazzo Muti with considerable splendour, from where she charmed Roman society.

As Charles declined further into dissipation, Louisa met and fell in love with a Roman poet, Alfieri. Charles, in a drunken rage, tried to strangle her. With Henry's help, Louisa fled to the nuns of S. Cecilia as her mother-in-law had done years before. For a time she lived in Henry's household, conducting her affair with Alfieri under the Cardinal's nose. Only on what Charles thought to be his deathbed did he reveal to Henry the full extent of his wife's dalliance. Eventually the lovers left Rome and settled together in Florence.

Charles Edward recovered some health and was joined at the Palazzo Muti in his old age and sickness by his illegitimate daughter Charlotte, Duchess of Albany, aged thirty-one. He had met her mother, Clementina Walkinshaw in Scotland during the 'Forty-Five and afterwards she had wandered Europe with him, passing as his wife. She fled after a series of violent quarrels and Charles rejected his daughter cruelly. When he later turned to her, she responded with kindness and brought order and sanity into her father's life, nursing him with great devotion. She brought dignity and peace to the last two years of his life at Palazzo Muti and Charles died there in January 1788. His daughter died only twenty months later from the cancer which had long afflicted her.

After the defeat of Charles Edward in the 1745 Rising, the continued claim of the Stuarts to the English throne became something of an embarrassment to English Catholics anxious to prove their Englishness, loyalty to the House of Hanover and capacity for assimilation. Even the Pope refused to acknowledge the claims of Charles and Henry to the English throne. Despite this, the number of Jacobite exiles in Rome increased. Writing in 1751, Horace Mann warned the Secretary of State about the influence of the Pretender and the growing numbers of English in Rome, staying for longer periods and coming under the dangerous sway of the Jacobites. He even spoke of the need to find some way of imposing limitations on travel by the English to Rome, but his idea was not taken up.[14] The period between the end of the war of Austrian Succession in 1748 and the start of the Seven Years War in 1756 saw the eclipse of the Stuart cause as an international political issue. For much of that time no one in Rome knew where Charles was, estranged from his brother and his increasingly ill and melancholy father.[15]

Henry, Duke of York was born in the Palazzo Muti on 6 March 1725, where Pope Benedict XIII arrived to baptize him personally. At the age of twenty-two, he decided on ordination, to his brother's distaste and fury. Not only was it likely to lose the Stuarts non-Catholic support in England, but it ruled out marriage and a dynastic contribution from Henry. Papal support was more enthusiastic and Henry was made cardinal four days after being ordained deacon by the Pope himself in the Sistine Chapel on 30 June 1747. He was given the titular church of S. Maria in Campitelli at the request of his father, and was allowed to keep it *in commendam* even after his ordination as cardinal priest of SS Apostoli. James had become especially devoted to Our Lady under this title as harbour of safety for Romans and special protectress of the city. Through an initiative of Henry and James a particular English devotion became established at the church of S.

[14]   Lewis, p. 145.
[15]   Lewis, p. 144.

Maria in Campitelli from 1751.[16] James asked that, every Saturday, thirty candles should be lighted on the high altar and the *Salve Regina* sung for the intention of the conversion of England. This predated by nearly a century the prayer campaigns for the same cause launched by Ignatius Spencer and Ambrose Phillipps de Lisle and presumably attracted English visitors and pilgrims to the church. In 1866 a triduum was held commemorating the Stuart establishment of this league of perpetual prayer. Pius IX himself composed a prayer 'on behalf of our brethren of England who live outside our unity of Faith'.[17] This church ranked third after S. Pietro and S. Maria Maggiore in a month of devotional visits to Roman churches instituted by the Pope. This tradition of prayer at S. Maria in Campitelli still continues, with special prayers being publicly offered after the 7 p.m. Mass every Saturday. In keeping with the ecumenical vision of our own age, the intention is for the reunion of Christians in England, and English visitors and pilgrims are made very welcome.[18]

Briefly between 1759 and 1763 Henry was titular cardinal of S. Maria in Trastevere. In the right apse of the church is a winter chapel restored by the Cardinal Duke who provided a new altar, chair and iron gates which are surmounted by the royal coat of arms. As papal chancellor his official residence was the Palazzo della Cancelleria, 'one of the most beautiful palaces in Rome'.[19] Built in the late fifteenth century on the gambling windfall of a papal nephew, it was confiscated by Pope Leo X (1513–21) who installed the Chancellery there. Three exiled Stuarts lived in the Palazzo della Cancelleria at various times, for Henry gave shelter to his sister-in-law Louisa Stolberg after she fled from his brother Charles Edward in 1781. After Charles's death in 1788 Henry took in Charlotte, Duchess of Albany, Charles's illegitimate daughter, until her own death.

[16] Kelly, p. 40.
[17] Guidebook/Prayer book of S. Maria in Campitelli.
[18] A second English Cardinal, Aidan Gasquet, Monk of Downside Abbey and historian of the English College was granted this title in 1914.
[19] Masson, p. 138.

When Henry was appointed Cardinal Bishop of Frascati in 1761, it seemed that the real work of his life had begun and he devoted himself unstintingly to it. There he lived the life of a zealous bishop, caring for his clergy and people. He lived in Frascati for forty years, 'in pious meditation, in vast charity and in princely entertainment'.[20] His genuine and lasting love for the town was returned by its people.

> Frascati was the scene of his greatest happiness. Here indeed he was a king. As a young and wealthy Cardinal Bishop, he lavished money on his see until it was said want and poverty had been abolished. He lived in great state, entertaining lavishly and was accessible to all. His travelling carriage drawn by superb horses was a familiar sight on the road to Rome, galloping at top speed.[21]

On 13 July 1761 the new bishop took charge of his see. All the inhabitants of Frascati gathered to welcome him and at the municipal hall he received an address from the magistrates, while at the episcopal palace of La Rocca the chapter canons were waiting to welcome him. The streets were decorated, the cathedral draped in crimson damask, feasting and rejoicing followed the enthronement ceremony and the fountain in the Piazza Maggiore flowed with wine. The evening ended with fireworks and bonfires across the hills.

When Henry took over the palace, it was in such a poor state of repair that at one banquet, he and his guests fell through the floor into the coach house beneath. The Cardinal was one of the lucky ones and was deposited gently on the roof of a coach. One of his tasks therefore was the complete restoration of the episcopal residence. His first project, however, was to summon a diocesan synod, which met in the autumn of 1763. He rented the Villa Aldobrandini for the purpose and lodged all his

[20] C. Harris, 'A Royal Bishop of Frascati', *The Beda Book: an Anthology* (1957), p. 46.
[21] Morton, p. 252.

clergy there at his own expense. The synod laid down guidelines in accord with the Council of Trent for the reform and ordering of clerical and lay diocesan life. He devoted immense energy to the reform of the seminary, founded in the mid-sixteenth century by Cardinal Cesi. It was moved to a new site, property acquired as a result of the suppression of the Jesuits in 1773, although Jesuits had been the first superiors. The Cardinal drew up stringent regulations, insisting as far as possible that students were natives of the diocese, and funding bursaries out of his own pocket. The full course of study lasted nine years, three of classical languages and literature, followed by philosophy and theology. The first rector was also the Cardinal's confessor and Vicar-General, Horatius Steffanucci SJ. In time the Cardinal endowed the seminary with one of the finest libraries in the Papal States, which became one of the targets of Napoleonic confiscation.

Among the first students at Frascati was Ercole Consalvi, a protégé of the Cardinal's, who went on to be papal Secretary of State to Pius VII. Consalvi played a major role in the restoration of the Papal States and in the development of cordial diplomatic relations with Britain. He was said to be the only man in Europe not afraid of Napoleon.

The Cardinal Duke of York's life expressed his character, a curious mix of ostentation and humility, of piety and worldliness. His daily routine was austere, the mornings spent in prayer and study in the seminary library and the afternoons in visitation of his diocese. Yet he maintained a lavish household of royal proportions and entertained widely. It was said that he kept sixty horses and always drove at breakneck speed, indifferent to the horses as long as he reached his destination on time. His carriage was drawn by six horses, preceded by running footmen, while a coach and four always followed in case of mishap. He continued to his death to maintain his claim to the British throne as Henry IX despite the refusal of the Pope to acknowledge it. He served the Pope loyally but deeply resented his refusal to support his royal claims. On the death of Charles in 1788 he had accession medals struck, bearing the inscription 'By the Will of God, but not by the desire of men'. In his own household he was always referred to as 'Your Majesty'.

The cathedral of S. Pietro in Frascati, restored by Henry, was the site of his brother's funeral and initial burial. Determined that Charles should have a royal funeral, Henry planned a ceremony of great pomp and solemnity. After lying in state at the Palazzo Muti, the body was removed to Frascati where a canopied catafalque bearing the royal coat of arms had been prepared. Huge crowds gathered inside and outside the cathedral, including British and Italian nobility – perhaps as much out of curiosity as respect. Charles was buried in the crypt and his brother erected a carefully-worded memorial which is preserved in the cathedral. It reads,

> Here is buried Charles Edward, whose father was James III, King of England, Scotland, France and Ireland; first born of James' sons, he was the successor and inheritor of his father's rights and kingly dignity. In his beloved Rome, where he lived, he was known as the Count of Albany. He lived 67 years and 1 month. He died in peace on 31 January 1788.

Charles remained buried at Frascati until Henry's death in 1807, when both brothers were buried alongside their parents in St Peter's in Rome.

In 1798 the Cardinal Duke, along with the rest of the cardinals, was forced to flee as Napoleon invaded Rome. The palace and seminary at Frascati were looted and the Cardinal was not able to return until the summer of 1800. He relinquished possession of the Palazzo Muti when he fled Rome in 1798 and gave the Pope much of his wealth to meet Napoleon's demands. A plaque just inside the entrance on the left of the courtyard commemorates the residence of the Stuarts in the Palazzo Muti, although the building is now given over to commercial use.

The Cardinal Duke followed the new Pope, Pius VII, elected at the conclave held by necessity in Venice, who re-entered Rome in July. While at the conclave, it came to the notice of King George III that the Cardinal Duke was impoverished due to the Napoleonic seizure of property and to the generous aid he had given to Pius VI. Lord Minto, the British Ambassador in Vienna, was dispatched to the conclave at Venice with £2000 and the promise of a pension of £5000. Though intended only to tide the Cardinal over his difficulties, the royal pension continued until he died.

In 1803, Pius VII appointed the Cardinal Duke as Dean of the College of Cardinals, which carried with it the *ex officio* appointment as Bishop of Ostia and Velletri. However, the Pope looked sympathetically on his request to be allowed to stay in residence at Frascati, though he ceased to be bishop of the see. He lived there until his death on 13 July 1807, on the forty-sixth anniversary of his election as Bishop of Frascati. His requiem was celebrated in the church of S. Andrea delle Valle, near his official residence, before burial in St Peter's. Cardinal Nicholas Wiseman, recalling his time in Rome as a student, wrote, 'The diocese of Frascati was full, when I first knew it, of recollections of the Cardinal Duke, all demonstrative of his singular goodness and simplicity of character ... for whatever else may have been wanting for his title, to a royal heart he was no pretender.'[22]

Among the Jacobite exiles who never left Rome was Sir Thomas Dereham, who died there in 1739 and was a generous benefactor to the English College. His memorial survives in the college church.[23] Dereham was a 'Notable Jacobite' who contrived to secure the appointment of a Catholic Jacobite as British Consul at Civitavecchia. Thomas Chamberlayne, Dereham's nominee, acted therefore as an unofficial Stuart representative at the main papal port.[24] Dereham had a successful diplomatic career before retreating to Rome, having represented the Medici interests in London during negotiations leading to the Quadruple Alliance of 1718 between England, France, Holland and the Empire. He also worked in Florence for a time. In Rome he was an assiduous opponent of Philip von

[22] N. Wiseman, *Recollections of the Last Four Popes* (1858), pp. 64–5.
[23] M. Williams, *Venerabile* 9, (1946) pp. 156–9.
[24] Lewis, p. 23.

Stosch who was appointed by the British government to spy on the Stuart court in Rome.[25] Charles Fane, as the British government diplomatic representative, wrote of his contact with Sir Thomas Dereham in 1734, who told him how he had befriended and helped Englishmen of late, since no British allies were lifting a finger to help them. He also explained that Dereham had a great correspondence in England and by means of the French Ambassador made a regular report on matters in England to the Pretender.[26]

In 1730, Charles Radcliffe, brother of the Earl of Derwentwater executed for his part in the 1715 rising, was in Rome. He also had been implicated in the rising and imprisoned in Newgate, escaping to the continent in 1716. His house in Rome became a regular meeting place for Jacobite supporters, with the added attraction of the beauty of his wife's (Lady Newburgh) two daughters by a previous marriage. Their parties became immensely popular in Roman society and it was said to be impossible therefore to distinguish in Rome who was loyal and who disloyal to the cause.[27] Part of their circle were Sir Marmaduke Constable and Francis Towneley, who was to be executed for complicity in the 'Forty-Five.[28] The long-term exiles in Rome included Andrew Lumsden who became James III's private secretary and whose sister was the wife of a celebrated Scottish engraver, Robert Strange, who had fought for the Jacobites at Culloden. In his spare time, Lumsden joined the growing fashion for studying antiquities. He ultimately was able to achieve a full pardon and to publish his book, *Remarks Upon the Antiquities of Rome and its Environs* in 1797.[29]

Eventually a son of one of the Jacobite exiles was to play a significant part in healing the breach between Britain and the papal court. Colin Erskine, a Jacobite Scot, settled in Rome and married Agatha Gigli, daughter of a noble Anagni family and they produced a son, loyally named

[25] Lewis, pp. 61, 86.
[26] Lewis, p. 109.
[27] Lewis, p. 86.
[28] Lewis, pp. 141–2.
[29] Lewis, pp. 144, 185.

Charles, in February 1739. The boy's father died when he was a baby and he was placed in the care of the Stuarts. At the age of nine he was placed at the Scots College but left at the age of fourteen with an ambition for the law rather than the priesthood. He went on to become a successful and well-respected lawyer and in 1782 entered the service of the papal court as an advocate. In the following year, his protector, the Cardinal Duke of York bestowed on him minor orders, which would enable promotion in the Curia. When the Pope made up his mind to improve relations with the Hanoverian Crown and to rebuild diplomatic links, Charles Erskine was the obvious choice. He was to follow up on private visits made to Rome by the Duke of Gloucester (George III's brother) and by the Duke of Sussex (George III's son) and in return for his services as a papal diplomat, he was given the dignity of Cardinal.[30] The British government gave permission for the papal mission provided it did not have a public character and Erskine left quietly for England on 4 October 1793.[31] He moved easily in London society and attended regularly at Court. Ironically, for a number of years after the Pope's exile, Erskine was running the affairs of the curial congregation of *Propaganda Fide* from London.[32] His tact and discretion (including his refusal to have a public announcement made of his cardinalate) clearly made him a popular success and 'his mission was a landmark in the evolution of England's relationship to the Holy See'.[33]

The English College by the eighteenth century was well established as a centre of training for the English priesthood and, as such, had entered the consciousness of English recusants. However, the college and its direction by Jesuit superiors was a source of disquiet to the English Vicars Apostolic. The 1739 Apostolic Visitation Report reveals a disturbingly small number of students and care-

---

[30] W. Maziere Brady, *Anglo-Roman Papers*, Memoirs of Cardinal Erskine (1890).
[31] G. Mooney, 'British Diplomatic relations with the Holy See 1793–1830', *Recusant History* 14 (1978), p. 195.
[32] Ibid., p. 196.
[33] Ibid., p. 196.

less bookkeeping and accounting. The influence of the English College in eighteenth-century English Catholicism in terms of priests was relatively small compared with the other foreign seminaries. 'Not only was there a general lack of enthusiasm for the college under its present management, but there was a lack of vocations.'[34] Yet the ancient pilgrimage connection and the role of the hospice in English piety survived. Despite a reputation for poor bookkeeping, the Pilgrim Book was generally assiduously maintained and a Prefect of Pilgrims appointed from among the small group of students.

Clearly there was a distinction between pilgrims and Grand Tourists and Rome itself knew the difference. The gentry and aristocracy may well have pursued elements of the traditional pilgrimage but could fend for themselves and often provided alms for the less wealthy. Successful Holy Years were held in 1725, 1750 and 1775, adding approximately 5000 to the recorded population totals in each of those years[35] (in addition to perhaps another 3000–4000 transient pilgrims).[36] As conditions for Catholics in England relaxed and travel became easier, less affluent people were able to recreate the pilgrim tradition. The eighteenth-century pilgrims, as recorded at the English College look very much like their pre-Reformation forebears and the traditional practices had survived. However, there are a number of distinctive characteristics about the eighteenth-century pilgrim, the first of which was that the general presumption ran against the idea of pilgrimage – even in the hospice. Pilgrims had to prove their credentials in a sceptical Rome. There was little, if any encouragement to pilgrimage in the tradition of recusant piety. Generally the pilgrims arriving at the hospice were not wealthy, mostly solitary or in pairs, only rarely female and virtually never clerical.

The 1739 Visitation Report makes mention of the pilgrim hospice, laying down that only English Catholic

---

[34] Williams, p. 54.
[35] H. Gross, *Rome in the Age of Enlightenment* (1990), table of population, p. 58.
[36] Gross, p. 64.

pilgrims were to be received who came to Rome for devotional purposes and bore a letter of recommendation from an English Vicar Apostolic. It reiterates the mediaeval convention of rich pilgrims receiving three days of hospitality and poor people eight days.[37] Both of these regulations were generally adhered to. Thus despite the difficulties and constraints of recusant life and the relative isolation from Europe for most ordinary Catholics, the ancient tradition of the English pilgrim hospice survived alongside the struggling seminary. Each year a handful of English Catholic pilgrims found their way to Rome and claimed the hospitality of the hospice. The recorded number rarely reached into double figures but this was in a period when the English Catholic population was numbered in tens of thousands.

The number of pilgrims recorded in the Pilgrim Books between 1654 and 1769 is erratic and a few years are missed entirely.[38] Certain years appear to have a 'bumper crop' of pilgrims, but these years in the decade before 1715 and in the early 1730s coincided with years of European war in which Britain was engaged. Thus it was not surprising that two successive Prefects of Pilgrims commented adversely on their intake.

As for pilgrims, during my troublesome reign I had but the two above mentioned that could properly be called so, but was pestered continually with such a riff raff of sailors and soldiers that the college seemed more like a man of war than anything else. [Following in a different hand], My condition during the time of my prefectship was like that of my predecessor to be eternally haunted with shipwrecked sailors ... I don't set down the precise time of their arrival here because not being truly pilgrims I thought it sufficient to let my successors know that the inhabitants of this house have got some few sparkles of charity left.[39]

---

[37] VEC Liber 292 Pilgrim Book, 1733–69.
[38] VEC Liber, 283 and 292.
[39] Liber, 292.

Rome in the eighteenth century had become the 'international capital of the poor as well as the rich'.[40] The poor and the beggars claimed citizenship in the city which devoted much of its energy to charitable sodalities and confraternities and where it was possible to survive on charity. It was not surprising, therefore, that institutions like the English College were wary when 'even the poor pilgrim, weighing the toil of earning a living by the sweat of his brow against the ease of obtaining alms, chose to remain in Rome and made begging his profession'.[41] Lines of demarcation became difficult to draw, but where possible were rigorously enforced. The papal authorities tried various methods of coercion to reduce begging and vagrancy, but the English hospice relied on a rigorous inquisition by the Prefect of Pilgrims. Careful differentiation was made by the English in the level of hospitality given according to the pious intentions of the visitor, and clear distinction was made at the hospice between pilgrims and mere visitors and indeed between Catholics and non-Catholics and English and other nationalities. In 1746, for instance, the Prefect of Pilgrims stated his determined refusal to record any in the Pilgrim Book who were not genuine pilgrims.[42] The hospice was clearly sectarian and distinctive, as laid down by the Visitation Report, and the administrators had no intention of it being used as a general lodging-house by all comers. The English College had established a new and clear identity which was related to the post-Reformation standing of English Catholicism and which it was not about to compromise. Pilgrims were lodged 'according to custom', with the overflow being accommodated at the nearby White Cross. Non-Catholic visitors were occasionally given basic charity, but at times complications arose.[43]

[40]   Gross, p. 198.
[41]   Gross, p. 198.
[42]   Liber 292, 'In 1746 came here many strollers, for the most part sailors, giving unto some a meal, or two, unto others more or less accordingly, for they not being pilgrims, had no right to any thing, and those who would be instructed in the Catholic faith were sent to the Convertiti, but I thought fit to omit writing them down, not being true pilgrims.'
[43]   Liber 292, 3 September 1734.

Edward Farly, printer of Exeter with his son Robert Farly, were admitted by Fr Rector's orders as pilgrims and had accordingly their diet and lodgings allowed them for about 8 days. They both of them fell sick a day or two before their time was expired. Thereupon they were advised to remove to the hospital of S. Spirito, but they, for certain reasons, which I'll immediately mention, not caring to remove to the hospital of S. Spirito, left the White Cross in Piazza Farnese, and went to look for themselves, but with their disease upon their backs, of which disease Robert Farly died three days after, and was buried at Monte Testaccio, and his father had like to have undergone the same fate. The reason therefore which hindered them from going to the hospital of S. Spirito, was that they both were Protestants. NB Fr Rector asked the father whether or no he were a Catholic and he answered in the affirmative. And here lay his equivocation. For being asked afterwards in the King's Court whether or no he had given himself out in our college for a Catholic, he answered that he had done so, and says he, I am a Catholic but not a Roman Catholic. Wherefore it would not be amiss if the future pilgrims are asked whether or not they are Roman Catholics.[44]

The hospice was evidently closely associated with the College of Convertiti originally founded for convert Jews and Muslims and opened to Protestants by Cardinal Howard in the 1680s. Any who expressed even moderate enthusiasm for the Catholic faith were hastily dispatched to the Convertiti for instruction. As the neophytes were lodged for up to six weeks while under instruction, this was obviously open to abuse and a number of those lodged at the hospice and the Convertiti clearly saw it as a free ride. For this reason the Prefect of Pilgrims was often rigorous in questioning new arrivals and records in detail their background and history before arriving in Rome.

[44] Liber 292, 3 September 1735.

Came, if I am not mistaken, for I have lost the schedule in which I marked it, a little shoemaker from the Island of Jersey (tis situate betwixt Normandy and small Britain) in quality of pilgrim. He was converted at Coln, and had his testimonials from thence ... His name was Isaac Neveu and had 40 years of age. Born of parents both Calvinists. He was treated as a pilgrim for 8 days because born in the English Dominions.[45]

However he abused not only the hospice charity but assistance given him to set up in business as a shoemaker in Rome and clearly got on the wrong side of the Prefect of Pilgrims.

... having got, as he said, a place to work in, but it was all, I fancy, a lie, for after that I never saw little Dapper make his appearance, whereas he had promised to come the Sunday following and give an account of his settlement. He seemed indeed to be very devout and very often I have found him upon his knees 'rapt up as it were in an ecstasy, but I am afraid 'twas fiction and dissimulation. He took particular care of his little paunch and would express in his broken English the great satisfaction he took in our meat and drink.

Such experiences caused the disillusioned Prefect of Pilgrims to bemoan the wickedness of the world. He remains unidentified for the period before the 1740s but is perpetually wishing to resign the post, as for instance he writes after one bitter experience with an Irish 'pilgrim',

... travellers, especially Irishmen, are very capable of playing the fool with young people and making them believe strange things. They have dealt so with me more than once, but bought wit, they say is the best: and one may know how to manage his affairs in this world the better, when he has had experience how full it is of misery, shifts and cheats. This office has

[45] Liber 292, 20 July 1733.

given me insight enough to be heartily tired of it, and before 8 months are over, I hope to be quite surfeited with it. God grant it.[46]

A considerable proportion of those who presented themselves for charity in Via Monserrato claiming the status of pilgrim were shipwrecked sailors (or so they said) from Civitavecchia or Livorno. The others who received charity were nearly all tradesmen or artisans of modest means. The wealthier pilgrims are not recorded and presumably joined their Protestant confrères in the albergi and apartments around the Spanish Steps. The Prefect was sceptical about many of those who arrived, describing John Storhill, a Yorkshire woolcomber, who came in October 1735 as 'the only true pilgrim that has been here of many years!' For that reason, dependence was placed on the recommendation of churchmen in other parts of Europe, and not everyone received full charity, some only a meal, some nothing at all. Pilgrims of other nationalities than English could not rely on English hospice charity. When on 27 May 1733 John Ronan arrived with his wife and daughter aged two and a half (unusual in itself as few women or family pilgrims are recorded), 'They were all three entertained (the wife being an Irish woman there was no *obligation* to receive her or the other because a child) out of charity.' However it would be no surprise that pilgrims from the tiny English recusant community were not as numerous as other nationalities, leading the Prefect to remark ruefully that 'one would be apt to think that our college was Irish, both by the numbers which come here and all the charity we give them'.[47]

One of the rare single female pilgrims was Catherine Stapleton, 'a strange, strolling old woman'. In 1737 she was on her third visit to Rome, having become a Catholic at the Convertiti in 1725.[48] Another elderly female pilgrim was Margaret Carder who received exceptional generosity.

[46] Liber 292, 26 October 1733.
[47] Liber 292, 28 December 1734.
[48] Liber 292, 4 April 1737.

... a poor Lancashire woman of three score and odd years ... in order to visit the holy places. She was detained in this hospital for two and twenty days with the usual charity of the college and had besides given her from the King a competent sum of money to return home; Rev Fr Rector also having compassion of her, through his great charity provided her of two shirts, two night gowns and at last she departed on 23 April.[49]

The remarkable Mary Bedfort, a Pennsylvania convert from Quakerism, arrived twice, the first time in 1738 with her two sons, who were taken up by James III, one being placed in a college and the other in an orphanage, while their mother set off for Santiago de Compostela.[50] She returned to Rome in 1747 having not only been to Santiago de Compostela but to Jerusalem and 'to all the holy places she could hear of'. Her extraordinary story, which conveys a wonderful flavour of the vagaries of eighteenth-century Roman life, is taken up by the Prefect of Pilgrims.

Now being somewhat disabled in her limbs she has a mind to end her days here in Rome, and for this end, I at her request, wrote a petition for her to His Royal Majesty, of whom she got 2 zecchines, besides what she got of the gentlemen at Court and several other pious persons. She has hired a little chamber which will just hold a bed, chair and herself and has bought also flints, steels and matches and other suchlike trinkets which she sells about the streets. But her merchandise going poorly on, she was forced to lay it all aside. This old woman was married to a middle-aged Frenchman who after some time ran away to Ancona from whence she brought him back but by reason of her following him. Not being able to get her basket for some time and he having run away again, she set out, as she said, towards England. At last died at Loreto.[51]

---

[49] Liber 292, 1 April 1740.
[50] Liber 292, 10 May 1738.
[51] Liber 292, 10 February 1747.

Pilgrims commonly headed to Rome via Loreto, the shrine of the Holy House alleged to have been miraculously transported there from Nazareth, and carried with them testimonial from the English confessor there. Edward Windell, a Yorkshire farrier (an example of the humble background of many of the pilgrims) arrived bearing a testimonial from Fr Atkinson, the penitentiary at Loreto, and was welcomed at both the English hospice and that of Santa Trinita and helped on his way by alms from the royal court and from 'some English gentlemen on their travels'.[52]

The eighteenth-century pattern of pilgrim behaviour was still built around the traditional circuit of the seven churches, but with an increased emphasis on the visiting of St Peter's to complete their devotions (usually confession and the reception of communion). A particular eighteenth-century addition to pilgrim behaviour was the seeking out of James III to be touched for the 'King's Evil'. The belief that the touch of the divinely appointed monarch would cure scrofula was immensely popular in seventeenth-century England and the tradition followed the Stuarts rather than transferring to the Hanoverians. Indeed, in England, the demise of the Stuart succession largely ended the practice. When in exile, neither James II or III ceased to perform the healing act, and the Jacobite supporters carefully fostered the old tradition as a mark of Stuart authenticity. In 1721 a polemical Jacobite writer brought out a purported letter from *A Nobleman of Rome, giving an Account of Certain Amazing Cures recently performed in the vicinity of this City*. Anti-Jacobite propagandists wrote furiously against it at various times in the 1730s and 1740s, provoked by the survival of the practice. Apparently Charles Edward carried out at least one healing rite at Holyrood Palace during the 'Forty-Five and continued the rite after his father's death on his return to Italy. It was a heavily symbolic act for both Jacobites and their opponents. After Charles's death his brother continued the tradition and the royal touch for scrofula or the 'King's Evil', which had survived from mediaeval

[52] Liber 292, 12 January 1737.

times, only finally died with him. Curiously, as late as 1901, items owned by the last of the Stuarts were credited with healing properties.[53]

However, there were English people in the eighteenth century, Protestant as well as Catholic, who remembered the tradition and sought out the Stuart Pretender in Rome. Such dedication in a Protestant was sufficient to override the hospice rules about the reception of Protestants. 'Came from England to be touched by the King's most Excellent Majesty, Matthias Woodbridge, born near Reading in Berkshire, about 16 years of age, a Protestant and on the day following was touched. He was entertained 8 days in the college and lodged as usual at the White Cross.'[54] Not all such visits ended happily. 'Came here Mr Brady who travelled purely on account of his child who had got the King's Evil and arrived safe to Rome but in going to Albano to the King, died on the road, and so the father departed with one only child for London.'[55] There were clearly close and frequent links between the hospice and the Stuart court. Charity normally extended to the giving of alms for the onward or return journey. Hospice charity was augmented by royal alms from the Stuarts and gifts from members of the papal household and other English people on the Grand Tour. Given the frequent duping of the hospice by convincing frauds, the rector of the English College forbade the students from giving alms, although there were instances of particular need when alms were given by the scholars. Charity was also forthcoming from the distinguished Jacobite exiles including Sir Thomas Dereham and Lord Derwentwater. Jacobite supporters were often among those who turned up at the hospice including Peter Whittle, a London watchmaker whose father had been fined £600 for drinking the health of His Majesty King James in the Old Bailey and who himself 'had suffered much on account of his being so stiff a Jacobite.'[56]

[53] M. Bloch, *The Royal Touch: Sacred Monarchy and Scrofula in England and France* (1973), pp. 221–2.
[54] Liber 292, 14 August 1737.
[55] Liber 292, 1 October 1751.
[56] Liber 292, 21 August 1749.

From such a detailed and extensive source it is possible to capture something of the diversity of English visitors to Rome in the eighteenth century, but also to sense the mixed motivations which brought the English to Rome, even those who might be called pilgrims. To take this source alone, however, would leave a jaundiced view of the relationship between England (Catholic and otherwise) and Roman institutions.

In 1748 and 1749 came here several strollers, according to custom, who for the most part were sailors. They get something here out of charity and so are soon dismissed, this place being only for true pilgrims, who come here only out of devotion's sake, or at least ought to come so. Poor old England, who has been the dwelling place of so many holy saints and martyrs, alas is now become, as I may say, a den of thieves! How many pilgrims?[57]

Some clearly did exist, but they could be difficult to differentiate. However, the question of differentiation of 'true pilgrims' only arises in the post-Reformation world. Distinctions began to be drawn and motives questioned which are identifiable to the historian in a way which was almost unknown in mediaeval society. There is a danger, therefore, of looking for 'true pilgrims' in the modern period and forgetting the hotchpotch of characters and intentions which peopled the mediaeval pilgrimage. Why should the motivation of the modern pilgrim be judged any more harshly than that of the mediaeval one? Yet his contemporaries did just that. The pursuit of pilgrimage and the claiming of the status of pilgrim was perceived as a mark of Catholic identity as against Protestant and was therefore something to be jealously guarded. The eighteenth-century English pilgrim was not exercising a common ritual of the society in which he lived. His pilgrimage was a statement of separation, not of community as it had been for his mediaeval forebears. Pilgrimage

[57] Liber 292, 21 August 1749.

to Rome for the English had taken on new associations and new meanings.

By the late 1790s, Rome was the target of the new French republican government and their brilliant young general, Napoleon Bonaparte. The papal states were already under occupation, with puppet governments in place all over the Italian peninsula. In February 1798 the cajoling and threats used by Napoleon towards the Pope were translated into action when Rome was invaded. The Castel S. Angelo was occupied by troops with arms trained on St Peter's and a Roman Republic was declared. Pius VI was imprisoned and exiled for the last months of his life, leaving Rome open to the sequestering of troops and pillaging of ne'er-do-wells. Britain had entered the war against France, and suddenly English pilgrims and Grand Tourists found themselves cut off from Rome, as from much of Europe. Curiously, Protestant England and the papacy became the staunchest of allies, with the Pope refusing to join the continental blockade against British trade and a Royal Navy frigate sitting off Civitavecchia in case the Pope needed immediate aid. Pius VII, elected in the Venice conclave of 1799–1800, became a great friend of Britain and built diplomatically on the ground laid by Erskine in the 1790s. Nevertheless, Pius VII found himself the helpless prisoner of Napoleon, and until 1815 and the final defeat at Waterloo Rome was bereft of the church institutions which gave it meaning and the visitors and pilgrims who sustained its economy. The French occupation depleted the population of the city of 180,000–200,000 by 20,000–30,000.[58] Fashionable artists like the sculptor Antonio Canova, who had depended on English patronage, found themselves on hard times, but they were not the worst off, for tradesmen in the city faced ruin and starvation as the economy collapsed and pillaging became routine. Rome was laid waste and was out of bounds for most of Europe, two successive popes had become prisoners of the French and Napoleon was determined to control or eradicate the power of the papacy.

[58] J. Chetwode Eustace, *A Classical Tour Through Italy* (1813), p. 255.

The English College was forced to evacuate, eventually only the agent Robert Smelt remaining. As he wrote stoically to one of the English bishops,

> We have property here and I am determined to stand by it if possible, as long as there is a prospect of keeping it, in case the French come and overturn the present government; after a time confusion may subside and I may obtain a passport to a neutral country, when I can be of no further use here; from thence I'll endeavour to find my way home.[59]

Eventually, Rome fell to the invading force,

> The old man [i.e. the Pope] left this city on Shrove Tuesday, arrived safe at Siena, where he will stay a few days, and then proceed to Pisa which is to be his residence – ours and the Scots college were sequestered in the name of the French republic.[60]

The survival of the college hung by a thread, as Smelt recorded:

> I have laid aside my intention of returning to England for the present, because times and circumstances may alter; in case peace takes place I hope our Government will interest itself to recover, at least, that part of our property originally purchased with English money as well as what belonged in ancient times to our national church and hospital before Gregory XIII gave it to the college. I am the only person acquainted with it, know every particular house, vineyard, garden etc. I even found means to obtain a copy of the book, containing the property called of the mission. Our property is advertised for sale throughout Italy, as well as all other confiscations; the good people of Rome say they can't

[59] Smelt – Douglass 7 February 1797, quoted in J. Kelly, 'Rome in 1797', *Venerabile* (1934), p. 382.
[60] Ibid., 2 March 1798.

purchase in conscience, and the bad ones have no money.[61]

Not surprisingly the pilgrim route to Rome as well as the Grand Tour came to an abrupt end. English pilgrims were once again cut off from Rome. A particularly turbulent sea change was shaking the English Catholic boat. The pilgrim hospice and college were sequestered and occupied by French troops just at a time when the desire for native seminaries in England had become stark necessity. Priests were being trained on English soil for the first time since the Reformation. The Jacobite cause was long dead and the last of the Stuarts had been forced to flee Rome with the Pope. Most significantly, there was evidence of a new attitude within English Catholicism towards Rome and the papacy. The Cisalpine movement urged a lessening of direct rule from Rome and the assertion of a distinctively English form of Catholicism. Perhaps English Catholics preferred to sail in their own rocky little boat than in the barque of Peter? Would English Catholic pilgrims ever find their way to Rome again?

[61] Ibid., 3 April 1798.

Chapter Seven

Friends and Relations

From the early nineteenth century Rome figured more vividly in the European and English Catholic spiritual landscape. The French Revolutionary imprisonment and exile of Pius VI and then of Pius VII at the hands of Napoleon wrought considerable sympathy in Catholic hearts for the person of the Pope. The persecution of the papacy and the final reinstatement of the Papal States in 1815 also contributed to a growing enthusiasm for papal authority and for the vision of Rome at the centre of European peace, the balance of power and true order. The image of Rome was kept alive for the English in the published travel accounts, and after the end of the war a stream of English visitors from an increasingly wide spectrum of society headed for Rome along the Napoleonic military roads which enabled quicker and more comfortable travel. Antonio Canova spent the winter of 1815 in London restoring his contacts in the world of fashionable artistic patronage, and on his return was able to obtain commissions for young artists in Rome, and did much to rebuild the artistic colony in the city. One of his pre-war patrons was the Catholic Henry Blundell of Ince Blundell, Lancashire. He was an indefatigable art collector who spent considerable time abroad forming a collection of paintings and sculpture.[1] Blundell's visits to Rome and his art collecting did not begin until he was a widower of over

[1] J. Gillow, *Biographical Dictionary of English Catholics*, vol. 1 (1885), pp. 244–5.

fifty, but he made four visits and collected nearly six hundred pieces.[2] However, by the end of the war Blundell was dead, and Canova and his compatriots had to find new patrons among the landed gentry who took up the Grand Tour again.

Cardinal Ercole Consalvi, protégé of the Cardinal Duke of York, convinced Anglophile and Papal Secretary of State, became (in 1814) the first Roman cardinal to set foot in England since the Reformation. He was also Cardinal Protector of the English College from 1818 until his death in 1824. He became great friends with the Prince Regent and his portrait by Sir Thomas Lawrence hangs in Windsor Castle. Part of the achievement of his diplomatic mission to England was that the British government paid the costs of Canova's operation to reclaim the art treasures of Rome removed to Paris during the occupation. The Pope's letter of thanks and the Prince Regent's cordial reply were the first exchange of royal and papal letters in centuries. After 1815, Consalvi embarked on an ambitious programme of restoration and embellishment of the papal city. In 1816, the Academy of St Luke and the old Institute of Archaeology were amalgamated, under the presidency of Canova, to create a new Academy of Arts.[3]

Among Consalvi's new developments was the completion of the Piazza del Popolo – sentimentalized by many English travellers as their first view of Rome arriving from the north through the Porta Flaminia. The adjoining Pincio Gardens were the setting for many of their leisure hours. Among the most powerful attractions in Rome for the post-war generation was the appearance of its ancient treasury, pagan and Christian, as never seen before. Classical Rome was revealed in greater glory. The views of Rome familiar from the Piranesi prints were disappearing.[4] Work begun before the imprisonment of the Pope, on excavating the Forum and restoring the Colosseum was continued, partly financed by Consalvi's English aristocratic friend the

[2]   J. Ingamells, *A Dictionary of British and Irish Travellers in Italy 1701–1800* (1997), pp. 101–2.
[3]   J. M. Robinson, *Cardinal Consalvi 1757–1824* (1987), p. 148.
[4]   J. C. Hale (ed.), *The Italian Journal of Samuel Rogers* (1955), p. 65.

Duchess of Devonshire.[5] She and other visitors enthused over the newly-reinstated Vatican Museum, including the newly-built Museo Chiaramonti, named after the Pope. This gallery was decorated with a series of frescoes recording Consalvi and Canova's achievements in the city. A further gallery, the Braccio Nuovo, was created specifically for the display of the classical statuary, both that newly excavated and the items returned from France.

Before the mid- and late nineteenth-century achievement of English Ultramontanism brought papal and Roman devotion into the heart of English Catholic life, there were many English Catholic families who visited Rome, often for extended spells. These visits were stimulated by a combination of poverty, devotion and artistic interest, and they joined large numbers of their countrymen and women. Many of them explored Rome clutching the works of the Rev'd John Chetwode Eustace (1764–1815), ordained at Maynooth around 1795, who published *A Classical Tour Through Italy* in 1813.[6] A number of Catholic priests accompanied young Catholic gentlemen as tutors and chaperones as Eustace did with George Petre who was his pupil. Eustace did the tour in 1802–3 and returned in 1814–15, but died in Naples of malaria. His book ran to eight editions by 1841.[7] Eustace's book was representative of a rather different English Catholic tradition from that which came to dominate in the nineteenth century. Eustace (and his employer Lord Petre) were part of the Cisalpine movement of the late eighteenth century which urged greater independence for the English from papal control in order to enhance their standing with their English contemporaries. His liberal Cisalpine views were expressed in his book and raised the fury of Bishop John Milner, the scourge of Cisalpines and Vicar Apostolic of the Midland District (to which Eustace was attached). Milner condemned the *Classical Tour* as 'insinuations of heresy, scandalous, schismatical, and the prevailing inducements to the indifference and irreligion

5   J. M. Robinson, p. 152.
6   D. A. Bellenger, *English and Welsh Priests 1558–1800* (1984), pp. 57, 206.
7   Barefoot, p. 146.

of the times.'[8] Eustace's expression of what were then regarded as liberal views, including recommending the use of the vernacular in liturgy and the reception of the chalice at communion, won him sympathetic non-Catholic reviews which commended his lack of bigotry. In the Preface to the *Classical Tour*, while proclaiming vigorously his Catholicism, he makes a remarkable call for tolerance and understanding between Christians.

> Yet with this affectionate attachment to the ancient faith, he [the author] presumes not to arraign those who support other systems. Persuaded that their claims to mercy as well as his own, depend upon sincerity and charity, he leaves them and himself to the disposal of the Common Father of All, who we may humbly hope will treat our errors and our defects with more indulgence than mortals usually show to each other. In truth, reconciliation and union are the objects of his warmest wishes, of his most fervent prayers: they occupy his thoughts, they employ his pen; and if a stone should happen to mark the spot where his remains are to repose, that stone shall speak of peace and reconciliation.[9]

The *Classical Tour* describes a Roman visit which was typical of its time in combining a passion for the remains of imperial Rome, many of them newly excavated, and a Christian pilgrimage. The first port of call, even before the hotel is found, is to St Peter's, but two out of eight chapters are given over to a detailed description of ancient Rome. The first full day of the tour is divided between a fuller visit to St Peter's and to the heart of classical Rome, the Capitol. This combination clearly appealed to the English of the early nineteenth century. By 1833 it was in its seventh edition and established as one of the best-known travel accounts of Italy, and was frequently referred to by other writers and plagiarized for descriptions.[10]

---

[8]   F. C. Husenbeth, *Life of Rt Rev John Milner* (1862), p. 403.
[9]   J. Chetwode Eustace, *A Classical Tour Through Italy* (1813), p. xi.

The widespread affection and sympathy for the restored papacy of the first generations of post-war visitors manifested itself in attendance at papal ceremonial and interest in the person of the Pope. Eustace's description of a papal blessing from the gallery of St Peter's conveys the popularity of such occasions and a sense of the English visitor's passion for spectacle and devotion:

His immediate attendants surround his person, the rest of the procession draws upon each side. The immense area and colonnade before the church are lined with troops and crowded with thousands of spectators. All eyes are fixed on the gallery, the chant of the choir is heard at a distance, the blaze of numberless torches plays round the columns and the Pontiff appears elevated on his chair of state under the middle arch. Instantly the whole multitude below fall on their knees, the canons from S. Angelo give a general discharge, while rising slowly from his throne, he lifts his hands to heaven, stretches forth his arm and thrice gives his benediction to the crowd, to the city and all mankind; a solemn pause follows, another discharge is heard, the crowd rises and the pomp gradually disappears. This ceremony is without doubt very grand and considered by most travellers as a noble and becoming conclusion to the majestic service that precedes it.[11]

The tone of that description, by one known for his liberal Cisalpine sympathies, indicates the enthusiasm for the restored papacy among post-war visitors to Rome.

Sir Thomas Gage, a Catholic gentleman from Suffolk, remarked in 1817 to a correspondent, 'Rome is crowded with English. I have filled my letter so much with other things that I have no room either for fine arts or antiquities which however occupy almost all our thoughts here'.[12]

---

[10] W.W. Meyer, *The Church of the Catacombs: British Responses to the Evidence of the Roman Catacombs 1578–1900*, Cambridge Ph.D (1985), p. 116.

[11] Eustace, p. 379.

If he is in any way typical of his English co-religionists, then they were part of the great 'cultural upgrading' of the post-war years which had precious little to do with piety. The *Gentleman's Magazine* of 1817 reported 1700 English families living in Italy. Two years later the Travellers' Club was founded in London, the criterion for membership being that the applicant had stood on the heights of the Capitol in Rome.[13] In the winter of 1818 it was estimated that over 2000 English were in residence – one-seventeenth of the total population of the city.[14] Rome had a curious familiarity to the English, yet it remains true that

> It is all but impossible nowadays to conceive of the impact of the South on travellers in the age of the Enlightenment. Nor can we share the tantalising prospect of the new and extraordinary sights that excited every quivering fibre of their imaginations ... For those condemned to live in the wet English shires and to pass their childhood in dull northern climes the miraculous effect of the Mediterranean light could scarcely be imagined.[15]

Clutching their copies of Eustace, thousands of visitors echoed his exhilaration on approaching the city from the north:

> We passed Monte Mario and beheld the city gradually opening to our view: turrets and cupolas succeeded each other, with long lines of palaces in between, till the dome of the Vatican itself, lifting its majestic form far above the rest, fixed the eye and closed the scene with becoming grandeur.[16]

---

[12] Jesuit Archives at Farm St., Foreign Correspondence No. 98, Sir Thomas Gage to ? 29 December 1817.
[13] Meyer, p. 107.
[14] Hale, p. 60.
[15] M. Sheridan, *The Romans: their Lives and Times* (1994), p. 55.
[16] Eustace, p. 202.

It is worth recalling the visual shock which Rome presented to the average English Protestant, as yet unfamiliar with the churches and cathedrals of the Catholic Revival in England, or the impact of Ritualism on the Church of England. 'I had been so much accustomed to whitewash in our churches at home, that the polished marble and gold of St Peter's were something new to me.'[17] To a Catholic visitor the impression was different and, despite the fact that Rome might be regarded in many ways as 'far inferior to our ideas',[18] they could scarcely help being impressed by the churches in comparison with their familiar recusant places of worship. Even the written accounts cannot fail to convey the sense of excitement and admiration, perhaps even of envy, in the first impressions of Rome's churches:

> No description can do justice to St Peter's. The mind is perfectly satisfied, the moment its interior strikes the eye. Its vast proportions, lightness, and the richness of the minutest part leave no point where the eye cannot rest with satisfaction ... There is scarcely a church but has some capital painting or venerable monument of religion and the present feasts are celebrated with great pomp at all the basilicas.[19]

The imagination was stirred by the completion in 1818 of Byron's enormously successful romance, *Childe Harold's Pilgrimage*, which may well have played an important part in the popular reclamation of the word pilgrimage. Childe Harold ends his pilgrimage in Rome and much of the fourth canto celebrates the city. Rome for Byron was the climax of all civilizations, embracing classical and Christian, yet he takes a morbid satisfaction in the loss of her glory.

---

[17] E. Bellasis, *Memorials of Mr Serjeant Bellasis* (1893), pp. 26–7.
[18] Jesuit Archives at Farm St., Foreign Correspondence No. 98, Sir Thomas Gage to ? 29 December 1817.
[19] Ibid.

> O Rome! my country! city of the soul!
> The orphans of the heart must turn to thee,
> Lone mother of dead empires![20]

Byron was not the only poet of his generation to be drawn to Rome and it became a magnet for Romantic writers, who became part of the sights of the city themselves. The Romantics headed for Rome as if under some strange morbid compulsion. For them it was not a place of refreshment or even a cultural curiosity, but a 'city of the dead'. Shelley, Keats and Byron became obsessed with Rome as the climax and paradigm of dead cultures, of the effect of history on human endeavour.[21] The more of Ancient Rome's past glory was uncovered by Consalvi's archaeologists, the more the past seemed to obliterate the present. To the Romantic imagination, Rome was associated with death and was an emblem of the passing of all human history. Rome became a metaphor for death. In that, it was a source of inspiration to a generation alienated from their contemporary society and Shelley in particular saw in it hope for the overthrow of corrupt and seemingly unshakeable political systems. It offered a posthumous life to those who already sensed their own death. Keats went to Rome as if already dead. 'I have an habitual feeling of my real life having passed, and that I am leading a posthumous existence.'[22] Rome was a site of physical and human desolation and the Romantic poets celebrate it in melancholy terms. Shelley's poem *Adonais*, written in mourning for Keats, has its climax in reference to Rome,

> Or go to Rome, which is the sepulchre
> O no of him, but of our joy: 'tis nought
> That ages, empires, and the religions there
> Lie buried in the ravage they have wrought
> ... Go thou to Rome – at once the Paradise,
> the grave, the city and the wilderness.

[20] Canto IV, verse LXXVIII.
[21] These themes are explored in an unpublished paper given by Dr Jennifer Wallace, entitled 'The sepulchre of our joy': Romantic Rome and Shelley's *Adonais*', given at a research seminar in the University in Bristol, 25 November 1995.
[22] Quoted in Stephen Coote, *John Keats: a Life* (1995), p. 319.

The Protestant cemetery near the Pyramid of Cestius became a Romantic shrine, even before it contained the remains of Keats, Shelley and his infant son. The Shelleys visited it soon after their arrival in Rome in the spring of 1819.

> I think it the most beautiful and solemn cemetery I ever beheld. To see the sun shining on its bright grass, fresh when we visited it with the autumnal dews and hear the whispering of the wind among the leaves of the trees which overgrow the tomb of Cestius … and to mark the tombs mostly of women and young people who were buried there, one might, if one was to die, desire the sleep they seem to sleep.[23]

The tombstone and the cemetery in *Adonais* signify the death which Rome seemed for the poet to express. Death and Rome are both grave and paradise.[24]

While rejecting formal Christianity, the Romantics' portrayal of Rome as the city of the dead played a part in recovering the ancient Christian meaning of Rome as both grave and paradise. Their descriptions and evocations of Rome were enormously powerful and influenced many visitors who saw Rome through their eyes. For Christian pilgrims, the image of Rome as a city of the dead was far from new. Those who sought the origins of Christianity in Rome were concerned with the 'posthumous existence' of the saints and martyrs. Rome's real city of the dead was being rediscovered in the form of the catacombs, which after centuries of neglect and misunderstanding, began to be excavated and interpreted for the first time by serious archaeologists. Catacomb archaeology was to play a vital part in the recovery of Christian pilgrimage in the nineteenth century, and in the emergence of Rome in the Protestant Christian imagination.[25]

[23] Quoted in Sheridan, p. 58.
[24] Wallace.
[25] Much of the material on the catacombs comes from the unpublished thesis of Dr W. W. Meyer, '*The Church of the Catacombs: British Responses to the Evidence of the Roman Catacombs 1578–1900*' (Cambridge Ph.D 1985).

Although Byron was partly responsible for their enthusiasm, the post-war travellers drove him to distraction, as he wrote in 1817:

> I have not the least idea where I am going, nor what I am to do. I wished to have gone to Rome; but at present it is pestilent with English – a parcel of staring boobies, who got about gaping and wishing to be at once cheap and magnificent. A man is a fool who travels now in France or Italy, till this tribe of wretches is swept home again. In two or three years the first rush will be over and the Continent will be roomy and agreeable.[26]

He was wrong. By 1820 the tide of British tourists to Rome had reached a peak and over the next ten years the literary market was awash with books on Italian travel.[27] Yet the Holy Year of 1825 drew relatively few pilgrims to Rome especially from beyond Italy. The Papal States were still rife with violence and poverty and the Holy Year failed to bring the expected benefits.[28]

Rome, like most other Italian cities had Pensione and Alberghi named 'di Londra' or 'd'Inghilterra' and the Caffe Inglese near the Spanish Steps was more popular than the famous Caffe Greco, despite the fact that the latter reserved a room for the English and served tea.[29] The area around the Piazza di Spagna had already begun to be colonized by the English in large numbers and became well established as the English quarter in Rome for much of the nineteenth century. As one observer wrote in the 1850s,

> English speech is the predominating sound and sturdy English forms and rosy English faces the predominating sight. Here are English shops, an English livery stable and an English reading room, where elderly gentlemen in drab gaiters read *The*

---

26 J. C. Hale, p. 60.
27 Meyer, p. 119.
28 N. Perry and L. Echeverria, *Under the Heel of Mary* (1988), p. 84.
29 Hale, p. 87.

Times newspaper with an air of grim intensity. Here English grooms flirt with English nurserymaids and English children present to Italian eyes the living types of the cherub heads of Correggio and Albani. It is, in short, a piece of England dropped upon the soil of Italy.[30]

However, the mood was about to change and the taste for art and antiquities was to be supplemented, even supplanted, by pious tastes for religious experience. Rome as museum and art gallery became for many visitors less important than Rome as shrine. It is notable that one English traveller passing south through Italy in 1825 commented that 'the roads from Genoa to Rome are crowded with pilgrims'. Interestingly, a horse-drawn *vettura* entered Rome only five minutes ahead of the footsore pilgrims whom its occupants had met on the road leaving Florence![31] For the generation of English Catholics who were beginning to emerge from the constraints of penal times and to assert their identity, the trend in the European church of restored confidence and renewal centred on papal authority was encouraging. Symbolic of the desire to restore Roman links with England after the defeat of Napoleon was the determination to reopen the English College, despite the logic that seminaries were flourishing on English soil by the end of the Napoleonic wars. Significantly, the English bishops were determined to have the college controlled by English superiors.[32] It took until 1818 to bring about the restoration under Robert Gradwell's rectorship. One of the first students was Nicholas Wiseman, author of a devoted and very personal volume of *Recollections of the Last Four Popes* (1858) recalling the period of his early familiarity with Rome.

He was at the centre of the circle of English Catholics who entered Rome as pilgrims or visitors of longer duration and had considerable influence on them and the ideal of the Church which was formative in England. In the early

[30] B. Barefoot, *The English Road to Rome* (1993), p. 181.
[31] Farm St., For. Corr. 234, Glover to Fr E. Scott, 14 May 1825.
[32] Williams, p. 75.

1830s he was described by one English observer as '. . . a young man, rapidly gaining a great reputation at the church Degli Incurabili on the Corso. He was a tall slim man of ascetic appearance, and not promising to be the very corpulent man he was in after years'.[33] The reputation he was gaining was as a preacher of English-language sermons for the Catholics (and anyone else interested) in Rome.

The great influx of English visitors (mainly Protestant) had led to the desire for Anglican worship to be available in Rome. In the winter of 1816–17 the Pope turned a blind eye when a series of Anglican services was arranged in the city. By 1823 an estimated 200 people were attending these services. After several temporary homes the Anglican chaplaincy settled in a deserted granary just outside the Porta del Popolo where it continued until the 1880s. From 1827 a salaried chaplain was installed (at £100 p.a.). One of the first incumbents was the Rev. Richard Burgess, who did not impress John Henry Newman on his first encounter in 1833.

> In spite of the multitudes of English here, there has been a Protestant chapel here only two years ... At Rome, Mr Burgess has a great name and has done (they say) much good – and is much followed – so we must say nothing. But we have just heard him, and *entre nous* he is one of the most perfect watering-place preachers I ever heard, most painfully so – pompous in manner and matter – what you might call an 'uncommon fellow' for want of better words, and a true specimen of the experimentally abortive style. And his doctrine mischievously semi-evangelical. He has already made overtures to me to preach him some sermons. I shall steadily refuse.[34]

Burgess joined the growing number of authors producing guides to Rome for the English market and published *The*

[33] S. J. Reid (ed.), *Memoirs of Sir Edward Blount* (1902), p. 35.
[34] John Henry Newman, *Letters and Diaries* 3 (1979) ed. I. Ker and T. Gornall, p. 227.

Topography and Antiquities of Rome in 1831. This work was not overtly polemical but his lectures delivered in the winter of 1832–3 (possibly the source of Newman's critique) and published the following year, drew a critical riposte from the Vice-Rector of the English College, Charles Baggs.[35] Relations between this unofficial congregation and the Catholic authorities were always problematic and the English chapel, providing a platform for Protestant sermons, was an irritant to the English Catholics in Rome.[36] Conversions to Catholicism, like that of 'Miss Trail, a celebrated miniature painter', caused antagonism, and in such situations 'the English nobility and gentry and clergy in Rome used all their influence to prevent her taking the fatalistic step'.[37] For this reason, Gradwell, Rector of the English College, was asked to provide Catholic sermons in English, and Wiseman proved the outstandingly successful answer. From then on the Sunday evening routine of the fashionable English Catholics seems to have been that recorded by one of the College students: '... in the evening went to the church to hear Wiseman preach, thence round Villa Borghese which fagged me exceedingly – abundance of English carriages in every drive ...'[38]

Newman's response to his first visit to Rome (as a member of the Church of England in 1833) reflects the ambiguity felt by Anglicans who were attracted by the power of Christian history and continuity of which Rome was the essence, yet repelled by what they had learnt to reject in modern 'Popery'. This grew into a painful tension for the men who became known as the Tractarians or Oxford Movement, just about to raise their voices within the Church of England as Newman was touring Catholic Europe. At the heart of the theology of the Oxford Movement was the belief that the Church of England shared the pre-Reformation origins and formation of Christianity. Rather than being viewed primarily as an adjunct to the State, which appeared to be

---

[35] Meyer, pp. 136–41.
[36] Meyer, p. 134.
[37] Farm St., For. Corr. 283, Glover to Fr Brooke, 6 August, 1828.
[38] St Laurence Papers, Ampleforth Abbey III (1995), *Mr Swale's Diary, Rome 1830–2.*

abandoning it anyway, the Church should be understood as part of the Universal Catholic Church. They talked and wrote openly of 're-Catholicizing the Church of England', by which they meant recovering its inner life and its Catholic spiritual dimension. To their opponents on the evangelical wing of the Church, this smacked of 'Popery' and they were accused of wishing to place the English church back under papal control. For some Tractarians, including of course Newman himself, the resolution of the tension was to embrace Catholicism in the Roman Catholic Church, and the influence of Rome itself was significant. Newman reached Rome for the first time in March 1833 and wrote to his friends with obvious enthusiasm for the artistic and cultural sites, but the conflict in his response to the city was immediately apparent. '. . . and as to the third view of Rome, the religious, here pain and pleasure are mixed; as is obvious'. His mind and heart were clearly divided, as he expressed in verse, 'How shall I call thee, Light of the wide West, or heinous error seat?'[39] Newman was quickly drawn to Rome, emotionally, and prepared to give it supremacy even over his beloved Oxford. Within two days of his arrival he was won over and, even reacting as a sound Protestant, to give it the benefit of the doubt.

> . . . And now what can I say of Rome, but that it is of all cities the first, and that all I ever saw are but as dust, even dear Oxford inclusive, compared with its majesty and glory. Is it possible that so serene and lofty a place is the cage of unclean creatures? I will not believe it until I have evidence of it.[40]

After a month in Rome and meetings with Wiseman and other members of the English College, he remained overwhelmed by the city but unconvinced by the tradition for which it stood and returned to England to launch the campaign for the soul of the Church of England.

As to my view of the Romanist system, it remains, I

---

[39]   *Letters and Diaries* 3, pp. 231–2.
[40]   *Letters and Diaries* 3, pp. 230–1.

believe, unchanged. A union with Rome, while it is what it is, is impossible; it is a dream. As to the individual members of the cruel church, who can but love and feel for them? I am sure I have seen persons in Rome, who thus move me, though they cast out our name as evil.[41]

As has been remarked by his most recent biographer, 'Newman's old Evangelical strain of judgment on Popery was shaken, but was alive and well.'[42] Newman returned to Rome twice in his life. In 1846–7 he prepared for ordination in the Catholic Church at the College of Propaganda Fide where he was ordained in May 1847 and evolved the plan for bringing the Oratory ideal of St Philip Neri from Rome to England. His final visit, during most of which he was indisposed with a heavy cold (at the age of 78) was to receive the dignity of cardinal from Leo XIII in 1879.

The Oratory of St Philip Neri in Rome offered Newman a model for his ministry in England. St Philip himself had formed the congregation in 1551 in the church of S. Girolamo della Carita opposite the English College. From there he would step out to bless the English priests as they left Rome for the English mission and likely death, with the words '*Salvete Flores Martyrum!*' Newman himself stayed for a time in the Cistercian monastery adjoining S. Croce in Gerusalemme and lived as a clerical student in the Collegio Propaganda Fide, but he is more closely associated with the Oratorian church of S. Maria in Vallicella (Chiesa Nuova). In 1879 Newman was created cardinal in recognition of his theological and pastoral labours in England and given the titular church of S. Giorgio in Velabro, where a portrait of him hangs in the sacristy.

Wiseman was sensitive to the new mood in Rome and in England and was anxious to see Catholic travel guides to Rome which would counterbalance those already flooding the market and 'resonate with proper spiritual

---

[41] *Letters and Diaries* 3, p. 277.
[42] S. Gilley, *Newman and his Age* (1990), p. 98.

and devotional tone.'[43] He wrote powerfully of this need in the *Dublin Review*.

> If we enter the precincts of the Eternal City, the power of religion, associated as she ever should be with the beautiful and the amiable, lays hold of our mind and heart and encompasses us with an inspiring influence which denotes the presence of the spirit of the place. A marvellous combination of splendid natural scenery, with grey and broken masses of ruins – the emblems of the enduring and of the perishable, of the works of God and of man – encircles and adorns those sacred temples, which seem to partake of the properties of both – erected of the frail materials composing the latter, yet apparently endowed with the immortal and unfading newness which is the prerogative of the former.[44]

Wiseman's desire to inspire people with the spirit of the place were fulfilled by W. J. A. Sheehy in 1838 (*Reminiscences of Rome: a religious, moral and literary view of the Eternal City*) and in 1842 by Jeremiah Donovan, (*Rome, Ancient and Modern and its Environs*). Works like these reflected and stimulated the growing confidence among English Catholics that the devotional and historical fabric of Rome clearly expressed its apostolic heritage, which was also theirs to reclaim. On his appointment as Cardinal Archbishop of Westminster in 1850, when he unwisely proclaimed the return of England to the Catholic firmament in his letter, *From Without the Flaminian Gate*, Wiseman was given the titular church of S. Pudentiana, reputed (though along with other claimants) to be the oldest Christian foundation in Rome. It was said to have been built in 154 on or near the site of the house of a Roman senator whose daughters Prassede and Pudentiana had a particular devotion to the Christian martyrs, and legend had it that Caractacus, a British chieftain, was imprisoned

[43] Meyer, p. 151.
[44] N. Wiseman, 'Religion in Italy', *Dublin Review* (1836), p. 468.

there, became a Christian and carried out missionary journeys to his native land. As H. V. Morton evocatively, if a little romantically, wrote:

> In this church Christian tradition goes back to the time of Pius I and the year 154 when old people were still living who had received first-hand accounts of the apostles from those who had known them 78 years previously. St Paul is said to have lived here too and it is claimed that St Mark may have written his gospel here.[45]

The church preserves a portion of a table once believed to have been used by St Peter (the rest being in St John Lateran). When Wiseman was titular cardinal he became interested in this tradition and had it compared scientifically with the wood in St John Lateran. It was concluded that both sections came from the same table, which was almost certainly of first-century date. Following the examination, Wiseman had the wood enclosed behind glass, but twentieth-century carbon dating has revealed the inaccuracy of the earlier dating and shown it to be mediaeval. S. Pudentiana was also the titular church of one of Wiseman's successors at Westminster, Cardinal Francis Bourne.

During the 1830s and 1840s Rome became a second home to a new coterie of devout affluent pilgrims who inherited some of the Romantic yearning for the city combined with newly-minted Catholic devotion. A large number were recent converts to Catholicism, but the striking feature of this period is the close interlocking network of families and friends which created a distinctive English Catholic community in Rome. Not untypical of the passionate devotion of that generation who sought and found reassurance and continuity of authority in Rome was Ambrose Phillipps de Lisle, who wrote on hearing Compline at S. Sabina:

---

[45] H. V. Morton, *A Traveller in Rome* (1957), p. 173.

I knelt down with a mixed feeling of heavenly awe and delight, and blessing God, that He had of His infinite mercy made me a member of His Holy Catholick Church, I thanked Him that He had brought me to hear at the threshold of the Apostles that 'New Canticle of the Lamb' the Divine chant of St Gregory: I besought Him to confirm my faith, which I felt strengthened by this living image of the Church of the fourth century, this Church which is the same yesterday, today and for ever.[46]

De Lisle was a remarkable convert, who made significant contributions to the shape of the English Catholic revival, including the erection of the first post-Reformation Cistercian Abbey, at Mount St Bernard, Leicestershire. Although influenced by the movement to restore the mediaeval English grandeur of Catholicism, led by Augustus Welby Pugin, he was also an ardent Romanophile. On his first visit in 1828 he wrote to a friend, 'I have been much delighted with my stay in Rome. How many profound and devout feelings are excited by a residence there ... it is impossible for me to be in a more edifying place ... the piety of the people is so great.'[47] He found the popular religion warm, exuberant and attractive – very different from what he had so far experienced in England.[48] His life was greatly affected by the contacts he made in Rome in the small close-knit society of wealthy English Catholics. Among these were the Earl of Shrewsbury, with whom he was to collaborate on church building projects in England, and Hugh Clifford (son-in-law to Cardinal Weld) whose cousin Laura he married. One of his early contacts was the 70-year-old Cornish gentleman, Sir Henry Trelawney, who arrived in Rome with his son and daughter (already a Catholic) in the winter of 1829–30 and was soon received into the Church.[49] In 1830 Cardinal Odescalchi ordained him in SS Giovanni e

---

[46] M. Pawley, *Faith and Family: the Life and Circle of Ambrose Phillipps de Lisel* (1993), p. 42.

[47] Pawley, p. 35.

[48] Pawley, p. 36.

[49] Farm St., For. Corr. 297, Ambrose Phillipps – Glover, 21 December 1829.

Paolo. He had been instructed by the Passionist Dominic Barberi and became part of Philipps de Lisle's circle. This led to Barberi meeting Ambrose Phillipps de Lisle and his friend George Spencer and began to give shape to his urgent desire to work on the English mission. Spencer was ordained in the nearby S. Gregorio.

George (later Ignatius) Spencer was in Rome for two years as a student in the English College, between 1830 and 1832. The son of Lord Althorp, ordained as an Anglican in the early 1820s, Spencer was one of the pre-Oxford Movement converts to Rome. He played an active part in the social circle of Rome's English residents. In his regular letters to his father, he wrote of the round of dinners and receptions.

> In the evenings I have been out very often; and have found a great deal of civility and kindness from both Italians and English. The week before last, Cardinal Weld gave two or three great assemblies, called, I think *ricevinientos* on his elevation. At one of these which I went to, I saw almost all the English in Rome I suppose; for he gave a general invitation to them. Another I was at, where there were only his own friends of the English, and the principal persons of Rome, among them about 15 cardinals. I have dined with Cardinal Odescalchi, with Torlonia, twice with Lord Shrewsbury, who lives in a great splendour in the Colonna Palace ...'[50]

Everard, tenth Lord Arundell of Wardour and his wife Mary, who were living in Rome to economize while Wardour Castle was closed up, were already resident in 1828 when Mary Arundell took Phillipps de Lisle as a surrogate son and constant companion on his first visit.[51] She had been brought up at the heart of the Irish Protestant ascendancy as

---

[50] 25 March 1830, quoted in J. Van den Bussche, 'The Honourable and Reverend George Spencer in the English College – his correspondence (1830–1832)', an unpublished paper given at a Conference on Rome and the English Church 597–1997, in the English College, Rome, in September 1997.

[51] Pawley, pp. 40–1.

the Viceroy's daughter and became a Catholic at the age of twenty-three, due to the influence of her secretly-Catholic mother. De Lisle was devoted to her but admitted that, 'her eccentricities and excesses would probably never have been tolerated had it not been for her exalted ancestry'.[52] Her letters reveal something of the life in Rome for the English Catholic community.

> At breakfast the carriage comes to the door. Now says Ev[erar]d, I shall not see you till dinner: of course you'll be till then in churches with *that boy*. Such masses at the Gesu! after which we adjourn to the outer sacristy and there such conferences with Padre Glover who is by the bye one of the dearest, most agreeable and delightful of men, and best of confessors. He will be one of the thousand things I shall deeply regret in leaving Rome.[53]

It was 'Padre Glover' who persuaded de Lisle that his vocation was as a layman and the two corresponded actively after de Lisle's return to England. Everard was a scholarly and pious man, but also restless and moody, and subject to bouts of ill-health, which travel helped to alleviate. He was also a High Tory, dreading the prospect of Parliamentary reform in 1832, which provided another good reason for staying out of England.

Having returned to Rome in 1834 after a year of travelling, Everard and Mary visited the church of the Gesu ...

> As they were leaving, Everard said in a whisper to Mary, 'I wish to be buried in front of the gate to the chapel of the Sacred Heart. Father Glover's confessional is close to it and he would remember to pray for me.' At the time he was quite well but he was taken ill that evening and a couple of days later it was clear that he was dying ... Everard remained conscious almost to the end and said calmly, 'We shall meet

---

[52] Pawley, p. 40.
[53] Pawley, p. 41.

again in a better world, and then Mary, we shall never be parted more and praise God together in happiness eternal'. Seeing that Mary was on the point of breaking down, he said cheerfully, 'Come, Mary, make no scene'. But when he breathed his last as morning broke, the Roman morning, with its brilliant blue sky, Mary's screams were terrible.[54]

In accordance with his wishes, Lord Arundell was buried in the Gesu, where a simple tablet (with his name misspelt as Warder) lies just inside the left aisle entrance.

The Jesuit church of the Gesu was held in particular esteem by the English Catholic community, not least because of the presence there of Fr Thomas Glover SJ, who acted as the envoy of the English Jesuits and as a valued English confessor from 1825 to 1848. Clerical as well as lay visitors like de Lisle found their way to the confessional of the 'gentle-hearted Father Glover' including the Benedictine William Bernard Ullathorne, in Rome in 1837 to report to the Pope on his work in Australia.[55] Glover, like the Pope himself, was forced to flee the revolutionaries of 1848. When Ullathorne returned to Rome to negotiate the restoration of the hierarchy for England, he found the rest of the Jesuits fled and 'the venerable Fr Glover' in hiding in the house of English friends, Mr and Mrs Englefield.[56] The Gesu was highly regarded not only because of its magnificent decoration and the English Jesuit presence but also because it was 'one of the best-regulated churches in Rome'.[57] It became the focus of devotional life for many of the English Catholic visitors and Glover became confessor to some of the notable converts who were drawn to Rome or who were received into the Catholic Church there, including George Ignatius Spencer.[58] Inevitably, several English Catholics found their

---

[54] C. Bence Jones, *The Catholic Families* (1992), pp. 145–6.
[55] William Bernard Ullathorne, *Cabin Boy to Archbishop*, (1942), p. 131. (Ullathorne was later Bishop of Birmingham for nearly 40 years.)
[56] Ibid. p. 288.
[57] Farm St., For. Corr. 98.
[58] Farm St., For. Corr. 300, Ambrose Phillipps de Lisle to Glover, 15 April 1830.

final resting place in the Gesu, including Sir Thomas Gage who died in May 1821 and was buried near the altar of St Francis Xavier.[59] The memorial to the seventh baronet of Heneage Hall, Suffolk was composed by the eminent English Jesuit, teacher of many recusant gentlemen at Stonyhurst, Charles Plowden.[60]

Also buried in the Gesu, near the altar of St Francis Xavier in the right aisle is Stephen Tempest who died at the age of only thirty-two. At the death of his older brother, Roger, Stephen's father had inherited the recusant estate of Broughton Hall, Yorkshire. He married Elizabeth, daughter of the Catholic landowner and art collector Henry Blundell of Ince Blundell, and in October 1816 they joined the post-war rush to take up the Grand Tour with their three eldest children. They spent two years visiting Rome, Florence and Naples and accumulating ornaments, paintings, glass etc. for their newly-restored home. Their eldest son Stephen continued to travel widely, not only in Italy, but to Vienna, Berlin and Constantinople. In the winter of 1821–2 he was back in Rome, accompanied by Mr Simon Scroope and a priest chaperoning his pupil on the Grand Tour. He became dangerously ill over Christmas and though recovered in the new year, died unexpectedly of consumption later that year.[61]

Also in Rome in the 1830s were the Cliffords, to whom Ambrose Phillipps de Lisle became related by marriage. Thomas Weld, son of the Thomas who had given Stonyhurst to the Jesuits, had married Lucy, a cousin of Lord Clifford. They were a 'pleasant, pious couple',[62] but she died in her forties in 1815. Soon after, Thomas began to consider the idea of ordination and left for theological studies in Paris, knowing that his only child Mary Lucy was about to marry her cousin Hugh Clifford, the son and heir of the sixth Lord Clifford of Chudleigh. He was described by one contemporary as a clever but eccentric man who wrote many entertaining letters to his friends.[63]

[59] Farm. St., Eng. Prov. Corr., vol. II, p. 406, letter to Glover.
[60] D. Mathew, *Catholicism in England 1535–1935* (1938), p. 140.
[61] M. E. Lancaster, *The Tempests of Broughton* (1987), pp. 104–9.
[62] Bence Jones, p. 114.
[63] S. J. Reid (ed.), *Memoirs of Sir Edward Blount* (1902), p. 36.

Thomas Weld was ordained priest in 1821 and made Lulworth Castle, the family home, over to his brother Joseph. His first priestly appointment was to St Mary's, Cadogan St, which had been built with Weld/Clifford money. From 1830, he and his daughter and son-in-law lived in Rome following his appointment as cardinal with the title of S. Marcello al Corso. It was a singular and unexpected honour – the first English cardinal since Howard in the seventeenth century. It was seen as a gesture of papal goodwill following the passage of the Catholic Emancipation Act in England in 1829. The Duke of Wellington (as Prime Minister) had proposed Weld's appointment as Bishop of Waterford; the Pope did not believe this to be appropriate but promised some mark of recognition of the achievement of Emancipation.[64]

His daughter and son-in-law lived with him in Rome – it suited her health and his finances. According to Wiseman, 'His apartments in the Odescalchi palace were splendidly furnished and periodically filled with the aristocracy of Rome, native and foreign, and with multitudes of his countrymen, everyone of whom found him always ready to render him any service.'[65] Between 1834 and 1837 Weld was Cardinal Protector of the English College. Mary Lucy died in 1831 and her father the cardinal looked after his two little grandsons and was often seen driving in Rome accompanied by them. He died in 1837 and divided the church plate between his grandsons and the churches of S. Clemente, S. Isidore and S. Patrizio. £3000 was left for charities in England and Italy.[66] The cardinal's funeral was a remarkable occasion with all the leading singers of Rome brought in to sing the Mozart Requiem. Thus it became a rare attraction to Italian culture seekers, who objected to the music being interrupted by the 'monotonous and harsh sounds of the English language' when Wiseman preached the panegyric. Such was the Italian impatience that after a few moments they began to hiss and had to be rebuked from the pulpit![67]

[64] J. Berkeley, *Lulworth and the Welds* (1971), p. 228.
[65] Wiseman, *Recollections*, p. 246.
[66] Berkeley, p. 234.
[67] *Cabin Boy to Archbishop*, p. 128.

Weld is buried and commemorated in a side chapel of S. Marcello. Beneath the chapel is a crypt where Lord and Lady Clifford are both buried. Their younger son William went on to be Bishop of Clifton at the particular wish of Pius IX and took an active part in the First Vatican Council.

The senior English Catholic family who lived in Rome was that of the Earl of Shrewsbury. The sixteenth earl, who beggared himself building Pugin's churches in England, retired to Rome to save money and died of malaria in Naples in 1852. His chaplain, who accompanied him to Rome, was Daniel Rock who in 1818, was one of the first group of half a dozen students, including Nicholas Wiseman, to colonize the newly-restored English College in Rome after twenty years of Napoleonic occupation and disruption. Whether he was one of the few who could be provided with surviving remnants of the 'old and hallowed costume of the English College' in order to meet the Pope, is not recorded.[68] His seven years in Rome were to be vital in forming his scholarly interests and enthusiasms, as well as in shaping his future career. There he developed a passion for the history of the early church and for collecting the evidence of its liturgical practice illustrated in the catacombs, which was to inform his later writings, and he also met while in Rome, John Talbot, later the sixteenth Earl of Shrewsbury. Rock made many visits to the catacombs while a student in Rome, which convinced him of their value and importance. His theological and historical opinions were strongly influenced by his encounter with these primitive cemeteries, and his *Hierurgia*, published in 1833, was the first English work to make extensive use of the evidence of the catacombs.[69] Talbot's meeting with Rock took place towards the end of an eventful Grand Tour, during which he fled from the hideous sights of the Peninsular War and was captured by pirates. On his return to England and succession to his brother's title he invited Rock (now ordained and working at St Mary Moorfields in London) to be his chaplain at

---

[68] N. Wiseman, *Recollections of the Last Four Popes* (1858), p. 11.
[69] Meyer, p. 144.

Alton Towers in Staffordshire. Shrewsbury's home was to be the centre of the Gothic-influenced Catholic Revival.[70] Rock's *Hierurgia* argued strongly that the monuments of Christian Rome were the tangible representations of the apostolicity of the Catholic Church and evidence of the connection between the primitive church and the present-day church. Rock 'sought to present doctrinal and historical support for the ceremonial and liturgical practices of contemporary Roman Catholicism',[71] and his work was designed to demonstrate the continuity between the primitive church and contemporary Roman Catholicism. In his later work, *The Church of Our Fathers*, he carefully and painstakingly set out the continuity between the practice of the early Roman Christian church, the Anglo-Saxon church in England and the practice of nineteenth-century Roman Catholicism. The point for Rock was the assertion and historical proof of clear continuity from apostolic times to the present day.

One of Lord Shrewsbury's daughters married a Doria Pamphili, creating one of the great Anglo-Roman families of modern times. The Dorias were among the most powerful of the Renaissance families, who ruled Genoa for four hundred years and in the seventeenth century married into the Pamphili family. In 1837, Domenico and Prince Filippo Doria went to London for Queen Victoria's coronation, and Filippo to visit the Earl of Shrewsbury. He returned with an English wife, Lady Mary Talbot. The Palazzo Doria Pamphili has a splendid eighteenth-century façade, but is much older, having passed through the hands of various papal families. It is the last of the great Roman palaces still in private hands, said to be two-thirds the size of St Peter's, and in its heyday to have housed a thousand people under its roof. Mary's sister Gwendolyn married Marcantonio Borghese in 1835 and became a legendary figure in Rome. During her short married life she was renowned among rich and poor alike for her great

---

[70] J. Champ, 'Goths and Romans: Daniel Rock, Augustus Welby Pugin, and Nineteenth-Century English Worship', *Studies in Church History*, vol. 35 (1999), pp. 290–320.

[71] Meyer, p. 144.

charity and generosity of spirit, as well as her personal beauty, charm and holiness of life. She knew Rome well from travels with her parents and was delighted to return there as a married woman. 'Unlike all other cities, Rome is a dwelling for the soul.'[72] Her charity was extensive and largely anonymous and her sudden and early death at the age of only twenty-two in 1840 stunned Rome.

> Her funeral procession to S. Maria Maggiore brought the city to a standstill. All the Roman poor, all inhabitants – and they were numerous – who had received kindness from the Princess, accompanied her remains to the church, Santa Maria Maggiore, which is three-quarters of a league from the Borghese Palace ... Countless charitable acts, only known to clergymen and physicians, were revealed; and secret thorns that sprung up in the path of fortunate worldings, who confided in, sought, and found sympathy from her, now became known.[73]

After her death, a story was told of a poor old woman, destitute, praying at her tomb. A young woman in black touched her on the shoulder and gave her a ring. When she tried to sell it, she was arrested as the ring was recognized as bearing the Borghese mark. When the prince was shown the ring he refused to take any action against the woman and maintained her for the rest of her days, for the ring was one which he had placed on his dead wife's hand before her burial.[74]

The poor of Rome were joined by the curious from England and the Princess's lying in state and funeral featured as one of the highlights of a Grand Tour in 1840.

> Went to the Borghese Palace to see the lying in state of the Princess Borghese, daughter to the Earl of Shrewsbury. She has died very suddenly of a quinsey –

[72] Diary quoted, Le Chevalier Zeloni (trans. Lady Martin), *Life of the Princess Borghese* (1893), p. 55.
[73] Ibid., pp. 162, 64.
[74] E. O'Gorman, *Our Islands and Rome* (1974), pp. 21–3.

and it is said here from bad treatment of the doctors. Last Sunday week we saw her with the Prince among the games in the park, all life and loveliness – she was taken ill of a cold and died in three days. At the Palace this morning there were at each entrance some of His Holiness' soldiers and four rooms were hung with black with stripes and festoons of gold. The first was an ante-room, the second with two altars – the third three altars – at each altar the priests were saying Mass – and in the fourth room was the corpse raised only a little from the floor and covered with a gold pall and a black velvet cushion or pillow at the head of the coffin. Round the coffin was railing on which was hung paintings of skeletons, death's heads etc – and on each side were eight monks chanting, two Capuchins with long beards and six Franciscans – the monks were relieved by their brethren – near here sat two women of the Princess in black veils – and some gentlemen of the household – there was an excellent picture of the Holy Family, or Madonna and Child from the collection over each altar – the candles were very large and altogether it was very solemn. She was buried at evening by torchlight – we went at half past seven and got the carriage drawn up so as to see the procession well. The whole of Rome was afloat for she was called the good English Lady, which gratified us much. In the procession – first came flambeaux – then the grand hearse with priests holding candles and in the midst of them the coffin covered with a gold pall – and a black velvet cushion – next carriages – then an innumerable number of monks of different orders chanting – as the procession went along the people strewed flowers upon the coffin. Alas poor Princess! We then drove to the church of Santa Maria Maggiore and witnessed the ceremony there – the church was hung with black and gold drapery – every window and between the pillars festooned – and the pillars about 50 bound round with braids of gold – the canopy (was) composed of black and gold and hung in four festoons from the top of the church. A great

number of priests received the corpse in the church,
and chanted a Requiem, when they left it for the
night in the care of the military guards – and next
morning Mass was to be performed for the deceased.
The crowd was great, but the people behaved well![75]

The description in the diary of an English Protestant traveller is the detailed and unemotional one of an onlooker,
recorded alongside the accounts of churches, tombs, art
galleries and the rest. It is valuable as an eyewitness
account of the richness and spectacle of Roman ceremonial and compares interestingly with the other account
written from the emotional perspective of Ultramontane
Catholicism. The same ceremonial which spoke of piety,
faith and religious emotion to the one, was to the other a
curious and fascinating spectacle to be observed like any
other, and as foreign as if in a mosque. This reflects two
extremes of reaction by English people in nineteenth-
century Rome – the disinterested and curious observer and
the passionate and committed participant. Each saw
different things in the same event.

A lesser-known member of the Weld and Shrewsbury
circle was Sir Edward Blount, the second son of Sir Edward
Blount MP for Steyning, Sussex and grandson of Sir Walter
Blount, the sixth baronet of Mawley Hall, Shropshire. He
unwittingly did more to advance the revival of popular
pilgrimage than almost any other Englishman. His was a
deeply religious family, producing a number of influential
lay Catholics, priests and women religious. He was
educated at Oscott College in the 1820s with many of the
rising generation of Catholic gentry and aristocracy. As a
young man he entered the Home Office as a civil servant in
the midst of the Emancipation crisis. In 1830, having left
the Home Office for the Foreign Office, he was appointed
attaché in Rome where he was made at home by the

[75] Journals of a Tour of Europe undertaken by Peter Brooke, Margaret
Antrobus and George Antrobus July–December 1840, pp. 123–4. A
typescript copy of this unpublished diary has been kindly made available to me by a descendant of Peter Brooke, The Revd Canon
Michael Ridley.

Shrewsburys and Welds. Cardinal Weld had reason to be grateful to his young friend when they were out riding at Frascati and the cardinal fell from his horse. Blount went rapidly and fetched medical help for what turned out to be a broken leg.[76] During his time in Rome, Blount witnessed the death of Pius VIII after only eight months in office, and the surprise election of Gregory XVI. He was not popular in Rome at a time when the Papal States were in a ferment of revolutionary plots. In spite of the tensions, the English enjoyed observing the Carnival of 1831 which culminated in the Corso where the traditional race of loose horses, terrified by fire crackers tied to them, was run. It ended with the *moccoletti*, a scuffle in which everyone sought to blow out his neighbour's candle. As Blount noted, 'the Romans felt they were dancing on a volcano and seemed to enjoy the fun all the more.'[77] In later life, Blount made an invaluable contribution to the accessibility of Rome to his fellow countrymen and women. On leaving the civil service he went into banking and invested heavily in the new French railways. He became chairman of Western France Railways for 30 years and among other projects he was the originator of the train line over the Mont Cenis pass between St Michel at the foot of the Alps and Modane on the Italian frontier and thence to Susa where it joined Italian lines. Thus he made possible modern high-speed pilgrimages across the Alps to Italy.[78]

Among the more eccentric English Catholic visitor/pilgrims at this time was Squire Charles Waterton, who as a young man was one of the earliest visitors to Rome just after the defeat of Napoleon. Along with two friends he 'mounted to the top of St Peter's, ascended the cross, and then climbed thirteen feet higher, where we reached the point of the conductor and left out gloves on it. After this we visited Castel S. Angelo and contrived to get on the head of the guardian angel, where we stood on one leg.'[79]

[76] S. J. Reid (ed.), *Memoirs of Sir Edward Blount* (1902), p. 34.
[77] Reid, p. 36.
[78] Reid, p. 87.
[79] Quoted in Anon. 'Squire Waterton comes to Rome', *Venerabile* 19 (1960), p. 518.

Some accounts suggest that Pius VII was furious at their behaviour and made them climb up again to retrieve their gloves, for fear that they would prevent the lightning conductor from working.[80] However, despite this, he was received in audience by Pius VII soon afterwards, along with his friend Sir Thomas Gage, and was able to tell the Pope of his travels up the Orinoco and the Amazon and of the 'miserable state of the Indians'.[81] Waterton was an extraordinary figure, born into a recusant household at Walton Hall, near Wakefield, which had withstood siege from Cromwell. His mother was a Bedingfield from Norfolk and his family claimed proud descent from Thomas More. His grandfather had been imprisoned for a time before the battle of Culloden and he himself refused to take the oath of allegiance attached to the Catholic Emancipation Act of 1829, thus debarring himself from public office. With such deep-rooted recusant tradition in his blood, it is perhaps not surprising that he continued the habit of a quiet and rather withdrawn life. However, the squire returned to Rome for eighteen months in 1840 and divided his time between religious devotions and his passion for ornithology. At the age of fifty-eight he walked the last twenty miles into Rome barefoot as an act of reverence. After his recovery from the horrific injuries to his feet (which took two months) he divided his time between the bird market at the Pantheon and the Gesu. He described Rome, surprisingly, as a quiet city but disliked the dirty streets and not overly hygienic kitchens. This did not stop him enjoying the food – 'If a man cannot get fat in this city at a very moderate expense, it must be his own fault'. He lodged in Palazzo di Gregorio near the Spanish Steps and enjoyed the hospitality of the English College and the Jesuit fathers at the Gesu. Though often critical of the behaviour of his fellow-countrymen, he befriended and tried to convert the novelist Thackeray.[82] He was visited by two Jesuit friends who had been schoolboys with him at Stonyhurst, Glover and Esmonde. Glover

[80] R. Aldington, *The Strange Life of Charles Waterton* (1949), p. 77.
[81] Farm St., For. Corr. 96, Fr Fortis – Fr C Plowden, 16 January 1818.
[82] Aldington, p. 166.

became spiritual director to the family and took his son Edmund Waterton under his wing. The squire left Rome on 16 June 1841 with a huge collection of eighty preserved birds plus other creatures, which is now preserved at Wakefield Museum.[83]

Thus the period after the Napoleonic wars was a period of rediscovery for the English in Rome. Not only did the English (particularly the Catholics) renew their acquaintance with Rome, but Rome began to rediscover itself. It began to take on a new significance and identity for Catholic and Protestant visitors alike and the process of clearly naming and recovering the pilgrimage tradition began. English visitors, whose Protestant and Catholic labels were becoming more distinctive, looked to Rome not only as a cultural centre but as a religious source and as the historical proof of their identity. Protestant and Catholic distinctiveness emerged and particularly among the Catholics, a new attitude to Rome appeared. Catholics became inclined to claim Rome physically and emotionally as a home. Loyalty to Rome and affection for it gradually became a benchmark of English Catholicism. The pilgrim and the visitor were beginning to become more clearly differentiated. Separate patterns of behaviour can be seen in accounts of Roman sojourns.

Europe and the Church began to regard Rome differently and to view it as central to religious and political life in a way not previously dreamt of for centuries. To many it quickly became a political anachronism, but to loyal Catholics it became the emotional heart and the authoritative source of truth and faith. In an age in which religious seriousness was becoming the fashion, especially in England, Rome was set for a new golden age.

[83] Aldington, p. 188.

Chapter Eight

Full in the Panting Heart of Rome

During the middle and later years of the nineteenth century, attitudes to Catholicism in England changed. The tolerant indifference of the eighteenth century and the often open co-operation of the early nineteenth century disappeared in a more hostile atmosphere. Catholicism for its part became more self-assured, more assertive, more distinctive – more Roman. This encouraged a desire among English Catholics, especially perhaps among the new converts of the 1830s and 1840s, who sought the assurance of papal authority, to forge even more concrete links between England and Rome. The Oxford Movement in the Church of England, dedicated to restoring the Established Church to its pre-Reformation Catholic roots, was a source of division within English Protestantism. To its advocates it led naturally to a positive reappraisal of the relationship between the Church of England and Rome and in many cases led individuals to seek membership of the Catholic Church. However, to the vast majority of Church of England members, supported by the Protestant Non-conformists, the Oxford Movement was a source of danger, undermining Protestantism from within and threatening the overthrow of English Christianity by papal authority. It did not take long for the latent anti-Popery in the English mentality to resurface. The reassertion of the 'Romanness' of Catholicism and the increased focus on the person and office of the Pope did not help, and the furore over Wiseman's Letter *From Without the Flaminian Gate* in 1850 was a prime case of how easily such fury was stirred.[1]

As Cardinal Archbishop of Westminster Wiseman presided over the 'Romanizing' of English Catholicism and the flowering of passionate papal devotion. Better known to most English Catholics of a certain age than his *Recollections,* is Wiseman's hymn 'Full in the Panting Heart of Rome':

> Full in the panting heart of Rome,
> Beneath the Apostle's crowning dome,
> From pilgrims' lips that kiss the ground,
> Breathes in all tongues one only sound:
> 'God Bless our Pope, the great, the good'.

He was a key figure in forging the connection between the rebirth of English Catholicism and the assertion of Roman spiritual authority. 'Not since Gregory Martin wrote of Rome in 1581 had an English Catholic been so sensitive to the historical and devotional value of the Christian monuments of Rome. Like Martin, Wiseman saw Rome as the heavenly Jerusalem, "the capital of spiritual Christianity".'[2]

The rediscovery of the catacombs and the attention which this brought upon the history of early Christianity played an important propaganda role. The history of the early Christian community in Rome, the 'Church of the Catacombs' was increasingly explained in polemical terms, by Catholics asserting the historic continuity and by Protestants arguing that theirs was the true heritage of the early church.[3] In the face of Protestant writers trying to proclaim the essentially Protestant simplicity of the church of the catacombs, cleansed of all the accretions of later centuries, Catholic scholarship (supported by the Tractarians) fought back fiercely and successfully.

---

[1] R. J. Schiefen, *Nicholas Wiseman and the Transformation of English Catholicism* (1984), pp. 187–92.

[2] W. Meyer, *The Church of the Catacombs: British Responses to the Evidence of the Roman Catacombs 1578–1900,* Ph.D. Cambridge (1985), p. 43.

[3] W. Meyer, 'The Phial of Blood Controversy and the Decline of the Liberal Catholic Movement', *Journal of Ecclesiastical History* 46 (1995), pp. 75–94.

Wiseman was an important figure in this campaign to reclaim the catacombs. He had been fascinated by them since his early years in Rome and used the evidence of them in his well-publicized lectures given in England in 1836. He wanted to capture and communicate the blend of history and devotion available in the archaeology of the catacombs and so turned to the most popular literary form in Victorian England – the novel. He published *Fabiola* in 1855 to immediate success. The first run of 4000 sold rapidly. The novel contains a great deal of church history and drew upon a wealth of archaeological evidence as well as imagination. A number of real historical figures are woven into the story and Wiseman used a number of individual and composite portraits to demonstrate forcefully the continuity between the church of the catacombs and the English Catholic Church of the nineteenth century.[4] Its success spread beyond England and it was translated into seven Italian editions as well as French, Spanish, Portuguese, Hungarian, German, Danish, Polish, Slavonic and Dutch. In England it ran through numerous editions and had widespread and lasting popularity.[5]

Wiseman saw the roots of nineteenth-century Catholicism in the catacombs, but also saw the catacombs in the contemporary history of English Catholicism. What else had the recusant communities done within living memory, but emerge anew from the catacombs? *Fabiola* marked the peak of Catholic presentation of the catacombs, provided Catholic apologists with a powerful tool and ensured enduring interest in the catacombs among pilgrims. However, even before the publication of *Fabiola*, the catacombs wrought a fierce emotional effect on at least one English pilgrim, Pauline de la Ferronays, the 20-year-old daughter of a French emigré count who became British Ambassador in Rome in 1829.

> We left the catacombs by the stair that had been used by the Christians. When I was on its steps, the

---

4   Meyer, pp. 269–71.
5   Meyer, p. 279.

different impressions I had received in succession broke upon me in their fullness. The steps were the same as the martyrs trod on their way to death. I longed to cast myself on the ground and kiss their footprints. I longed to stay and weep without stint. I felt there I could have given utterance to the feelings with which my heart was full. Then I thought that the young girls who went up those slopes to die heroically saw me from their height in heaven and prayed for me who was so little like them ... I could not resist the satisfaction of kissing those sacred stones before I returned to the church. When again in it, I knelt down and longed to remain there. I had felt emotions never before experienced by me. I owed to them the religion in which, happily, I was born. I felt the need of thanksgiving and of prayer to God that all my life should be an expression of my gratitude and of my love towards Him.[6]

This overheated emotionalism was to become a feature in Catholic piety in the nineteenth century and to play a part in the reclaiming of a direct, immediate and personal relationship between the present-day Catholic and the saints and martyrs of the past.

The archaeological work on the catacombs was in part done by Englishmen, influenced by both Wiseman and the Tractarian search for Christian history and continuity. James Spencer Northcote was educated at Corpus Christi, Oxford, where he formed a lifelong friendship with Newman. After graduation in 1841 he married and was ordained in the Church of England. He worked as a curate in Ilfracombe, Devon, where he became close friends with the other leading Tractarian, Edward Pusey. In 1845 his wife and three sisters converted to Catholicism and he was not long in following. After a brief period as a teacher, he moved to Rome in 1847 and spent three years there, during which time he wrote a series of articles for *The Rambler*. In the first article he wrote

---

[6] M. C. Bishop, *A Memorial of Mrs Augustus Craven* (Pauline de la Ferronays) (1895), pp. 16–17.

of the attractions of Rome and critized English visitors who never set foot in the catacombs.

The history of the Church may record its triumphs; antiquaries and tourists may enumerate its treasures; all its churches and palaces, museums and galleries, may be traversed by the hurrying foot, and scanned by the curious eye; but not all these taken together will suffice to give an adequate idea of the indescribable charm of a residence within its walls, or even a faithful representation of what it really is. Rome is pre-eminently a place to be lived in, not learnt from books; and in which the longer you live the more you learn, and the more you learn, the longer you will desire to live in it; I might add too, if you would not think me too enthusiastic and too tiresome, that the more you learn, the more you will find is yet to be learnt; for when you have exhausted your studies of that Rome which is before your eyes, you have yet an equal task remaining in that Rome which is beneath your feet. Roma Sotteranea is hardly less extensive, and certainly not a whit less interesting, than the Rome in which we live; and if it be true that time and labour are necessary for the understanding of the latter, still more are they required for the under-standing of the former ... Yet many of our countrymen – some too who spend a considerable time in Rome, and devote themselves most assidu-ously to the task of lionizing – have been known to go away without having paid even a single visit to these most interesting Christian antiquities; and many more, after a rapid walk through some of the subter-ranean galleries and an impatient peep into two or three of the principal chapels, having too (it may be) a very imperfect comprehension of the *lingo* spoken by their guide, come away with a satisfactory convic-tion that they have *done* the catacombs, and that after all there is not so very much in them.[7]

---

[7]   J. S. Northcote, 'The Catacombs', *The Rambler* 2 (1848), p. 124.

Not only were the visitors often dismissive of the real value of the catacombs, but the archaeologists faced the incomprehension and greed of the locals.

Last week I crawled through some mighty queer places, I assure you, and all I got for my pains (besides the knowledge, which is what I went for) was a terracotta lamp or two, and a shell that had been fastened into the mortar of an old Christian's grave about 1500 years ago. The man under whose property we were grubbing, gave us some breakfast before we went down, put two men with their spades and pickaxes at our command, and plodded after us most industriously for three or four hours, under the idea that we should find a treasure of crowns for him somewhere. Indeed he would not have taken the trouble under any other supposition, poor fellow, for he has always refused admission to the Government diggers to enter at all, being firmly assured that silver and gold lie hid there, and wishing to appropriate this spoil to himself.[8]

Northcote's ambition was to write a straightforward but thorough account of the catacombs and to this end he accompanied the leading archaeologist John Baptist de Rossi day after day into the catacombs. 'Half an hour spent with him is always a greater treat to me, and teaches me more of what I am interested in, than hours of study or conversation with other less gifted persons.'[9] In the midst of the political revolutions of 1848, Northcote and his companions were 'grubbing about underground with our little wax tapers, almost as contentedly as if there were not this sea of revolution rolling over our heads when we come up again'.[10] His extensive first-hand knowledge enabled

[8] J. S. Northcote to G. B. Northcote, 22 January 1849 (Oscott College Archives).
[9] J. S. Northcote to G. B. Northcote, 5 January 1856 (Oscott College Archives).
[10] J. S. Northcote to G. B. Northcote, 18 December 1848 (Oscott College Archives).

him to write creatively an appealing image of the life and worship of the early Christians. Northcote's were among the most popular and successful items in the early editions of *The Rambler* and kept the catacombs in the forefront of English attention for two years. His was the first treatment to take full account of the scientific and scholarly break-throughs. He created a popular image of the catacombs which would enkindle a devotional response, demon-strating the Catholic character of the evidence and portraying the early church as the progenitor of modern Catholic faith. In 1854, in response to demand from the English for tours of the catacombs, Northcote published his *Roman Catacombs*, revised in 1859. This remains the most detailed and scholarly account of the catacombs to have appeared in English.

This passionate interest in the life of the early Christians in Rome also contributed to a recovery of the close link between martyrdom and pilgrimage. The stories of Roman martyrs again became familiar to Catholic pilgrims visiting Rome (and the armchair pilgrims, through the written word). Martyrdom and pilgrimage were again intercon-nected and in the English mind took on a new level of interest. Wiseman was not the only one to idealize English Catholic history in the image of the early church and the stories of Catholic martyrdom associated with the life of the 'Recusant Catacombs' began to be popularized for the first time. In the second half of the nineteenth century, English writers including Georgiana Fullerton, Frances Taylor and Dom Bede Camm began to collect together the evidence of the English Catholic martyrdoms of the sixteenth and seventeenth centuries and to tell their stories for historical and devotional purposes. Alongside this it became more important to remind English readers of the continuity of the pilgrimage tradition to Rome, to which the beatification of the Reformation martyrs later in the century was to give fresh impetus.

The reception of pilgrims at Rome has lasted since the earliest times. At the feasts of SS Peter and Paul, Corpus Christi and Portiuncula, many pilgrims come to Rome. During Holy Week the number amounts to about 5000. During the year of the Jubilee it amounts to a still greater number. In the Jubilee year of 1825, the numbers amounted to 273,299, the last time of a public Jubilee.[11]

Not only martyrs but inevitably, the relics of martyrs underwent a resurgence in interest in the nineteenth century. The physical 'home' of the relic and the ritual of veneration were important elements of pilgrimage. The showing of relics was the highlight of mediaeval pilgrimage. Pilgrims were not expected to make private homage to the relic, but to attend special rituals, some of which took place only rarely, according to Gregory Martin's account. 'Even so in Rome at this day, there be certen dayes in the yeare when the principal relikes are shewed in certen churches, where there is greatest concourse of people, namely at Easter.'[12] Gregory Martin's graphic account of the liturgical ceremonial to which the showing of relics had been raised by the late sixteenth century was an advertisement which could not fail to whet the appetite of English would-be pilgrims and stir the blood of persecuted Catholics cut off from Rome.

The notion of relics had never entirely forsaken the lands of the Reformation, and in England relics continued to haunt the imagination of reformed clergy. Both Donne and Herrick used the imagery of relics in their love lyrics.[13] The carrying of portable altar stones containing relics by travelling recusant missioners kept alive the association between relics, martyrdom and the Eucharist in English Catholicism, and the rediscovery of hidden or lost relics like those of St Chad were a source of triumph. The

[11] W. H. Nelligan, *Rome: its Churches, its Charities and its Schools* (1858), p. 313.
[12] Parks, p. 52.
[13] Bentley, ch. 7.
　　e.g. '... As well a well wrought urn becomes
　　　　The greatest ashes, as half-acre tombs,
　　　　and by these hymns, all shall approve
　　　　Us canonized for love ...' (John Donne, 'The Canonization').

veneration of relics of Reformation martyrs began rapidly among English recusants, as Allen's preserving of Campion's bones suggests.[14]

The direct, interventionist power of relics was reasserted vigorously at the Council of Trent in the face of the Reformers.

> But whom would not the wonders wrought at their tombs convince of the honour which is due to the saints and of the patronage of us which they under-take? The blind, the lame-handed and the paralysed restored to their pristine state; the dead recalled to life and demons expelled from the bodies of men! Facts which St Ambrose and St Augustine, most unex-ceptionable witnesses, declare in their writings not to have heard, as many did, not to have read, as did very many grave men, but to have seen. But why multiply proofs? If the clothes, the kerchiefs, if the shadow of the saints before they departed life, banished disease and restored strength, who will have the hardihood to deny that God wonderfully works the same by the sacred ashes, the bones and other relics of the saints?[15]

The Ultramontane Church asserted Tridentine ideals and emphasized the direct relationship which the Catholic Christian could have with the divine, particularly through devotion to saints. It was due in part to this emphasis that holy men and women such as Bernadette Soubirous and John Vianney were quickly canonized and that visionaries and mystics were popular devotional figures. As part of the Ultramontane development of the Church, the authority of Rome in the discernment and authentication of saints and their relics became increasingly important. Roman approbation of holy people, sites and objects was a vital part of the centralization which characterized the Ultramontane vision of the Church. One particular contro-

---

[14] See p. 77.
[15] Catechism of the Council of Trent, Part 3, ch. 2, q 15.

versy over relics reflected the English determination to become part of this vision. The controversy emerged in the early 1860s over the supposed phials of blood which were found at the tombs in the catacombs and were taken as an authentic sign of the martyrdom of the dead person. Thus they were venerated as important relics. When questions were raised over whether this was in fact the case, Wiseman was horrified and Northcote (while sharing some of the scholarly reservations) was concerned about the effect of the controversy on devotional life. The phials represented the cult of martyrs and the validity and necessity of the use of relics in English devotional life. What would be the effect if the faithful thought that they had been venerating relics improperly identified? More worryingly, what would be the effect on Roman authority in relation to the relics which it authenticated and distributed worldwide and on its control of devotional practice? The phial controversy illustrates the growing intransigence and assertion of Roman rule in the face of intellectual advance, and the hostile use to which intellectual advance could be put by opponents of Roman authority, in an effort to undermine it.[16] The anxiety for the faithful may have been unfounded, as one pilgrim expressed a healthily pragmatic but nonetheless religious attitude to relics, in the light of the controversy.

> We are also eager to venerate relics, as were the early Christians, even though we may mistake the identity of the relic which we think we possess. After all, what does it matter in God's sight what we venerate, if we sincerely believe the authenticity of what is under our eyes? Be there error in that or not, still our homage is offered to the true object, whatever it may be?[17]

The conscious recapturing of the tradition of pilgrimage (rather than cultural education or curious tourism) reached a peak in the 1850s and 1860s along with fervid

---

[16] Meyer, *Journal of Ecclesiastical History*, op. cit.
[17] M. C. Bishop, p. 199.

devotion to Pius IX and anxiety among pro-papal Catholics about the threat to him from the *Risorgimento*. Travel became cheaper and easier and allowed greater numbers of less-affluent people to make the journey, but for rich and poor alike the purpose and conduct of the visit took on ever-deeper religious significance. As a consequence, Northcote in the mid-1850s (by then widowed and back in Rome preparing for ordination in the Catholic Church) found his role as guide for English pilgrims to the catacombs 'quite oppressive'.[18]

Pauline de la Ferronays, while hardly a typical pilgrim, gives us a glimpse of the pattern of English pilgrimage in the 1850s and 1860s. Having first encountered Rome as a passionate young woman, she returned many times after her marriage to Augustus Craven. Her husband, grandson of the Margrave of Anspach and for a time attaché to the British Legation in Naples, became a Catholic in Rome in 1836, two years after his marriage to Pauline. He fell in love with Rome as his wife had done and wrote of its effect on him, 'As I approach Rome I feel my heart warmed and my intelligence enlarged and the longer I remain, the more the feeling increases.'[19] There is no doubt from Pauline's recollections of their times spent in Rome that they regarded them as religious pilgrimages. Holy Week 1858 made a deep impression on her. 'There were none (impressions) that did not help to make me better, and after experiencing them I understood that for me a pilgrimage to Rome was more helpful to my intelligence that any book, and of more service to my soul than any sermon.'[20] She also gives a clue to the continuity and resurgence of ancient pilgrim traditions. Pauline and her friends enrolled in an ancient confraternity (almost certainly that at Pellegrini della S. Trinita mentioned by John Evelyn in the seventeenth century) which cared for poor pilgrims. On several occasions they joined the 'men and women of the highest rank (who) attend to the

---

[18] J. S. Northcote to G. B. Northcote, 5 January 1856 (Oscott College Archives).
[19] M. C. Bishop, p. 93.
[20] M. C. Bishop, p. 174.

personal wants of the hundreds of pilgrims who come, poor and travel soiled, from the wildest regions of Italy'.[21] The most vivid description is that of Easter 1870, when her biographer accompanied Pauline to the pilgrim hospice. She describes a scene which could have taken place at any time since the ninth century, but was probably being enacted for the last time before the loss of papal Rome to the new secular state of Italy.

> The crowd was great, but the pushing and fussy strangers were railed out from the long table on which the simple supper was laid. It was very largely made up of salad and bread. The waiting ladies, wearing the uniform pinafore of the association, bustled about in a very practical fashion, pouring oil and vinegar on the salads, apportioning the figs and finocchi on the plates and filling the bowls of soup. With genuine pleasure Mrs Craven flitted here and there. Having done her task of washing pilgrims' dusty feet, she went from seat to seat, supplying the wants of her half-dozen clients, and no doubt carefully non-observant of their furtive appropriation of loaves or salads which they thrust into their wallets with a view to future feeding. The contrast was great between her and the massive mothers, many of whom had infants at the breast; between her eager rapidity and dexterity of motion and the stolid and ruminant peasants, dignified and ignorant. The great variety of local costumes interested the monotonous upper class who crowded to see the show; but nothing seemed to disturb the pious gravity of the pilgrims.[22]

This is not the only account of Rome to suggest that the pilgrims themselves had become part of the sightseeing routine.

At St Peter's on Sunday we saw many pilgrims,

---

[21] M. C. Bishop, p. 174.
[22] M. C. Bishop, pp. 281–2.

evidently from the country, with their scrip and staff
come on pilgrimage to the shrine of St Peter – they
first went to the statue of the saint and kissed his toe,
touching also their brow and chin – and then some of
them took their beads and rubbed them on his foot –
those who were too little were lifted up by the others.
Afterwards they went and knelt round the tomb of St
Peter which is before the high altar.[23]

The defensive attitude taken up by proponents of the
Ultramontane Catholic view had become the norm.
English pilgrims were encouraged to see Rome, not only as
the heir of the early Christians but as embattled by hostile
forces of liberal politics, Protestant polemic and scientific
rationalism. Hence the tone of one typical Catholic guidebook published in 1858.

The circumstances of the present times render it
more necessary than ever, that the journey to Rome
should now bear the character of a pious pilgrimage,
when the anti-Christian spirit of the writers and so-
called foreign correspondents of too many journals,
seek to fill their letters with all that is calculated to
throw ridicule on the manners, customs and social
regulations of the Eternal City. More than ever
should she be surrounded with love and respect, for
she has more than ever become the stronghold of
faith and liberty and the centre of civilization. The
railroads and steamers, and the desire to travel, which
seems to be the grand characteristic of the times,
have made the pilgrimage to Rome easier and more
frequent than in days gone by. A work which will
embrace both a religious and a scientific view of the
Eternal City, must be calculated to assist the pious
pilgrim in his accomplishing his longed for object,

[23] Brooke diary, vol. 1, p. 89. The 'scrip and staff' was more likely the
usual travelling accompaniment of the Italian peasant, than any
conscious retention of mediaeval tradition. However, it is a reminder
that southern Italy and Rome itself in mid-nineteenth century still
retained many elements of the mediaeval feudal world.

Medal commemorating the marriage of James III and Maria Clementina Sobieska, 1719.

Touch piece distributed by James III *c.* 1720, as part of the rite of 'touching for the King's Evil'.

Coronation medal struck by Henry IX, 1788.

Courtesy of Oscott College

Commemorative medal of Cardinal Philip Howard, 1683
(see pp. 92–6).

Courtesy of Oscott College

TOUR THROUGH ITALY,

EXHIBITING A VIEW OF ITS

SCENERY, ITS ANTIQUITIES, AND ITS MONUMENTS;

PARTICULARLY AS THEY ARE OBJECTS OF

CLASSICAL

INTEREST AND ELUCIDATION:

WITH AN ACCOUNT OF THE

PRESENT STATE OF ITS CITIES AND TOWNS;

AND OCCASIONAL OBSERVATIONS ON

THE RECENT SPOLIATIONS OF THE FRENCH.

BY THE

REV. JOHN CHETWODE EUSTACE.

VOL. I.

Hæc est Italia diis sacra, hæ gentes ejus, hæc oppida populorum.
Plin. Nat. Hist. III. 20.

LONDON:

PRINTED FOR J. MAWMAN, 39, LUDGATE-STREET.

1813.

Title page of John Chetwode Eustace's travel guide to Rome, the first in the nineteenth century, often reprinted and much imitated (see pp. 139–42).

Courtesy of Oscott College

Medal struck to commemorate the nineteenth-century restoration of Peter's Pence, symbolizing the revival of pilgrimage and the increasing emphasis on the person and office of the Pope (see pp. 26, 201).

Courtesy of Oscott College

Portrait of James Spencer Northcote, the leading English
authority on the catacomb archaeology of the nineteenth
century (see pp. 171–4).

(see pp. 171–4).

Courtesy of Oscott College

HOLY YEAR CEREMONIES IN ROME.

Special Excursions to . .

ARCH OF CONSTANTINE, ROME.

ROME

for

£15 15s.

Via Dover, Calais, Bale, Lucerne, St. Gothard, Milan, Genoa, & Pisa.

Leaving LONDON, FRIDAYS, SEPTEMBER 14th and 21st, 1900.

ITINERARY.

FRIDAY.—Leave London (Charing Cross Station) at 9·0 p.m. for DOVER and CALAIS.

SATURDAY.—The Train leaves CALAIS at 12·30 a.m., and reaches LAON at 4·15, CHALONS at 5·47, GRANMONT 7·26, BELFORT 10·10, arriving at BÂLE at 12·47 p.m. Plain breakfast served en route, and luncheon on arrival at Bâle. Leave Bâle at 2·40 p.m., and arrive at LUCERNE 5·57, in time for dinner.

SUNDAY.—To be spent at Lucerne, splendidly situated on the loveliest lake in Switzerland and surrounded by lofty mountains.

MONDAY.—Leave Lucerne at 10·50 a.m. by the celebrated St. Gothard Railway for MILAN. Lunch at GOESCHENEN, arriving at MILAN in time for dinner.

TUESDAY.—Leave Milan after breakfast at 8·30 a.m. by day express via Genoa, the lovely Italian Riviera, Spezia and Pisa to ROME, arriving 11·30 p.m. Lunch and dinner en route.

WEDNESDAY to MONDAY to be spent at Rome. Members of the party will be at liberty to make their own arrangements for visiting the various Monuments, Galleries, Churches, etc., but they are strongly advised to take advantage of the Excursions we have arranged with DR. RUSSELL FORBES at the specially reduced charge of 20/- each person for the three days. Tickets for these must, however, be taken before leaving London.

Accommodation consists of breakfast, lunch, dinner and bedrooms, commencing with bed on the 6th day and ending with lunch or dinner on the 11th day.

The following Itinerary is suggested for the Return Journey:

MONDAY.—Leave Rome by convenient train for Genoa.

TUESDAY.—At Genoa, leaving by afternoon train for Milan.

WEDNESDAY.—Milan to Paris.

THURSDAY.—Arrive Paris, leaving for London via Calais and Dover by Day or Evening Service.

First Class Travel ... ... Four Guineas extra.

The above Fares include Travel Tickets London to Rome and back, meals on outward journey, Two Days at Lucerne, One Day at Milan, Six Days at Rome, and Two Days' Hotel Coupons for use on Homeward Journey. The accommodation to consist of bedroom, lights, and service, meat breakfast and dinner (at Rome lunch is provided at the Hotel in addition), and services of Conductor on Outward Journey to Lucerne and Goeschenen, and of Cook's Interpreters at Milan, Genoa and Rome.

Cook's Ten Guinea Tours to Rome recommence for the Season on

Wednesday, October 3rd. The Fare includes Second Class Travel Ticket London to Rome and back, together with Six Days' Hotel Accommodation. viz., Five Days at ROME, and One Day at either GENOA or TURIN on the outward journey. The accommodation consists of breakfast, luncheon, and dinner, bedroom, lights, and service. HOLDERS OF THESE SPECIAL TICKETS HAVE THE PRIVILEGE OF ACCOMPANYING ON THE OUTWARD JOURNEY, FREE OF CHARGE, THE THIRTEEN and SIXTEEN GUINEA CONDUCTED PARTIES TO ROME, which leave London on the same dates. They have the privilege of joining our Carriage Drives in Rome, and of attending the Explanatory Lectures of Dr. Russell Forbes on reduced terms; and also the option of prolonging their stay for any number of days not exceeding Twenty-five by simply purchasing the necessary Hotel Coupons for the extra time it is desired to remain in Italy or Paris. Excursions from Rome to Naples, Pompeii, Vesuvius, Florence, Venice, Milan, &c., have also been arranged at Special Rates in connection with these Tours.

OTHER DEPARTURES FOR 1900 are, October 31st, November 28th, and December 19th.

Advertisement from Thomas Cook's *Excursionist and Tourist Advertiser*, for his 'ten-guinea tour' to Rome for the Holy Year of 1900 (see p. 205).

Courtesy of the Thomas Cook Archives

The joint diocesan pilgrimage of the diocese of Clifton, Plymouth and Nottingham in Holy Year 1950, photographed in front of St Peter's.

Courtesy of Fr J. A. Harding

A group of 1990s pilgrims with Pope John Paul II at Castelgandolfo.
Courtesy of Anthony Coles

and will aid him in his walks through this sacred city.[24]

Such defensiveness was encouraged by the often hostile attitudes of English Protestantism. English travellers to Rome throughout the century shared something of Newman's ambivalence, without his theological sophistication. As one author has expressed it, 'Nothing in the Mediterranean was so enticing, nor yet so repulsive as the religion of Papal Rome'.[25] Fascination with the exotic 'foreignness' of Catholic ceremonial drew visitors to St Peter's and the other great churches as to some curious ritual of an alien race. Eustace's strictures to his fellow countrymen to 'keep up the national reputation of candour and of good sense by conciliatory and forbearing conduct' were not always heeded.[26] Their behaviour at times embarrassed even their own countrymen who commented on the crassness of English reaction to Catholic services. Ruskin 'had no conception that English women could be such brutes, or exhibit themselves so contemptibly',[27] and a Catholic observer 'actually saw an Englishman in St Peter's on Easter day square his fists up at the Captain of the Swiss Guard, who required him to obey one of the Halberdiers, who was keeping him within his own proper circle'.[28] The well-known story of three young Englishmen encountering Gregory XVI out walking and forcing him to take the muddy portion of the path became a source of considerable embarrassment to the more courteous of their countrymen.[29] Some Protestant authors, however, delighted in telling their correspondents and readers of the horrors of popery encountered in Roman churches, which in their eyes took on something of the mesmerizing horror of Madame Tussaud's. The theatrical style of liturgical devotions and the overtly pious behaviour

---

[24] W. H. Nelligan, p. 9.
[25] Pemble, *The Mediterranean Passion* (1987), p. 212.
[26] J. C. Eustace, *A Classical Tour Through Italy* (1813), p. xxiii.
[27] Pemble, p. 212.
[28] William Bernard Ullathorne, *Cabin Boy to Archbishop*, p. 129.
[29] Ibid.

of the local population both produced distaste. The impressions of one Protestant clergyman at the Holy Week Tenebrae service in the Sistine Chapel in 1866 was not untypical:

> The solemn and dolorous chanting was most artistic and impressive, the voices rich and magnificent, but the whole service was too long and became exhaustive in the extreme ... Only one of the ambassadors seemed to take the smallest interest in the service; the rest were laughing and staring at the gorgeously dressed belles of beauty collected there from every part of papal Christendom.[30]

Worst of all was the appearance of English Catholicism in all its enthusiastic Ultramontanism in Rome. One Presbyterian visitor refused to visit the English College, fearing that the Rector would bestow on him 'the same help the wolf gives to the lamb'.[31] A Baptist minister in 1868, having experienced Protestant worship at the meeting room outside the Porta del Popolo, 'cast out and crucified without the gates of Rome, as its great prototype was outside the gates of Jerusalem', left Rome in disgust at its squalor, political oppression and false religion. He described it as 'a gigantic prison, where liberty lies bleeding in chains'.[32]

Converts to Roman Catholicism were seen by some Protestant polemicists as traitors to the Church of England and were in some cases rejected by their family and friends. Conversely, they were regarded by some Catholics as 'scalps' won in the battle to convert England back to the 'true faith'. Wiseman was criticized by his fellow bishops for making too much of the new converts and neglecting those who had borne the brunt of difficulties under penal legislation. Both in Wiseman's time and later, converts from the Church of England were drawn to the certainty and authority which Rome seemed to offer, and like

[30] *Cook's Excursionist and Tourist Advertiser*, 26 February 1866.
[31] J. Lethbridge, 'Sheep among the Wolves', *Venerabile* (1960), p. 343.
[32] *Cook's Excursionist and Tourist Advertiser*, 6 May 1868.

Northcote, to the continuity with the ancient Church which was built into the very fabric of the city. The converts themselves even became one of the attractions on a Roman pilgrimage.

... But perhaps one of the most interesting sights on Saturday evening may be witnessed outside the room of the English confessor [at the Gesu]. There, on a bench, waiting for their turn to go to confession, the converts, some of whom, when they were Protestants, held distinguished places of honour and trust in their own country, but now they are seated as humble penitents waiting to receive graces which hitherto they had been strangers to. There sits one, venerable in appearance, who for twenty years was a bishop, but in obedience to the workings of divine grace, he became a Catholic and gave up his all in this world, and now knows not how he will maintain himself during the remainder of his days; but his faith fails not for he knows God will take care of him. There is another who has been a fellow of his college at Oxford – his father, a man of large income, has devoted much of this to his education, and has provided him with a comfortable maintenance for the rest of his days. Accustomed to the comforts of an English home, he is now an exile, for his father has refused to receive him and told him he preferred to see him a felon in a common gaol than to hear of his being Catholic ... but it would be weary to go on through the list. All feel happy and all would willingly again tomorrow renounce home and friends, relations and wealth and their station in society to become a member of the Church, and to be made a partaker of those joys which the world knoweth not of.[33]

Among the Tractarian converts drawn to Rome was Robert Wilberforce, son of the evangelical slave trade reformer and brother of the later Bishop of Oxford. He

[33] Nelligan, pp. 188–9.

was educated at Oriel College, Oxford, where he became fellow and tutor alongside the leaders of the Oxford Movement, Newman and Froude. He became a learned and able defender of the Tractarians, as well as pursuing a successful pastoral career in the Church of England and was an eminent sacramental theologian. Wilberforce did not, like some other Tractarians, 'succumb to the seductive attractions of Romanism',[34] but somewhat reluctantly found the Church of England untenable. In him the natural fears of slipping all his moorings and beginning again at the age of fifty were more evident, but in October 1854 he resigned his benefice and was received into the Catholic Church in Paris. He was a widower by then and began to study at the Accademia Ecclesiastica in Rome for the priesthood – a sign of special favour from the Church.[35] He was not in good health on his arrival and shortly before his ordination he died at Albano from an attack of gastric fever, aged 54. He is buried in S. Maria Sopra Minerva, where two plaques, one in the floor, one on the wall of a side chapel on the right, commemorate him. The tablet in the floor reads, 'In this chapel of S Raymond, the body of Robert Isaac Wilberforce rests in peace: a man learned, devout and humble, who, about to ascend the steps of the altar in his priestly office on this earth, passed to the lamb that is slain from the beginning of the world. 3 February 1857'.

Pius IX encouraged the attachment of converts to Rome through the Collegio Pio (now known as the Collegio Beda), founded in 1852 in Piazza Scozza Cavalli, in the area associated with the Saxon hospice. The property was reputed to have once been partly owned by Sir Thomas Dereham, an English Jacobite exile, buried in the English College chapel. From 1855 to 1918 the Collegio Pio shared the English College property, but then moved to 67 Via S. Niccolo da Tolentino where it remained until moving to its present modern home near S. Paolo fuori le Muri. Roman contacts became essential for the advocates of Catholic revival in

[34] D. Newsome, *The Parting of Friends* (1966), p. 371.
[35] Newsome, p. 408.

England and a foothold on Roman soil became a useful base. One particularly influential convert, Scottish by birth, but a product of English society was Fr Edward Douglas. His wealth provided the resources to build the church of Our Lady of Perpetual Succour (the only neo-gothic church in Rome apart from All Saints Anglican church), which became the Generalate of the Redemptorist Congregation. Douglas was born in 1819 in the wealthy and aristocratic Scottish family of Queensberry, which was shocked by his conversion in 1842. Although he was a student at Christ Church, Oxford until 1841, he does not seem to have had much contact with the Tractarians. More significant influences were his mother, who brought him up alone, and a family friend, Lady Herbert of Lea, later a convert herself. He visited Rome late in 1841 and was rapidly received into the Catholic Church. Ordained in Italy in 1849, he returned to England and lost no time in joining the Redemptorists, who were just starting their missionary work in England. He studied at the Redemptorist Institute in Trond, Belgium, along with Francis Weld (a nephew of the cardinal). They were the first British vocations to the Redemptorist way of life.

Douglas's mother died in 1850 and left him a vast fortune, which he proposed to devote to the purchase of a Roman house for the Congregation. He worked in the Redemptorist house at Clapham for a couple of years, but then was dispatched to Rome to help in the search for a suitable headquarters for the Superior General. He was to remain in Italy from 1853 till his death in 1898, rarely ever leaving Rome. For the first nine years he was superior of the Roman Province of the Congregation. He seems to have been a quiet, uncontroversial man, but with considerable determination and a great warmth and gift for friendship with a reputation as a 'winner' of converts.

Between 1855 and 1861 Douglas supervised and paid for the building of the church. It was built close to the site of St Matthew's church which had been destroyed during the French occupation. St Matthew's had contained a fifteenth-century icon of Our Lady, from Crete, credited with miraculous powers, which survived the destruction.

The Redemptorists gained permission to enshrine the icon in their new church, which was solemnly dedicated on 16 January 1866. From then on, the church of Our Lady of Perpetual Succour became a centre of Marian prayer and devotion and every Redemptorist house and church contains a replica of the famous icon.

The common room at the house adjoining, the Villa Caserta, was the gathering place for many of the prominent supporters of papal infallibility at the First Vatican Council, including Cardinal Manning, with Douglas's enthusiastic encouragement. As the Italian troops invaded Rome in September 1870, much ecclesiastical property was occupied. Douglas tried to protect the Villa Caserta by claiming it was British property and hoisting the Union Jack over it. Neither the Foreign Office in London nor the Italian courts were impressed with Douglas's arguments and the Union Jack had to go. However, through the influence of a friend (the wife of the French Ambassador), King Victor Emmanuel was persuaded to declare the Redemptorists' property an international institute and therefore exempt from suppression.

The Redemptorists were only one example of the burgeoning number of modern religious orders and congregations of men and women for whom a house in Rome was seen as a vital asset. This was true not only of orders of continental origin, like the Redemptorists, but also of those founded in England, specifically to work on the English mission. The Little Company of Mary (Blue Nuns) founded by Mary Potter were just such an order. Their foundress, herself a sick woman, went to Rome in 1882 to seek formal approval for her new institute. Leo XIII not only gave his approval, but invited her to stay in Rome and work there. This she did and in fact when the constitutions were finally approved in 1893, Rome was chosen as the mother house. A site was purchased on the Coelian Hill next to S. Stefano Rotondo and Mary Potter's dream of a hospital built in the shape of a cross with the chapel at the intersection was achieved within four years. The chapel was dedicated with special permission of Pius X to the Maternal Heart of Mary. Mary Potter died on 7 April

1913 and was buried in Campo Verano (the Rome cemetery next to S. Lorenzo fuori le Muri), but was translated in
1917 to the crypt of the hospital chapel.[36] In 1997 her body
was returned to her native Nottingham.

Another English female congregation which made a
lasting impact on Rome was the Poor Servants of the
Mother of God, founded in 1870 by Frances Taylor to work
among the poor of London. The founding of their Roman
house, the Mater Dei Institute, in 1887 came about in a not
dissimilar way to that of the Blue Nuns. Frances Taylor was
born in 1832, the daughter of a Lincolnshire vicar. In 1854
she went to the Crimea as a volunteer with Florence
Nightingale and while there, was received into the Catholic
Church. Returning from the Crimea, she devoted her
energy to charitable work among the poor of London and
to writing. From 1862 she was proprietor of *The Lamp* and
was the first editor of *The Month* in 1863.

She published an account of her experiences in the
Crimea and also *Tyburn and Those who Went Thither* – the
first attempt at a systematic account of the Elizabethan
Catholic martyrs. This brought Frances to the attention of
Lady Georgiana Fullerton, herself an accomplished writer
and published novelist. She was a member of the
Cavendish family and married a Guards officer with lands
in Ireland. To the astonishment of Georgiana and her
family, he became a Catholic in 1843. She followed suit in
1846. Alongside charitable work and her other writings,
she collected material on the English Catholic martyrs to
aid their recognition and if possible advance the cause of
their beatification – hence her interest in Fanny Taylor's
book.

The two women met and became firm friends and allies.
By 1868 they had begun to evolve plans for a religious institute of women, taking the model of a Polish congregation
of Little Servants of the Mother of God. The little community began in London in 1870 in a cottage near Farm
Street, where the women took in sewing and laundry to
maintain themselves and their work. By 1872 the order had

---

[36] F. Ripley, *The Mary Potter Story* (1954), *passim*.

a distinct identity from the Polish root, as the Poor Servants of the Mother of God. The idea of a house in Rome did not emerge till the 1880s, when a chance conversation of Fanny Taylor (now Mother Mary Magdalen) while in Rome in 1885 sowed the seed. Things moved quickly. A flat in a house in Via San Sebastianello was rented, but Mr Fullerton quickly took steps to purchase the entire property for the sisters. His wife had died in January 1885 but he continued to support the sisters and the Rome convent was in part a memorial to his wife.

Magdalen and two companions moved into the house in January 1886, beginning with laundry and charitable activity among the poor. Soon after, the sisters began an English-speaking school, which at its peak had 600 pupils and lasted for over a century till 1992. The chapel of St George and the English Saints was built as a memorial to his wife by Mr Fullerton and was opened on the anniversary of her death in January 1887.

The story of the chapel of Mater Dei and the replica which it contains of the earliest known fresco of Our Lady and the Holy Child in the Catacombs of S. Priscilla draws together a number of nineteenth-century threads. The convent was the result of the ardent *Romanitas* of English converts and reflects the determination of religious founders to have a base in Rome. This picture, given the title of Our Lady, Queen of Prophets, was solemnly enshrined in the chapel on 14 December 1995, bearing witness to the revived consciousness of the catacombs. The chapel dedication suggests the importance in the late nineteenth century of drawing together devotion to English and Roman saints, and it became a new shrine on the revived pilgrim trail.

The catacomb of S. Priscilla was not rediscovered until May 1578 and much of the scholarly work was not done on it until the nineteenth century – among others by the Englishmen Northcote and Brownlow, authors of *Roma Sotteranea*. The fresco is believed to date from before the fourth century. Writing in 1863, the distinguished archaeologist of the catacombs, John Baptist de Rossi assessed it thus:

Everyone can see that the scene depicted in the catacomb of Priscilla is quite in the classical style and is a
work of the best period of art. The form of the
clothing points to remote antiquity; the cloak thrown
over the nude, the figure of the prophet with the right
shoulder bare, and still more the tunic with short
sleeves worn by the Virgin. The beauty of the compo-
sition, the dignity and grace of the features, the
freedom and power of the drawing, give to this fresco
the impress of an age so cultivated and flourishing as
to the fine arts, that when I first beheld it I seemed to
see before me one of the oldest specimens of
Christian painting which are to be found in our cemeteries.

While the nineteenth-century copy cannot imitate the
fragile delicacy of the ancient fresco, it is still possible to
see from the painting the source of the archaeologist's
passionate excitement. For many years, a Jesuit archaeologist from the Gregorian University, Fr Bonavena, had
wished to see this oldest known fresco of the Mother of
God reproduced and honoured publicly. He first voiced
this desire in 1893 and action to find the right church for
this was triggered by Leo XIII's letter *Ad Anglos* of April
1895. The Guild of Our Lady of Ransom had been canoni-
cally erected in the chapel of St George at Mater Dei in
1890, to pray for the conversion of England. Thus it
seemed an appropriate location for a shrine to Our Lady
which was both Biblical and Prophetic. Papal approval of
the copy made on canvas was obtained and the picture was
solemnly enshrined in December 1895. In 1896 Leo XIII
instituted the feast of Our Lady Queen of Prophets on 27
January and the 'English Convent' became widely known
as a centre of prayer for the reunion of Rome and
Canterbury. Thus in more recent years it has become a
barometer of the changing nature of relations between
England and Rome.
    The middle years of the nineteenth century witnessed an
immense revival in the desire and capacity of English
people to go to Rome, for cultural and spiritual reasons.

The pattern of revival had strong echoes of the mediaeval tradition, but also took on new characteristics. Travel facilities improved and enabled larger numbers of less wealthy pilgrims to rediscover the tradition. The martyr tradition, which had given rise to Rome's pre-eminence, was recovered in new guise. The 'city of the dead' of the Romantic imagination took on different meaning in the nineteenth century as the catacombs were explored and stories and legends of martyrs pieced together. Yet the Rome of the early Christian martyrs was becoming identified with the Rome of contemporary martyrdom. The Pope as victim, as persecuted father of an ungrateful family, as spiritual hero, came to predominate in the imagination. For the English, the emotional and spiritual power of Rome and the Pope became either the magnetic attraction or a repugnant manifestation of all that was misguided about Catholicism. This gave a particular shape to both English Catholic life and non-Catholic attitudes towards it.

Chapter Nine

Roma Capitale

That Rome underwent a dramatic change in 1870 is undoubted. It became the capital of the new Italian State and Pius IX ended his long reign as the self-styled 'prisoner of the Vatican'. The Quirinale Palace became the residence of the new King of Italy and huge numbers of religious buildings and churches were taken over by the new secular authorities. The Pope's role as the governor of Rome and the Papal States had gone, though he occupied an almost divine status in the hearts and minds of many Catholics. A deputation of English residents and visitors to Pius IX in April 1871 to express sympathy with the Pope was howled down by the Roman press, and 'members of the deputation cut their former friends, and never called to see them; in fact avoided them, or if they met them in the street they gave them a distant bow, which is worse than not seeing them'.[1] The British government had supported the arrival of democratic government in Italy and had given shelter to its prophet in exile, Giuseppe Mazzini. There was little sympathy among English Protestants for the loss of papal temporal power, so the continued support for the papal cause by Catholics was a further irritant in Catholic/Protestant relations in England. Indeed, as one author has suggested, the liberation of Italy from papal rule became an obsession of English Protestants in the middle years of the nineteenth century, 'its greatest

[1] Michael Dwane [a student at the English College, Rome 1865–71] to William Greaney, April 1871 (Oscott College Archives).

crusade since the campaign against slavery'.[2] When in 1875 Thomas Cook organized a 'Baptist Pilgrimage to Rome' to celebrate the opening of a chapel there, the party was given 'a hearty welcome' by Garibaldi.[3] English Catholics, by contrast, were among those who responded to the Pope's call for a volunteer force to defend the Papal States. Among the English Zouaves were two young brothers, Julian and Wilfred Watts-Russell, the former of whom was killed in battle at the age of seventeen. His memorial can be seen in the chapel of the English College. His funeral took place there and he was regarded by the English Roman community as a contemporary martyr.[4]

Members of the English College recorded the dramas of 1870, both the invasion by Italian troops, and the Vatican Council brought to an abrupt halt because of it. William Barry, an English priest and popular novelist was a student at the college in those dramatic days. He described Rome in 1868 as 'a vast world of institutions, perplexing to the stranger'.[5] His Rome was 'the older Rome, not yet modernized, while the main thoroughfares were paved with cobblestones, the Tiber was not embanked, and the street lighting was very dim, largely dependent on the lamps before the Madonna burning at every street corner'.[6] The Vatican Council was, for the two dozen or so residents of the English College, a source of great excitement as several of the leading English bishops (including Cardinal Manning) lived there during the Council. Bishop Thomas Grant of Southwark fell victim to the effects of prolonged illness while in the college. The Council opened on 8 December 1869, 'a dull, rainy winter's day on which the spectators who thronged St Peter's had but clouded glimpses of the procession in which, as though it were a moving pageant, all the Catholic hierarchy passed along'.[7]

[2] J. Pemble, *The Mediterranean Passion: Victorians and Edwardians in the South* (1987), p. 10.
[3] *Cook's Excursionist and Tourist Advertiser*, 9 December 1875.
[4] J. Johnston, 'Julian Watts-Russell', *Venerabile* 6 (1932), pp. 54–5.
[5] W. Barry, *Memories and Opinions* (1926), p. 68.
[6] Barry, p. 68.
[7] Barry, p. 82.

The students evidently enjoyed the sights of Rome at such a historic moment, not only the bishops of the Universal Church, but many of the deposed crowned heads of Europe – Spain, Bavaria, Naples. As members of a papal institution, the students were often called upon to assist at the great liturgical events and thus to become part of the spectacle themselves. When the Council closed prematurely on news of the impending invasion of Rome, the English College and its occupants found themselves surrounded by drama of a different kind. The diary of a college student, William Kirkham, recalls the excitement, bravado and despair at the fall of Rome to Italian Nationalist troops.

Sept 18. Went round to the gates most threatened: viz those to the east of the city. They are fortifying them as best they can, but what *can* they do? ... The Papal troops have had a few skirmishes in which they killed about 30 *Bersaglieri*; one shot at the Porta Pia bowled over 8 lancers at an Osteria not far from S. Agnese ...

Sept 19. Expect an attack today. Artillery were firing but they appeared to be only testing their guns. Rifle bullets were flying about our ears like angry wasps on the Lateran steps ...

Sept 20. This a.m. I was awakened shortly after 5.00 by the sound of a heavy cannonade which seemed to come from the direction of St John's. It continued without intermission and shortly after was taken up seemingly with heavier guns at Porta Pia and then became general in that quarter ...

About 8.30 I was standing at my window on the top *piano* looking out when I was startled by a shell hitting an opposite house a little to the right and bursting on the roof. The inhabitants on the balcony rushed in which a shriek ... The shelling was coming on pretty thickly, for we could hear nothing else but heavy explosions and the rattling of stones and broken glass. I was standing by the pulpit in the refectory getting rather queer, but not afraid, when bang went a shell. It seemed as if it had burst in the middle of us. We heard bricks falling and windows crashing into the garden.

By the following morning the shelling had ceased and the students and rector emerged from the cellar where they had taken shelter and examined the (limited) damage to the college buildings, and looked across to St Peter's to see the white flag of surrender flying from the basilica.

> That night was something awful! There were a lot of murders committed, no lights in the streets, and I saw a long procession going down the Monserrato with torches, the dregs of Rome with camp followers of the Italian army, any amount of women with them, waving swords and singing 'Viva Garibaldi!' and other such songs. It all reminded me of what I had read of the French Revolution. Poor Pio Nono![8]

The English passion for Italy and Rome in particular was affected by outbreaks of war and changing tastes in art, culture and travel which took them further afield. Protestant piety was satisfied more by the prospect of pilgrimages to the Holy Land, Bible in hand, which became possible in the second half of the century. Nevertheless upwards of 10,000 English visitors colonized Rome each year in the later nineteenth century and brought to the city the fashions and society habits of London.[9] The peak of Anglican converts seeking the assurance and religious culture of Rome had passed. For the pilgrims, the capital of the new Italy was not what they wanted to visit, and while they continued to pour into the city, it became more difficult to do so and to experience what their parents had found in the 1850s and 1860s. At least one passionate devotee of the papal city refused to return after the end of papal rule.

> When I last saw it in 1870 it was already changed and no longer the calm, majestic place of those days, the

---

[8]   *Venerabile*, April 1928, 3, pp. 321–7.
[9]   Pemble, pp. 41–3.

shadow of coming events was already upon it ... Now I
have no wish to see it as it is, and even if I could go to
Roma Capitale I should refuse to do so; I wish to keep
my old thoughts undisturbed. For you who are young
and belong to the present, you will still find, I know,
much to venerate and to delight in. I should not be
surprised if even now you found it difficult to sit down
quietly elsewhere after you have lived at Rome for
some time.[10]

Lord Acton, the historian and no real friend of papal
Rome, was nevertheless moved by the change in atmosphere in post-Unification Rome. As part of the liberal
Catholic group which published *The Rambler* in the 1860s,
Acton opposed the extreme Ultramontane political and
religious viewpoint. He had little taste for the drive
towards defining papal infallibility and was not enthusiastic about defending the Papal States. Nevertheless he was
beguiled by Rome itself and mourned aspects of its disap-
pearance.

Travellers' Rome is what it was; but in the real city the
change is like the work of centuries. The religious
activity and appearance that were of old are gone, and
their place is usurped by things profane. The state has
so thrown the Church into the background, that the
Leonine city sleeps like a faded and deserted suburb,
and one must look behind the scenes for what used to
be the glory and the pride of Rome.[11]

He was not alone among the English literati in
mourning for papal Rome. 'The changes carried out in
Rome after it had become the capital of Italy raised a
chorus of regret ... This note of nostalgia frequently
recurs, for the temporal power of the papacy and the cere-
monials of the Roman Church were, like so much else,
enhanced by death.'[12] Rome became the haunt of literary

[10] M. C. Bishop, p. 284.
[11] H. Paul (ed.), *Letters of Lord Acton to Mary Gladstone* (1904), pp. 79–80.
[12] Pemble, p. 173.

pilgrims, while remaining something of a second home for fashionable English gentry in the winter. The passionate excess and eulogy was not the preserve only of those nostalgic for papal Rome. Even contemporary observers noted the English tendency to abandon their traditional reserve under the warmth of the Italian sun: 'The majority of English tourists seem to think it essential to dress themselves in their finest intellectual clothes before they pass the Alps; and nine out of ten of them ... either gush or cant.'[13] Rome featured largely in the increasingly popular and influential literary form of the nineteenth century, the novel. Its influence on English popular and intellectual culture was immense, and so it became a place of pilgrimage for those yearning for an enlarging of the spirit and intellect which was not necessarily religious. For writers whose talents went well beyond 'gush or cant', such as George Eliot, Rome was the key to enlightenment, as in the case of Dorothea Casaubon in *Middlemarch*.

> To those who have looked at Rome with the quickening power of a knowledge which breathes a growing soul into all historic shapes, and traces out the suppressed transitions which unite all contrasts, Rome may still be the spiritual centre and interpreter of the world. But let them conceive one more historical contrast: the gigantic broken revelations of that Imperial and Papal city thrust abruptly on the notions of a girl who had been brought up on English and Swiss Puritanism, fed on meagre Protestant histories and on art chiefly of the hand-screen sort ...[14]

This spiritual enrichment articulated by artists but shared by many is the clue to the continued claim of Rome on the hearts and minds of those of the late nineteenth century and twentieth century who would call themselves pilgrims. For Dorothea, Rome was the means of discovering not only a wider intellectual and artistic world, but of discovering

[13] George Augustus Sala, quoted in Pemble, p. 65.
[14] George Eliot, *Middlemarch*, ch. 20 (Penguin edn.), p. 225.

passion, love, honesty and ultimately her true self. She can be read as an icon of the modern pilgrim whose experience of formal religion is limited or even negative, but who is striving to nurture their own spiritual life.

After 1870, the unsettled state of Rome made the work of the archaeologists more difficult. The government controlled the excavations and the previous authority and resources of the Sacred Congregation of the Vatican were greatly curtailed. The unsettled mood made the raising of funds for archaeology more difficult, and even the leading excavator, John Baptist de Rossi, was forced to rely on donations. Northcote helped by publishing a popular work in 1877, *A Visit to the Roman Catacombs*, but interest in England in the catacombs was fading from its earlier peak. Many of the English abhorred the determined restoration by the government of works of art, buildings and classical ruins. Archaeologists were blamed for the ruin of the familiar decay and vegetation around buildings which had appealed to the Victorian taste.[15] A new Rome began to emerge – the secular modern city, in which the pilgrim was arguably less at home.

English Catholic interest shifted towards the cause of the martyrs of the Reformation and penal times, whose stories became part of the popular culture of English Catholicism. The cause for beatification by the Church of the first group of martyrs was opened by Cardinal Manning in June 1874, although as early as 1860 Wiseman had petitioned the Pope (unsuccessfully) to institute a feast in England in honour of the martyrs. In 1886, fifty-four martyrs were beatified and a further 261 were honoured as Venerable. The source of information for many of these was a printed book of engravings of frescoes which, until the French Revolution, could be seen in the English College. They were painted by Circignani in the late sixteenth century, recording those martyred between 1535 and 1583. (He was also responsible for the frescoes in S. Stefano Rotondo.) The engravings of the college frescoes played an important part in the process and were specifically mentioned in the documentation of the

---

[15] Pemble, p. 178.

cause as the main evidence. The lives of the martyrs, written by various Jesuits and Oratorians, were compiled and published in 1904 by Dom Bede Camm OSB.[16] The archival material necessary for this process was compiled partly from material gathered in the early 1870s in the Vatican archives by Fr Joseph Stevenson. He was one of the most surprising English visitors to post-Unification Rome.[17]

Stevenson had trained as an archivist in the British Museum and had also been vicar of Leighton Buzzard. He became a Roman Catholic in middle life and was ordained priest in 1872. The archives of the Vatican, like all papal offices, had been walled up after the occupation of Rome, to prevent the new state getting its hands on them. The English historian Lord Acton, who had worked in the Vatican archives, knew of the valuable material contained therein for the history of England, and had suggested that the British government request access to papers relevant to English history for copying. After Acton's opposition to the majority view at the Vatican Council he was *persona non grata* in Vatican circles, so the British government turned to Stevenson, whose archivist friends in London had pleaded his case to Gladstone. From 1872 to 1876, Stevenson worked on English papers from the reign of Henry VIII onwards in the Vatican archives, paid by the British government. For most of the time he was the only person apart from the Vatican officials to enter the archives and was given total freedom. Thus he could also obtain material for his own interests. He sent copies of Elizabethan material to his great friend John Morris SJ who was working on that period and who was one of the first group of compilers of lives of English Catholic martyrs and first Postulator of the causes for Beatification.[18] Reference is made in Camm's edition to the transcripts of martyr papers by Stevenson and his successor William Bliss.[19] The fact that many of them were alumni of

[16] B. Camm, *Lives of the English Martyrs Declared Blessed by Pope Leo XIII in 1886 and 1895*, 2 vols (1904).
[17] The extraordinary story is told in detail in O. Chadwick, *Catholicism and History: the Opening of the Vatican Archives* (1978), pp. 76–86.
[18] Camm, Intro., p. 50.
[19] Camm, Intro., p. 54.

the English College in Rome, and that all had died in defence of papal authority over the English church, fired a new enthusiasm for pilgrimage among late nineteenth-century and early twentieth-century English people. The cult of the English martyrs was really born in the later nineteenth century and was part of the aggressive reassertion of English Catholic identity in the face of Protestant hostility.

In 1929 the first of those beatified martyrs whose relics were now preserved and venerated in England, were canonized by Pius XI, and among the thousands of English witnesses to the event was G. K. Chesterton, who caught the mood of patriotic fervour in his account of the occasion,

I heard the very long list of those English heroes who resisted the despotic destruction of the national religion, read in due order; and listened to a number of names that sounded like Smith or Higgins pronounced with a perfect Italian accent ... What moved me very much, as an Englishman, was that he (the Pope) spoke with peculiar warmth and vividness of England, and like one who had seen it rather than heard of it. He dwelt even more strongly on the words 'so beautiful a country' than on the words 'so great a nation'. He also emphasized strongly the fact that the last witnesses in England were men of every class and condition, poor as well as rich, and agricultural labourers as well as the first noble of the land.[20]

This sense of the ordinary, everyday character of many of the martyrs captured the imagination of English Catholics and helped to repopularize pilgrimage to Rome. It was also echoed in the rapidly growing popularity of church dedications in England to the English Martyrs.

The English, not just the rich nor even just the pilgrims, were yet again rediscovering Rome. By 1872 they could approach Italy via the newly completed seven and a quarter mile Mont Cenis tunnel. English visitors came from a wider social spectrum, especially the rising commercial middle

[20] G. K. Chesterton, *The Resurrection of Rome* (1930), p. 321.

classes who aspired to elements of both the Grand Tour and the pilgrimage. By 1858 most of the journey could be done by rail and steamer in a matter of days. At Easter 1866 Thomas Cook escorted the first organized party of English tourists to Rome by railway and steamer. Augustus Hare's *Walks in Rome* ran to sixteen editions between 1871 and 1903. In 1887 the church of S. Silvestro in Capite was granted to the use of the English-speaking Catholics and in the same year the Mater Dei convent near the Spanish Steps opened its English-speaking school. Thomas Cook, despite his staunch Baptist credentials, was much involved in making travel arrangements for pilgrim groups, not only from England, but from across the Atlantic as well. Indeed, he expressed great pride in having 'a high-class party of English visitors entrusted to our management' for the 'season of unprecedented attraction to the Catholic community', celebrating the priestly jubilee of Pius IX in 1877.[21]

The number of English visitors to Rome in the nineteenth century had become so numerous that regular courses of English sermons were given at S. Andrea delle Fratte, Holy Trinity in the Via Condotti and S. Salvador in Onda near the Ponte Sisto. Moves were already afoot for an English-speaking church by the middle of the century. Fr William Whitmee, a convert, got the support of Archbishop Edmund Stonor who lived in Rome from 1861 to his death in 1912 and Cardinal Edward Howard, who was a member of the same family as the seventeenth-century Cardinal Howard and, like him, was Protector of the English College (1878–92).[22] He became a papal diplomat and Cardinal Bishop of Frascati.

Both were friends of the influential Mgr George Talbot and enlisted his co-operation in Whitmee's projected use of S. Silvestro in Capite as an English church. Whitmee was superior of the Pallottine fathers who ministered to the Italian population in London. As St Vincent Pallotti had built St Peter's Clerkenwell as the 'Italian Church' in

[21] *The Cook's Excursionist and Tourist Advertiser*, 21 May 1877.
[22] M. E. Williams, *A History of the Venerable English College, Rome*, (1979), p. 137.

London, this seemed an appropriate ministry to undertake in Rome. The Poor Clare sisters who had built S. Silvestro left in 1876 and after lengthy negotiations, Leo XIII granted the Pallottines permission to take it over. The property had been expropriated by the state, so it took a further two years to obtain the church and for Fr Whitmee to begin work as the first Rector. The Pallottine Order continue to serve S. Silvestro as an English-speaking church and the adjoining English Centre was opened in 1949 in time for the Holy Year.

One of the key features of Roman pilgrimage to emerge strongly in the nineteenth century was the papal audience. Increasingly in the Ultramontane church, attention was drawn to the personal authority and the personal cult of the Pope. The long papacy of Pius IX (1846–78) in the middle years of the century and his 'heroic' battles with the forces of liberalism, nationalism and unbridled progressivism enhanced both his personal stature and that of the papacy. The atmosphere in which the Vatican Council of 1869–70 defined the dogma of papal infallibility encouraged his supporters to bestow on Pius IX almost divine qualities.[23] The consequence of this enhanced papalism was that not only bishops, diplomats and churchmen craved an audience with the Pope, but pilgrims of all sorts and conditions. Early in the century, aristocratic Catholic visitors and notable converts would often be presented to the Pope by one of the English clerics resident in Rome. This was a phenomenon of the nineteenth century, and by the 1860s the papal audience for large groups of pilgrims had become *de rigueur.*

The year 1867 saw the celebration of the eighteenth centenary of the martyrdom of St Peter and despite the political conditions, it was kept with great solemnity in Rome with 90,000–100,000 visitors in the city. This was the first great papal occasion in many a long year and the scale of travellers to Rome had exploded. The centenary brought 490 prelates and bishops, all the patriarchs of the East and about 1400 priests. 'The railroad incessantly

---

[23] C. Butler, *The Vatican Council 1869–70* (1930), vol. 1, pp. 76–7.

disgorged black bands into Rome. The Italian press spoke in derision of the flight of crows – *il passagio delle cornacchie*. Rome became quite dark. All the hotels, cafés, dwelling houses were filled during this invasion of priests'.[24] This may be the first time when the modern practice of issuing tickets for papal audiences and ceremonies was employed.[25] Four times as many people applied for tickets as were available. On an intensely hot 29 June, St Peter's was packed with pilgrims and disaster was only narrowly averted as the tapers set fire to the silk hangings, and candles themselves drooped in the heat and ignited the wooded scrolls on the sconces.[26] This was but one of a series of celebrations during June and July, culminating in the canonization of St Paul of the Cross (founder of the Passionists) among others, and the beatification of 205 Japanese martyrs. The huge gathering of bishops, priests and laity, the magnificence of the ceremonies in which the Pope demonstrated his hold on the keys of heaven gave a clear message to the Italian nationalists, who at the same time were drafting legislation for the confiscation of church property. A flavour of the religious sentiment of this time towards the Pope, evoked by such an event, can be gleaned from the English commentator's quasi-divine description of the papal procession 'radiating from and centring in him'.

> For the ordinary faithful is reserved a joy which is not for him [i.e. the Pope]. It is the vision of the extreme sweetness and placidity of the common father. The encouraging sight of one who, amid all the swerving waves of doubt, represents the perfect embodiment of the special Messenger of the One Unseen – who, with utter good faith, and therefore without a shadow of ostentation, shows you that he believes in himself, and convinces you he is what he believes himself to be.[27]

[24] F. Gregorovius, *Roman Journals 1852–74* (1907), pp. 278–9.
[25] *Contemporary Annals of Rome* (Articles reprinted from the *Westminster Gazette*) (1870), p. 88.
[26] Ibid., p. 92.
[27] Ibid., p. 101.

It was still possible for visitors who had contacts with the resident English clerics to obtain private audiences, which followed a familiar pattern.

When our turn came we were called by Mgr Talbot, and at once introduced into a long room, where stood His Holiness at a little table at the end, and then Mgr Talbot, having mentioned who we were, left us alone. We knelt at the door on entering, again in the middle of the room, and again when we were close to him; he put out his hand and tried to prevent us from kissing his foot, but we persisted and he permitted it. The Pope at once commenced in a cheerful and familiar tone. Mamma talked French, and got out what she wanted to say well. I then chimed in Italian and asked his blessing for my own family and that of my sister, and amongst others for my three boys at school under Dr Newman at the Oratory and for Dr N. and his school. This he gave, quoting a passage out of Ecclesiasticus. He then talked about Dr Newman, as the first English convert he had ever seen, and of his first coming to Rome; then about Fr St John and Fr Faber. Our interview lasted about ten minutes, during which we got all our rosaries blest. He looked well and in good health, his eye was bright, his voice clear, and we all came away charmed.[28]

Another account of a pilgrimage made in the mid-1870s indicates that the ticket routine was by then well established. 'We had a meeting today, to receive our tickets for the audience at the Vatican tomorrow. Rome is in a ferment; the excitement is very great – pilgrims running over each other everywhere.'[29] This was clearly a large-scale nationally-organized pilgrimage and the published account speaks of 'the programme of sights and functions marked out day by day for the pilgrims'.[30] National groups and various sodalities and associations obtained audiences.

---

[28] Bellasis, pp. 172–3.
[29] W. J. Anderdon, *To Rome and Back* (1877), p. 49.
[30] Anderdon, p. 54.

The age of the popular national, diocesan and parish pilgrimage embracing clergy and laity of all walks of life had arrived. It was not only pilgrimage on a different scale but highly organized, controlled 'official' pilgrimage, which was a clear sign of the increasing centralization of the Church. The Ultramontane influence which now dominated Catholicism took control of many aspects of popular piety, including pilgrimages, and turned them into expressions of loyalty to the Pope and to Rome. Many of the English pilgrimages were placed in the hands of Thomas Cook, who had the monopoly of travel business, and was agent for all the steamship companies and railways of Europe. In 1887 he was offering reduced fares for parties of forty or more and specially-chartered trains for groups of over 300 who wished to participate in the priestly jubilee celebrations for Leo XIII.[31] In 1893 he was appointed by the Catholic Union of Great Britain to make arrangements for an English and Scottish pilgrimage to be led by the Duke of Norfolk. Clearly and consciously, Thomas Cook was playing a major part in the recovery of the tradition of pilgrimage as a communal activity for all classes of people.

> Thanks to the conveniences and facilities afforded by the modern system of locomotion, thousands of pilgrims are enabled to travel hundreds of miles in comfort, by train or steamer in the course of a day or two, instead of on foot or horseback from the Tabard Inn in Southwark as our forefathers accomplished their pilgrimage in the days of Chaucer.[32]

The Irish pilgrimage of that year consisted of 344 people led by four Bishops, the English and Scots raised 533 pilgrims led by the Duke of Norfolk and the Bishop of Nottingham. All the arrangements were made by Thomas Cook and 'everything was carried out with satisfaction and success'.[33] Costs were kept to a minimum and by the time of the Holy Year of 1900,

---

31 *Cook's Excursionist and Travel Advertiser*, 14 November 1887.
32 *Cook's Excursionist and Travel Advertiser*, 18 March 1893.
33 Ibid.

'to suit the convenience of those who are not able to spend so much time' (i.e. those who have to work!) a special cheap six-day, ten-guinea tour to Rome was planned.[34]

What differed in the revival of the Roman pilgrimage tradition was that Rome was no longer simply the shrine for the relics of SS Peter and Paul and other early martyrs which historical accident had determined. Rome itself, and particularly the Pope, was the martyr. As the proclamation of the Official Holy Year pilgrimage from England put it, 'Of late years the spoliation of the Holy See, by sacrilegious invaders of Church property, has given a new motive and impulse to Roman pilgrimages from all parts of Christendom.'[35] At no point in the previous history of popular pilgrimage had such attention and devotion been focused on the Pope, nor had it entered the pilgrim's mind to seek an audience with the Pope. Pilgrimage to Rome in the late nineteenth century, while it continued to pay homage to the fathers of Christianity, was increasingly about corporate or communal expressions of loyalty, homage and obedience to the present Holy Father. That phrase in itself, which became common-place among the English (even among sympathetic non-Catholics) in this period, was a telling expression of a Victorian understanding of paternal relationship.

> The audience of the English pilgrims took place today at 7.30. A special Mass was said for them by Cardinal Howard. Most of them had assembled by the time we arrived, and the spectacle was most impressive ... When it was over, we went into the crypt, where Masses were going on. It is difficult to get there but our pilgrims' tickets admitted us everywhere, even to the Council chamber; and with sorrowful interest we gazed on its vacant seats. 'How long, O Lord, how long.'[36] At noon we assembled for the audience at the

---

[34] *Cook's Excursionist and Travel Advertiser*, 10 September 1900.

[35] Cardinal H. Vaughan, *The Pilgrimage to Rome for the Solemn Homage*, 16 November 1900 (Oscott College Archives).

[36] The reference is to the anticipated resumption of the Vatican Council, abruptly prorogued on the invasion of Rome and long expected to be recalled.

Vatican. For many of us, it was the first time in our lives; a precious privilege, to be ever gratefully remembered. It was impossible to realize beforehand how deeply impressed one would be by the presence of the Holy Father. We had a long time to wait, and the large hall was crowded. At last there was a murmur at the opposite door, the Cardinals then formed a circle round the throne; the Holy Father was carried in, and we all knelt. He is just like his pictures; only, no portrait could give the saintly beauty of his expression; and though feeble in body, he is youthful in soul, and seems as full of vigour and spirit as if he were forty! The address was read by the Bishop of Clifton, and he listened with great pleasure and attention, making little gestures of approval. When it was ended, some of the principal gentlemen, the Duke of Norfolk, Lord Denbigh etc. went up to kiss his hand and say a few words. Then the names of a few of the principal ladies were called out by Cardinal Howard for presentation; but the number was limited, as the Holy Father was becoming fatigued and had to speak ... Everyone near him was seized with emotion. I shall never forget that moment as long as I live, and must always thank God for having lived to see it.[37]

During the rest of their pilgrimage, some of the English were able to gatecrash the Scottish audience and one for 'Roman ladies'. Each of them was packed with people and proved to be, as the author commented. 'A severe trial, with all one's loyalty and enthusiasm'.[38]

The only Holy Year of the nineteenth century was the unsuccessful one of 1825, after which the military and political situation in the Papal States made it impossible until 1900. The first jubilee of the new century took place in the strange conditions of the continued refusal of the papacy to recognize the nation within which it lived. However, by then tensions had eased, the sequestering of

37 Anderdon, pp. 50–2.
38 Anderdon, p. 61.

religious property by the state had ceased and a kind of *de facto* recognition had been exchanged between the religious and secular authorities. Leo XIII's encouragement of the Catholic Workers' movement brought tens of thousands of pilgrims in the last decade of the century, especially after the publication of his encyclical *Rerum Novarum* (1891) which was nicknamed 'The Workers' Charter'.[39] While Pius IX's death in 1878 could not even be officially reported to the unrecognized Italian state, by the time of Leo XIII's death in 1903 Italian troops (unofficially) formed a guard of honour.[40] As the opening of the Holy Year approached, 2000 Italian troops were on parade in the Piazza S. Pietro on festivals, with the express purpose of showing honour to the Pope.[41] The crowds and excitement generated by the opening of the first twentieth-century Holy Year, on Christmas Eve 1899, was intense and an English College student, who went on to be Bishop of Portsmouth and a noted historian of English recusancy, recorded the occasion vividly.

> After a deal of dodging we got into the portico [of St Peter's] where we stood for two hours packed like sardines. We were talking to some English ladies most of the time. A gallery had been built along the outer wall and this was reserved for the 'few'. About 11.30 the procession began to come in from the Vatican end – Monsignori, Abbots, Bishops, Primates and Cardinals amidst some chanting by the Papal choir. Then the Pope arrived whilst the silver trumpets were being played and took his place on the throne close to the Porta Santa. I could see very little of the ceremony that followed. The Pope sung the prayers in a wonderful strong voice and then (I suppose) the door fell down for he disappeared and after him followed the rest *seniores priores* and then the other doors were opened and we found ourselves shot up the steps and

[39] Perry and Echeverria, *Under the Heel of Mary*, p. 142.
[40] A. Rhodes, *The Vatican in the Age of Liberal Democracies 1870–1922* (1983), pp. 172–3.
[41] VEC Liber 825, *Diary of John Henry King*, 24 December 1899.

into the basilica in seconds. Bamford had his wings [i.e. of his cassock] torn off in the mêlée. Half way up the aisle we found our way blocked by the barriers but on seeing two nuns clear it gracefully, I wasn't going to be left behind so over I went and made my way towards the dome. In the other transept were hundreds of banners presented by pilgrims. After a good hour's wait the Pope came into the space in front of the Confessione. He wore his tiara this time. Then he gave his solemn blessing to the crowd and we retired for dinner about 1.30.[42]

Large-scale English pilgrimages took place in 1900 for the Holy Year and in 1901 to mark the opening of the new century. The latter laid claim to being the first in the new century, as Leo XIII himself proclaimed: 'To you Catholics of Great Britain falls the honour of having organized the first pilgrimage which has come this century to lay in the hands of the successor of Peter the testimony of your unquenchable love for the Church and the Apostolic See'.[43] Accounts of both events reveal the extent to which pilgrimages had become part of the ecclesiastical system and were carefully organized by lay and clerical leaders. The presence of clergy and the celebration of sacraments dominated the conduct of the pilgrimages, which traditionally had been largely expressions of lay piety. While the traditional circuit of the seven churches remained a feature, it is clear that St Peter's now dominated even more. It was the heart of Catholic Christianity, the object of loyalty, the Pope's basilica in which every Catholic felt at home, the symbol of Catholic power confronting the secular world, all of which seemed as important as the shrine of Peter and Paul.

There were two distinctively English features. Firstly, the English class system was perpetuated within the pilgrimage. The organization for the 1900 pilgrimage, 'was conducted by the Catholic Association and was under the

[42] VEC Liber 825, King, 24 December 1899.
[43] VEC Liber 871, Newscuttings.

immediate care of Fr Bannin RSM and Mr Dunford, secretary. The pilgrims came in two groups. Section B comprised the industrial classes who were lodged at Santa Marta, while the better class stayed at the Minerva.'[44] In 1901, the pilgrimage was headed by the Duke of Norfolk, who presented an address to the Pope 'offering the Pope the loving homage of British Catholics'.[45] The other particular English feature was the active involvement of students from the English College in the care of pilgrims from their home country. The tradition of the pilgrim hospice had not been forgotten, but the scale of the Holy Year pilgrimages made it impossible for the college to offer hospitality. The alternative was for students to do duty as hosts and guides but along carefully supervised lines.

Throughout the Holy Year, pilgrims poured into Rome. 'Having deposited our luggage at the College we went up to the Pincio and saw some of the 10,000 pilgrims who had just come in.'[46] However, pilgrim duty for the students was strictly limited to the 'official' English pilgrimage which did not arrive until October. They were formed into pairs and allocated to certain hotels where the English pilgrims were due to arrive. They were expected to take groups of anything up to eighty pilgrims on carefully-planned itineraries (to avoid overcrowding). The intention was evidently to enable the whole party to complete the traditional 'seven churches', catacombs, and papal audience. The timing and transportation for the visits was evidently somewhat chaotic but the audience in St Peter's was a mix of order and informality which has become familiar to modern pilgrims. A formal dress code was observed, with ladies in black and wearing a veil, but informality broke in with the prolonged cheering for the arrival of the Pope and spontaneous hymn-singing. It was clearly the highlight of the pilgrimage, and when the programme was completed in the space of four days the 'industrial classes' began the long train journey back to England. The more leisured classes who could afford to stay longer were then

---

[44] VEC Liber 825, King, 11 October 1900.
[45] VEC Liber 871, Newscuttings.
[46] King, 21 April 1900.

able to turn their attention to the other sights of Rome, and did the rounds of churches and museums. For the students it was an exhausting round of guided tours, carriage drives and hospitality which they were forced to accept, despite the strictures of the college authorities. Naturally by 1900 the tide of pilgrims was joined by a large number of non-Catholics, for some of whom the emotional power of Rome in Holy Year overwhelmed their reservations. One such was Charles Rose Chase, an Anglican Ritualist with a taste for all things Roman except papal infallibility and primacy. 'As far as worship and the system of praying is concerned, I am thoroughly Roman Catholic. But as to the jurisdiction and Church rule, I am thoroughly Anglican.'[47] By the end of the nineteenth century the High Church party was a strong force in the Church of England and ritualist practice was widespread, so to find such ideas expressed and practised by one of her clergy-men was not unusual. On his visit to Rome at Easter 1900 Chase met up with his former curate in the Church of England, E.A.P. Theed, now a Catholic priest, who guided him around the city. The pilgrimage experience enthralled him:

> I don't remember when I have been so touched before. 30–40,000 in St Peter's and then that wonderful old man carried in – ninety years old, but with clear complexion and bright eye and such a look of interest in everything ... I could not speak for crying, and the tears come into my eyes every time I think of the sight of that perfect Holy Father. One certainly believes in him personally, if one cannot believe in the system he represents.[48]

However, Chase was wise enough to know the emotional power of such occasions and while clearly drawn to Catholicism, remarked that 'It is easy to be a Papist in Rome. What one feels when one gets home remains to be

[47] H. P. Russell, *From Hussar to Priest: a Memoir of Charles Rose Chase* (1913), p. 126.
[48] Russell, p. 128.

seen.'[49] In his case the spiritual and emotional experience of the pilgrimage had set the seal on his intellectual enquiries and by November 1900 Chase was back in Rome as a student of the Beda College. A more unlikely pilgrim was Oscar Wilde. Ostracized by English society both home and abroad, he travelled to Genoa to visit the grave of his wife, and on to Rome where he became an habitual attender at papal occasions and was mesmerized by Leo XIII. 'I have seen nothing like the extraordinary grace of his gesture, as he rose, from moment to moment, to bless – possibly the pilgrims, but certainly me.'[50] Within a few months Wilde was dead in Paris, but not before he had been received into the Catholic Church. Such diverse accounts of pilgrims illustrate that the perennial possibilities which pilgrimage held out, of life-changing experience, had survived into the twentieth century.

Further National Pilgrimages took place in 1925 and in 1950 which followed similar patterns. The English College students again played their part as guides and general helps. In 1925 the National Pilgrimage took place in May, led by Cardinal Bourne, the Archbishop of Liverpool and the Bishop of Leeds, with 1200 pilgrims and 110 priests.[51] It becomes clear from accounts of 1925 that papal ceremonies (including the increasingly frequent canonizations of saints) and liturgical extravaganzas ranked high on the list of sights to be seen by pilgrims.[52] Papal audiences gave rise to the usual frenzy of excitement and outpouring of emotion, of which this is but one example: 'What a wonderful thing the Papacy is! Those faithful guardians of the inheritance of the past, and prophets and guides of the future, the binding link between earth and heaven. Oh! the joy and gratitude to belong to Peter and his successors through these long years of continuity.'[53] Nevertheless, the circuit of basilicas still had to be completed before all else and one account indicates that at least some pilgrims

---

[49] Russell, p. 135.
[50] J. Glorney Bolton, *Roman Century 1870–1970* (1970), pp. 148–9.
[51] *Venerabile* (1925), p. 217.
[52] V.E.C. Liber 859, 1925 – *A Jubilee Year. A Glimpse.*
[53] V.E.C. Liber 859, p. 25.

adhered to the ancient Holy Year tradition of visiting the basilicas each day to gain the full indulgence. 'May 25, Monday. Made our Jubilee visits as usual. St. Paul's outside the walls seemed full of pilgrims; German, Alsace-Lorraine and French too, headed by their Bishops.'[54] The behaviour of pilgrims in relation to the Christian sites in Rome and the conscious rehabilitation of the formal routine of visits was striking even in 1950.

> They [the churches] began to fill up with pilgrims, at least the main ones did – the absence of curiosity among the mass of pilgrims for anything off the prescribed beat was very striking, not only with regard to pagan Rome; they missed half of Christianity. For the first time one seemed to be seeing the big basilicas as they were meant to be, swarming not just for the big event now and then but all day every day. It drastically changed one's sense of their origin and of their art.[55]

Thus it is clear that by this time the ecclesiastical organized pilgrimage was a feature of life all over Europe, and diocesan and national pilgrimages to Rome, and increasingly to Lourdes, were readily and cheaply enough mounted to enable a large number to participate. The large numbers of pilgrims and the constant flow of different groups clearly placed a strain on the college students who were constantly in demand for guiding. By 1950, there is evidence that this was apparently getting almost out of hand and disrupting the life of the college.[56] Recollections of those involved suggest that a firm hand had to be taken by the Rector at times. At S. Sylvestro (the English-speaking church), a social centre had been opened in time for the Holy Year to offer cups of tea and home-made cake, maps, directions and an escape from the hurly-burly for the bewildered English pilgrims. It did not take the college students long to find the source of tea and

[54] V.E.C. Liber 859, p. 20.
[55] E. Clark, *Rome and a Villa* (1953), p. 199.
[56] V.E.C. Liber 833.

cakes, which led to a severe reprimand from the Vice Rector. 'If there's any mothering to be done round here, I'll do it!'[57]

Despite this emphasis within Catholic culture on the organized pilgrimage there were still many, in fact in increasing numbers, who made the pilgrimage to Rome alone. However, there were signs that the ancient tradition was being submerged in the tide of tourism, that the ritual associated with pilgrimage was waning and that a broader understanding of pilgrimage and the impact of Rome on the human soul was gradually emerging. Even by 1900 the arrival in Rome of a pilgrim on foot from England was a remarkable event. The young John King encountered such a man who had walked from Oxford and was going on pilgrimage 'in the old style to Jerusalem'[58] (a telling phrase). The pilgrim, by name Newberry, was a convert and Professor at Prior Park, whose prospects had been ruined by his conversion to Catholicism and by prolonged ill-health. 'He walked to Dover and then having crossed the Channel he set out on foot to Lourdes and from there came into Italy and crossed to Loreto and finally reached Rome on July eighteenth, seventy-five days after leaving Calais. After his stay here he goes on to Brindisi to take ship to Palestine.'[59]

By 1950, the tone of Holy Year was irrevocably changing and the pattern of pilgrimage with it. Political conditions had changed as well and the chill of the Cold War was already settling over Europe. Among those who were exempted by the Church from making the pilgrimage to Rome were those 'unfortunate inhabitants of those countries in which conditions prevent their journeying to the Eternal City'.[60] Elements of the tradition survived to be translated into the language and behaviour of the second half of the twentieth century, but some aspects were gone for ever. While pilgrims were uniformly urged to go 'as

---

[57] I am grateful to Fr J. A. Harding of the Diocese of Clifton for this story.
[58] V.E.C. Liber 825, 23 July 1900.
[59] V.E.C. Liber 825, 23 July 1900.
[60] Perry and Echeverria, p. 243.

humble pilgrims, in a spirit of penitence', they were also warned to examine carefully what they were offered by travel agents 'in order to be sure that the facilities offered are quite adequate and the fares quoted strictly inclusive'.[61] A dramatic aspect of Holy Years up to the nineteenth century was the huge amount of charity given to pilgrims by various religious organizations. This did not appear to be the case in 1950 – nothing was free.

> On the pilgrim side, whatever the financial sacrifice, the signs and attitudes of the old-time penitents – sackcloth, tears, bleeding feet – had gone quite out of date. It was front-page news when a pilgrim arrived on foot or, as one did, on horseback; many came by plane; the eleven-mile trek to the basilicas, to which only one visit was now required, was done by bus or taxi; one heard nothing of the once traditional humiliation of the powerful before the poor. It was rare to see middle class or rich pilgrims departing in any way from the customary foreign scorn of Rome's great natural charity, they were as apt to be as harsh towards the beggars as any other tourist; and a good many seemed less bent on the 'reform of life' that Holy Year was supposed to induce than on the other possibilities of the trip.[62]

Such observations, while at one level accurate, ignore the changing pattern and meaning of pilgrimage and forget that mixed motives have always taken pilgrims on the road to Rome. By the mid-twentieth century not only had habits of travel changed but so had the intentions and expectations of those who travelled. Pilgrimage had also changed its meaning, losing some of the formal ritual and gaining a broader and perhaps deeper meaning associated with the increasingly complex search for – what? Self-fulfilment? Faith? Reassurance? In the post-Hitler, post-Holocaust, post-Hiroshima world religious certainties were less secure

[61] Abp J. Masterson, *Letter to the Clergy of the Archdiocese of Birmingham on the Holy Year*, 24 December 1949 (Oscott College Archives).
[62] E. Clark, p. 204.

and religious practice less satisfactory for many. Pilgrimage became increasingly a journey into the unknown.

1950 was arguably the last of a particular style of Holy Year, the final triumphant salvo of the Ultramontane Catholicism of the nineteenth century, soon to be revolutionized by the Second Vatican Council. There were many who felt that by 1975, Holy Years had become outmoded expressions of religiosity. The practicalities of coping with thousands of visitors and the consequent traffic, accommodation, food and facilities for the Holy Year seemed to defeat the Rome administration. Despite those who argued that this sort of papal jamboree did not fit with the spirit of the post-conciliar church, Paul VI decided to press ahead after consultation, in the hope that the Holy Year

> might not only be inserted within the spiritual guidelines of the Council, whose faithful implementation is very close to our heart, but that it may also be able to support and relate in the best way to the untiring and loving efforts of the Church to burden itself with the moral hardships and with the profound longing of our era.[63]

That was a hugely significant statement about one aspect of the Church's life and the way in which it might be brought to reflect the spirit of the Council.

Alongside the disciplined diocesan pilgrimages of the twentieth century came another style of pilgrim, of a type illustrated by the author Anthony Rhodes. He journeyed through the Sabine Hills on a donkey called Pepe, accompanied by the beast's owner Giuseppe Masceri, to reach Rome in the Holy Year. Though expressing no overt religious intention he caught the atmosphere of Holy Year and 'considered myself, in a sense, a pilgrim, for I wanted to see the Pope at the end of our journey, and I hoped to meet other pilgrims on the way'. He did meet a colourful variety of other pilgrims and felt himself to be part of a

[63] E. M. Jung-Inglessis, *The Holy Year in Rome, past and present* (1997), p. 268.

great tradition, the purpose and meaning of which was often confused,

> ... In the Middle Ages when the pilgrimages started, to come on foot was obligatory of course. The journey was then long (ninety days from Paris). And many dropped by the way, from exhaustion or the violences they received; or in extreme cases, even reaching Rome, and then falling beneath the blows of the Devil, who lay in wait up a nut tree outside the gates, above the grave of Nero. But nothing discouraged the faithful, and the pilgrimages never flagged ... Of course there were a good many imposters, pilgrims who were really, like ourselves, only glorified tramps.[64]

He encountered monks walking overland from Dalmatia with a cross which was borne by the villagers along the way as it had been for centuries, French pilgrims at a convent hostel which had 'never refused hospitality to a pilgrim for 500 years', and, in the queue for tickets for the papal audience, 'men and women by whom one half expected to be importuned, whose general insalubrity and odour contrasted strangely with this magnificent waiting room'.[65] This was the modern experience of a centuries-old tradition busily adapting itself yet again to new conditions and demands. It was an experience which demanded an openness and willingness to accept Rome and its pilgrims on their own terms, as Rhodes suggested.

> I sat nearby, at the opening of the Via della Conciliazione, listening to the shouts for the waiters, who hurried forward balancing trays with cups of coffee and wine; the clinking of glasses and the harsh klaxon of the buses that ploughed their way through this crowd, ever adding human fuel to the masses in the square. Who would have thought, in this vast congeries of sound and profane humanity, that this

[64] A. Rhodes, *A Sabine Journey* (1952), pp. 116–17.
[65] Rhodes, pp. 115–16, 119, 190.

was a great Sunday of Holy Year before St Peter's –
had he not understood something of the Catholic
Faith?[66]

How has the modern rediscovery of pilgrimage reinter-
preted its practice? It has placed greater emphasis on the
devotional than the penitential and ascetic, though there
remained a recognizable distinction in modes of travel and
accommodation which were deemed appropriate. The
pattern of devotional practice once seen in Rome changed,
though the emphasis remained on the basilicas and catacombs. The communal aspect of pilgrimage remained
important, indeed became enhanced. Diocesan, parish
and associational pilgrimages increased in popularity,
echoing the footsteps of the mediaeval pilgrim bands from
guilds and villages. However the modern pilgrims were not
in groups so much for physical protection but in recognition that the Christian life is one lived in communion.
Pilgrimage, particularly to Rome, remained a vivid experience of true Catholicity. At the centre of this experience of
the Church Universal was the shifting emphasis on to the
person of the reigning Pontiff. Kneeling at the feet of the
present Vicar of Christ came to be as important as kneeling
at the tomb of St Peter.

Relics underwent a revival in the nineteenth century
alongside pilgrimage, despite the losses and despoilations
of the Reformation and French Revolution, but the
emphasis had shifted. More attention became focused on
the life of saints rather than the death. Pilgrimage in the
modern period became less tied to relics *per se* and more to
holy sites, hallowed by the lives and deaths of saints but
also, as importantly, by centuries of prayer and devotion.
Less emphasis was placed on the physical contact with
relics and the specifically intercessory power of the saints
and more on the desire spiritually and imaginatively to
enter into the lives of the saints. The 1994 *Catechism of the
Catholic Church* reflects this later view in treating the veneration of relics, pilgrimages, etc. as proper expressions of

[66] Rhodes, pp. 194–5.

the 'religious sense of the Christian people'.[67] They are to be treated with respect, but are not the benchmarks of Catholic loyalty as was clearly the case in the sixteenth-century *Catechism of the Council of Trent*.

There is no doubt that the reinterpretation by Paul VI brought about a huge shift in the meaning of Holy Year or Jubilee, which was borne out in the preparations for the one of 2000. The shift is from an emphasis on personal repentance and forgiveness, overlaid with pro-papal cheer-leading, to an emphasis on reconciliation between God and humanity and within humanity itself. 'This reconciliation should be the fruit of the common experience of the Holy Year. The pilgrims in Rome ought to be and are the representatives of Christians everywhere in the world.'[68] The theme of the Holy Year of 1975 was 'Renewal and Reconciliation', which carried with it a spirit of ecumenical and interfaith understanding, newly flowering in the 1970s.

Thus as the Church celebrates the Jubilee of 2000, the highlighted themes are those of reconciliation, justice for the poor, freedom for prisoners and dignity for the disabled, disenfranchised and discarded. They are modern themes, flowing from the rethinking of the role of the Church in the world which flows from the Council. It is no accident that the present Pope, therefore, has seen the Council and its aftermath and his entire papacy as a preparation for the Great Jubilee. 'From this point of view we can affirm that the Second Vatican Council was a providential event, whereby the Church began the more immediate preparation for the Jubilee of the Second Millennium.'[69] The Holy Year of 1975, and the extraordinary Holy Years of 1983 and 1987 are also seen as part of this preparation. This portrayal of the purpose and ideal of Holy Year is nothing less than a rein-vention of an ancient popular practice in the life of the Church. However, that in itself is nothing new – the Counter-Reformation reinvented it to carry forward the ambition of reconverting Protestants and confronting paganism; the

[67] *Catechism of the Catholic Church* (1994), No. 1674.
[68] Jung-Inglessis, p. 269.
[69] *Tertio Millenio Adveniente*, para. 18.

Ultramontane church of the nineteenth and early twentieth centuries reinvented it as a means of reinforcing the centrality and authority of the popes in the life of the Church. Nevertheless, ever since 1300, the Holy Year has, in its various guises, been an exercise in the assertion of papal authority. Its reinvention tells us as much about the preoccupations of successive popes as about the Church's developing understanding and practice of repentance and charity.

Pilgrimage to Rome continues to have meaning. It has reflected the changing life of western Europe and, latterly, of the entire world. Thus its meaning is that which the world, the lost, the seeking, the uncertain as well as the faithful give it through their lives. From the mid-twentieth century onwards that meaning has perhaps been less clear and readily identifiable. Relics have become less attractive to seekers of blessing and healing, but sites hallowed by centuries of prayer still attract and the ancient symbols of journey still speak to the twentieth-century soul. Rigid patterns of pious observance have largely been abandoned, and few modern pilgrims would even be able to name the 'seven churches' and the relics associated with them. Yet as the Millennium approached the prospect of a Holy Year had the power to excite, to attract, perhaps for much the same reasons as one author reflected in 1950.

When Pius XII opened the Holy Door at St. Peter's, open only for one year in every twenty-five, he was repeating a gesture established through the ages of such peril and crisis, the fact of there now being any door to open might convey less a sense of the Vatican's practical genius than of its truth in the matter of miracle. Today's peril and crisis, not at all dimmed by any analogy, were meeting a power mercifully transcending today's confusion, even regardless of any transcendence in the creed. The opening of a door is the natural symbol of such consolation, most of life being a wish to find some door or other that will open: to get out, to be let in, to find elbow room that is not lonely and meaningless.[70]

[70] Clark, p. 195.

Bibliography

Books

Letters of Lord Acton to Mary Gladstone, ed. H. Paul (1904)

R. Aldington, *The Strange Life of Charles Waterton* (1949)

W. J. Anderdon, *To Rome and Back* (1877)

M. Andrieux, *Daily Life in Papal Rome in the eighteenth century* (1968)

B. Barefoot, *The English Road to Rome* (1993)

E. R. Barker, *Rome of the Pilgrims and Martyrs* (1913)

W. Barry, *Memories and Opinions* (1926)

D. Baxter, *England's Cardinals* (1903)

M. Beard, *Faith and Fortune* (1997)

J. Berkeley, *Lulworth and the Welds* (1971)

Bede, *Ecclesiastical History of the English People* (1990 edn)

The Beda Book

E. Bellasis, *Memorials of Mr Serjeant Bellasis 1800–1873* (1893)

D. A. Bellenger, *English and Welsh Priests 1558–1800* (1984)

H. Belloc, *The Path to Rome* (1902)

C. Bence Jones, *The Catholic Families* (1992)

J. Bentley, *Restless Bones: the Story of Relics* (1985)

M. C. Bishop, *A Memoir of Mrs Augustus Craven* (*Pauline de la Ferronays*) (1985)

J. Black, *The British and the Grand Tour* (1985)

M. Bloch, *The Royal Touch: Sacred Monarchy and Scrofula in England and France* (1973)

D. Birch, *Pilgrimage to Rome in the Middle Ages* (1998)

R. Brentano, *Rome Before Avignon* (1990)

G. F. Browne, *The Venerable Bede, his life and writings* (1919)

C. Butler, *The Vatican Council 1869–70* (1930)

B. Camm, *The Lives of English Martyrs declared blessed by Leo XIII in 1886 and 1895* (1904)

J. Capgrave, *Ye Solace of Pilgrims,* ed. C. A. Mills (1911)

Catechism of the Catholic Church (1994)

Catechism of the Council of Trent

N. K. Chadwick, ed., *Studies in the Early British Church* (1958)

O. Chadwick, *Catholicism and History: the Opening of the Vatican Archives* (1978)

E. Chaney, *The Evolution of the Grand Tour* (1998)

G. K. Chesterton, *The Resurrection of Rome* (1930)

J. Chetwode Eustace, *A Classical Tour through Italy* (1813)

E. Clark, *Rome and a Villa* (1953)

B. Colgrave, ed., *Life of Bishop Wilfrid of Hexham by Eddius Stephanus* (1927)

S. Coote, *John Keats: a Life* (1995)

F. M. Crawford, *Ave Roma Immortalis* (1903)

J. G. Davies, *Pilgrimage Yesterday and Today: Why? Where? How?* (1988)

R. David, tr., *The Lives of ninth century Popes* (Liber Pontificalis) (1995)

Diary of John Evelyn, ed. W. Bray (1818)

Dictionary of National Biography

E. Duffy, *The Stripping of the Altars; Traditional Religion in England 1400–1580* (1994)

E. Duffy, *Saints and Sinners: a History of the Popes* (1997)

A. Dures, *English Catholicism 1558–1642* (1983)

G. Eliot, *Middlemarch*

H.O. Evennett, *The Spirit of the Counter-Reformation* (1968)

D. H. Farmer, *The Oxford Dictionary of Saints* (1987)

D. Fenlon, *Heresy and Obedience in Tridentine Italy* (1972)

Michael Finch, *G.K. Chesterton: a biography* (1986)

R. C. Finucane, *Miracles and Pilgrims; Popular Beliefs in Medieval England* (1977)

B. Foley, *Some Other People of Penal Times* (1991)

H. Foley, *Records of the Society of Jesus* (1875–93)

A. Gasquet, *Obit Book of the Venerable English College* (1929)

A. Gasquet, *A History of the Venerable English College, Rome* (1920)

J. Gillow, *Biographical Dictionary of English Catholics* (1885)

S. Gilley, *Newman and His Age* (1990)

J. R. Glorney Bolton, *Roman Century 1870–1970* (1970)

P. Granfield, *The Papacy in Transition* (1980)

F. Gregorovius, *Roman Journals 1852–74* (1907)

H. Gross, *Rome and the Age of Enlightenment: the Post-Tridentine Syndrome and the Ancien Régime* (1990)

P. Gunn, *The Actons: remarkable people* (1978)

J. R. Hale, ed., *The Italian Journal of Samuel Rogers* (1955)

M. Harvey, *England, Rome and the Papacy 1417–1464: the study of a relationship* (1993)

M. J. Havran, *The Catholics in Caroline England* (1962)

C. Haydon, *Anti-Catholicism in Eighteenth-Century England* (1993)

P. J. Helm, *Alfred the Great* (1963)

B. Hemphill, *The Early Vicars Apostolic of England 1685–1750* (1954)

C. Hibbert, *The Grand Tour* (1969)

C. Howard, *English Travellers of the Renaissance* (1914)

D. R. Howard, *Writers and Pilgrims: medieval pilgrimage narratives and their posterity* (1980)

P. Hughes, *The Reformation in England* (1950)

F. C. Husenbeth, *Life of John Milner* (1862)

J. Ingamells, *A Dictionary of British and Irish Travellers in Italy 1701–1800* (1997)

E. M. Jung-Inglessis, *The Holy Year in Rome: Past and Present* (1998)

B. Kelly, *The Life of Henry Benedict Stuart, Cardinal Duke of York* (1899)
J. D. Kelly, *The Oxford Dictionary of Popes* (1986)
The Book of Margery Kempe (Penguin Classics 1985)
Thomas à Kempis, *Imitation of Christ*
R. Krautheimer, *Rome: Profile of a City, 312–1308* (1980)
M. E. Lancaster, *The Tempests of Broughton* (1987)
R. Lanciani, *New Tales of Old Rome* (1901, reissued 1967)
L. Lewis, *Connoisseurs and Secret Agents in eighteenth-century Rome* (1961)
P. Llewellyn, *Rome in the Dark Ages* (1971)
C. B. Lucas, ed., *The Letters of Horace Walpole* (1904)
S. G. A. Luff, *The Christian's Guide to Rome* (1990 ed)
F. McLynn, *The Jacobites* (1985)
A. Marrett Crosby, *The Foundations of Christian England* (1997)
Gregory Martin, *Roma Sancta*, ed. G.B. Parks (1969)
G. Masson, *The Companion Guide to Rome* (1965)
D. Mathew, *Sir Tobie Mathew* (1950)
D. Mathew, *Catholicism in England 1535–1935* (1938)
W. Maziere-Brady, *Anglo-Roman Papers* (1890)
J. Miller, *Popery and Politics in England 1660–88* (1973)
R. J. Mitchell, *John Free: from Bristol to Rome in the fifteenth century* (1955)
Fynes Morison, *An Itinerary Written by Fynes Morison, Gentleman* (4 vols, 1907–8)
H. V. Morton, *A Traveller in Rome* (1957)
Anthony Munday, *The English Roman Life*, ed. P. J. Ayres (1980)
B. Navarra, *Filippo Michele Ellis* (Rome 1973)
B. Navarra, *Guide to the Cathedral of Segni*
W. H. Nelligan, *Rome: its Churches, its charities and its Schools* (1858)
J. H. Newman, *Letters and Diaries*, vol. 3, ed. I. Ker and T. Gornall (1979)
D. Newsome, *The Parting of Friends* (1966)
E. O. Carragain, *The City of Rome and the World of Bede*, Jarrow Lecture 1994
E. O'Gorman, *Our Islands and Rome* (1974)
M. Oliver IBVM, *Mary Ward 1585–1645* (1959)
Veronica Ortenberg, *The English Church and the Continent: Cultural, Spiritual and Artistic Exchanges* (1992)
G. B. Parks, *The English Traveller in Italy* (1954)
M. Pawley, *Faith and Family: the Life and Circle of Ambrose Phillipps de Lisle* (1993)
J. Pemble, *The Mediterranean Passion* (1987)
N. Perry and L. Echeverria, *Under the Heel of Mary* (1988)
H. Peters, *Mary Ward: a life in contemplation*, trans. Helen Butterworth (1994)
R. T. Petersson, *Sir Kenelm Digby: the Ornament of England 1603–65* (1956)
G. Phelps, *Squire Waterton* (1976)
S. J. Reid, ed, *Memoirs of Sir Edward Blount* (1902)
C. Roberts, *And So To Rome* (1950)
A. Rhodes, *A Sabine Journey* (1952)
A. Rhodes, *The Vatican in the Age of Liberal Democracies 1870–1922* (1983)

F. Ripley, *The Mary Potter Story* (1954)
J. Martin Robinson, *Cardinal Consalvi 1757–1824* (1987)
M. Rubin, *Corpus Christi: the Eucharist in Late Medieval Culture* (1991)
H. P. Russell, *From Hussar to Priest; a memoir of Charles Rose Chase* (1913)
J. J. Scarisbrick, *The Reformation and the English People* (1984)
R. Schiefen, *Nicholas Wiseman and the Transformation of English Catholicism* (1984)
G. Scott, *Gothic Rage Undone* (1992)
M. Sheridan, *The Romans: their Lives and Times* (1994)
David Sox, *Relics and Shrines* (1985)
J. Stoye, *English Travellers Abroad 1604–1667* (1989)
J. Sumption, *Pilgrimage: an image of medieval religion* (1970)
E. Swinglehurst, *Cook's Tours: the story of popular travel* (1982)
V. and E. Turner, *Image and Pilgrimage in Christian Culture* (1978)
W. B. Ullathorne, *Cabin Boy to Archbishop* (1942 ed)
H. Vidon, *The Pilgrim's Guide to Rome: discovering links with past English-speaking pilgrims and residents* (1975)
M. Wade Labarge, *Medieval Travellers: the Rich and Restless* (1982)
M. Walsh, *A Dictionary of Devotions* (1993)
B. Ward, *Miracles and the Mediaeval Mind* (1982)
W. E. Wilkie, *The Cardinal Protectors of England: Rome and the Tudors before the Reformation* (1974)
A. Williams, A. P. Smyth and D. P. Kirby, *A Biographical Dictionary of Dark Age Britain: England, Scotland, Wales c. 500–1050* (1991)
M. E. Williams, *A History of the Venerable English College, Rome* (1979)
A. Wilson CP, *Blessed Dominic Barberi* (1967)
N. Wiseman, *Recollections of the Last Four Popes* (1858)
Le Chavalier Zeloni, trans. Lady Martin, *The Life of Princess Borghese* (1893)

Periodicals
B. Bolton, 'Received in His Names', *Studies in Church History,* vol. 31, 1994, pp. 153–67.
J. F. Champ, 'Philip Howard OP, Rome and English Recusancy', *New Blackfriars* no. 76, June 1995, 268–79.
J. F. Champ, 'Goths and Romans: Daniel Rock, Augustus Welby Pugin, and Nineteenth-Century English Worship', *Studies in Church History,* vol. 35 (1999), pp. 290–320.
J. M. Cleary, 'The Carne Monument in Rome', *Cardiff Naturalists' Society Reports and Transactions,* vol. 80, 1948–50, pp. 12–15.
M. L. Clark, 'British Travellers to Rome in Tudor and Stuart Times', *History Today,* vol. 28, November 1978, pp. 746–51.
E. Duffy, 'William Cardinal Allen', *Recusant History,* 1995, pp. 265–90.
G. Gurtler, 'Deceptis Custodibus or Liberty Lost – Liberty Regained', *Royal Stuart Papers,* no. 25, 1990.
J. R. Hulbert, 'Some Medieval Advertisements of Rome', *Journal of Modern Philology,* vol. 20, 1922–3, pp. 403–24.

G. Mooney, 'British Diplomatic Relations with the Holy See 1793–1830', *Recusant History* no. 14, 1979.

Glanmor Williams, 'Poets and Pilgrims in 15th and 16th century Wales', *Trans. Hon. Soc. Cym. 992–3, 69–98*

Cook's Excursionist and Tourist Advertiser passim.

The Venerabile passim.

Contemporary Annals of Rome (1870), Articles reprinted from the *Westminster Gazette.*

M. Foster Farley, 'Adrian IV: England's only Pope 1154–9', *History Today* vol. 28, Aug. 1979, pp. 530–6.

F. P. Magoun, 'The Rome of Two Northern Pilgrims', *Harvard Theological Review,* vol. 33 (1940), pp. 267–89.

N. Wiseman, *Dublin Review* 1836.

J. Spencer Northcote, *The Rambler,* vol. 2, 1848, p. 124.

Theses Etc

W. Meyer, The Church of the Catacombs: British Responses to the Evidence of the Roman Catacombs 1578–1900, Ph.D. Cambridge 1985

W. J. Moore, The Saxon Pilgrims to Rome and the Schola Saxonum, Doctoral Thesis, U. of Fribourg 1937.

G. Anstruther, 'Philip Howard OP' (Unpublished Life in Dominican Archives)

Archives

Jesuit Archives, Farm St, London.

Archives of the Venerable English College, Rome.

Archives of St Mary's College, Oscott

Thomas Cook Travel Archives

Dominican Archives, Edinburgh.

Index

225

Printed in the United Kingdom
by Lightning Source UK Ltd.
127810UK00001B/58-348/A

9 780852 443736